UNIVERSITY OF NORTH CAROLINA AT CHAPEL HILL
DEPARTMENT OF ROMANCE LANGUAGES

NORTH CAROLINA STUDIES
IN THE ROMANCE LANGUAGES AND LITERATURES

Founder: URBAN TIGNER HOLMES
Editor: CAROL L. SHERMAN

Distributed by:

UNIVERSITY OF NORTH CAROLINA PRESS

CHAPEL HILL
North Carolina 27515-2288
U.S.A.

NORTH CAROLINA STUDIES IN THE
ROMANCE LANGUAGES AND LITERATURES
Number 266

THE LEPER IN BLUE

THE LEPER IN BLUE

Coercive Performance

and the

Contemporary Latin American Theater

BY
AMALIA GLADHART

CHAPEL HILL

NORTH CAROLINA STUDIES IN THE ROMANCE
LANGUAGES AND LITERATURES
U.N.C. DEPARTMENT OF ROMANCE LANGUAGES

2000

Library of Congress Cataloging-in-Publication Data

Gladhart, Amalia
 The leper in blue: coercive performance and the contemporary Latin American theater / by Amalia Gladhart.
 p. – cm. – (North Carolina Studies in the Romance Languages & Literatures; no. 266).
 Includes bibliographical references.
 ISBN 0-8078-9270-X
 1. Latin American drama – 20th century – History and criticism. 2. Theater – Latin America – History – 20th century. 3. Theater – Political aspects – Latin America. I. Title. II. Series.

PQ7082.D7 G543   2000
862'.60998 – dc21

00-031869

Cover design: Heidi Perov

© 2000. Department of Romance Languages. The University of North Carolina at Chapel Hill.

ISBN 0-8078-9270-X

Depósito legal: V. 2.368 - 2000

Artes Gráficas Soler, S. L. - La Olivereta, 28 - 46018 Valencia

CONTENTS

	Páge
ACKNOWLEDGMENTS	9
INTRODUCTION: THE BLUE LEPER	11
1. PERFORMANCE, TEXTUALITY, AND THE NARRATION OF HISTORY	29
2. FEIGNED PARALYSIS: PERFORMANCE AND GAMES	75
3. PLAYING GENDER	111
4. TORTURE ON STAGE	154
5. NOTHING'S HAPPENING: PERFORMANCE AS COERCION	192
CONCLUSION: DISPLACEMENT, REPLAY	217
WORKS CITED	228
INDEX	238

ACKNOWLEDGMENTS

I have incurred numerous debts in the course of completing this study. This book has its origins in my doctoral dissertation, and I am especially grateful to John W. Kronik, my committee chair, for his meticulous and insightful readings. Debra A. Castillo and Timothy Murray, members of my committee, were generous with their time and assistance. I also thank Priscilla Meléndez for her teaching and her friendship. The intelligence and generosity of colleagues and classmates at the University of Oregon and at Cornell have been invaluable.

A New Faculty Award from the University of Oregon provided time for initial revisions. I am also grateful for the support of the Oregon Humanities Center. A Mellon Fellowship in the Humanities greatly eased my time at Cornell. A bequest from Delcie Mae King supported a trip to Ecuador in September 1994. In Ecuador, Nora Ramírez and Raúl Salgado kindly opened their home.

Julian Weiss, Linda Kintz, and Kirsten Nigro read and commented upon portions of the manuscript. Two anonymous readers for the Series made numerous helpful suggestions. Amanda Holmes provided able assistance with many of the translations. I am grateful to all of these readers. Any remaining awkwardness is, of course, my own.

Earlier versions of chapters 3 and 5 appeared in the *Latin American Literary Review* and *Gestos,* respectively.

A special thank you to my parents for that first trip to Ecuador, and to my brother for sharing the ride. This book is dedicated to my husband, Sean Hayes, without whose encouragement and forbearance it would not have been completed, and to our daughter, Katherine.

Introduction

THE BLUE LEPER

My first experience of Latin American theater was a truly amateur production in northern Ecuador–the actors and producers were local, at any rate; I don't know where the script originated. My Spanish at the time was still provisional: the only word of the play I clearly understood was "leprosa, leprosa," shouted vigorously by a girl in a blue dress. My father explained she had found pus on her hotel sheets and believed herself infected. There was something about a place she'd visited some time ago, a danger she didn't fully notice at the time. None of it made much sense. It was a school performance, in honor of the local patron saint–another fiesta, La Santísima Virgen de la Caridad–and an auspicious beginning, I suppose, to my study of theater.

The disgust of that image of pus-smeared sheets, and the absolute confusion of a play performed in Spanish barely six weeks into our stay in Mira, eclipsed all other aspects of the spectacle. I have a clear picture of the girl, dressed to represent a woman twice her age–I say girl, but to my eleven-year-old's eyes she looked fully grown, sophisticated in that close-gathered, shiny blue dress. And I can see the dress, the wavy hair just past her shoulders, can hear her crying "¡Leprosa, leprosa!" as she rushes across the stage (and me whispering to my father, "That's leprosy, right, Dad?"), but I have no memory of how the play turned out, whether she became ill, whether the hotel management was to blame, who she was, anyway.

It was the only time I went into that school auditorium, in all the fifteen months we lived there. Nor have I returned on later visits. The locked gate across the entrance–somewhat separate from the school, outside its patio walls–was a place for boys to congregate, a gauntlet of whistles to run in pursuit of an errand, not a place to enter. It was, in effect, a space of contagion, a private quarantine demanded by the character's apparent illness and, more significantly, by the privacy of the nuns who ran the school, the girls (my friends) who had to stay indoors or risk their parents' wrath. It was one of the boundaries that, despite my privileged status as a guest in town, I was unable or unwilling to traverse.

The isolation of that stage, entirely cut off from the rest of my life in Mira, resonates with the weird image of the screaming leper. The blue leper, as I think of her, is joined by five or seven other offset memories retained from the time before the village began to make sense, before I had my own internal map and the words with which to talk about it. Images, for me, of what I have since come to associate with the instability of performance: a sense of repetitive motion that is never quite the same, of slippage from one version to the next as each teller reshapes the tale in her own image. Those unassimilated memories reflect as well the stubborn demarcation of the stage, and not only the concrete stage of the nuns' *colegio*. Despite all efforts to erase the boundaries between the theater and whatever might take place "out there," the simple need to mark *this, here* as stage, as something else, establishes a separation.

The girl's dress is a fixed star, a point of reference that echoes the distorted femininity of Lupita in Rosario Castellanos's *El eterno femenino* (Mexico, 1974) [*The Eternal Feminine*], the desperate reinventions of Él and Ella in Sabina Berman's *El suplicio del placer* (Mexico, 1978) [The torture of pleasure], and Gabriel's stymied performance in Isaac Chocrón's *La revolución* (Venezuela, 1971) [The revolution]. That blue dress is doubled in the blue cape worn by the final Mama Negra of Latacunga's annual fiesta. I will return to the Mama Negra in my conclusion, in order to consider the connections between staged performances—of which the blue leper is emblematic—and the theatricality represented by the procession of the popular Ecuadorian celebration. Like the school girl's exuberant performance, the fiesta pushes the borders of theatricality, drawing that which had been offstage into the precincts of the performance. In both, the play of unassimilated excess is unavoidable.

The blue leper is a number of things: a point of reference in my own observation of myself seeing, the inevitable self-reflexiveness that conditions all writing about performance just as it shapes the performance being viewed. A reminder that the audience is always vulnerable, that the auditorium is a narrow room filled with live bodies, audible (even when attempting a polite silence) in the involuntary hiss of breathing or the deliberate reproduction of a soundtrack broadcast across the show. Or a rejoinder that things aren't always what they seem, that repetition breeds contempt but equally brings comfort, reassurance, and that the sense of no first time means no first danger, either. The girl stands trapped in the nonperformance of this observer's faulty memory–as I've noted, I couldn't say what happens next–unable to escape the pull of a dimly recalled hotel. Like a video loop on interminable playback, she hurtles across her stage toward the agent of infection, her voice bound in the single word of a desperately truncated text, stalled by an audience that won't quite hear but can't quite leave.

My individual difficulties as spectator at the school play had to do with language, with imperfect simultaneous translation and my own inability to grasp local speech. But in a somewhat similar manner, the audience is always in some way separate from the stage, divided, different. And there is nearly always something that remains only partially understood. I was only provisionally part of that community, but an audience, as community, is intrinsically provisional, because it is constituted by an immediate and unique event. The episode further suggests that the performance space is potentially dangerous for both performer and spectator.

The blue leper's reduced text (¡*leprosa!* ¡*leprosa!*) also points to the link between the dramatic text and its eventual (or possible) performance. Such texts are rewritten in performance, but also in each individual reading, in each night's rendition and in each spectator's recollections of the show. There is no last word, no definitive version, and this contingency is deeply tied to the problems of compulsion and of staged violence that arise in so many plays. The play as oppositional mechanism is inexact, and it is difficult to know what has been or will be said. The escape offered by the performance is at best provisional, even if the violence is (at some level) illusory.

The blue leper is but one example. Coercive performance, however, is evident in many contemporary Latin American plays. Playwrights such as Vicente Leñero, Sabina Berman, Mariela Romero, Griselda Gambaro, Eduardo Pavlovsky, and Rosario Castellanos, among many others, depict the freedom of performance within a framework of compulsion. Performance is invoked to address social realities, such as the production and interpretation of history, ritual game playing, and gender identity, which can be thought of as a series of performances. A phenomenon at once liberating and coercive, performance is not limited to the theater space but may be used in strikingly similar fashion on and off stage. The plays I will discuss reveal a distinct ambivalence toward the theater. On the one hand, the theater works as a space of freedom and oppositional action, but on the other, it may mimic the operations of power and compulsion that characterize extra-theatrical reality.

Performance is a broad concept that goes beyond the play within the play or self-referentiality of metatheater to encompass individual actions and social realities. In her introduction to *Radical Street Performance*, Jan Cohen-Cruz writes that performance "indicates expressive behavior intended for public viewing" (1). This definition provides a useful point of departure for the representations of performance I will address, all of which require an audience and entail conscious action. The viewing public, however, is often highly circumscribed, and does not in all cases recognize itself as audience. Performance is intrinsically contingent and unstable, and citational in the widest sense–that is, citing not only the (a) text, but social norms, gender roles, cultural in-jokes, and historical narratives. As Elin Diamond argues, "Every performance, if it is intelligible as such, embeds features of previous performances: gender conventions, racial histories, aesthetic traditions–political and cultural pressures that are consciously and unconsciously acknowledged" (1). Performance may be imposed or freely chosen and is not automatically playful or liberating. It is therefore a double-edged figure with which to critique social elements such as gender, game playing, and state terror that themselves contain (outside the theater) elements of theatricality. The group of plays I will study foreground performance within the dramatic text in order to critique the theater itself.

By forcibly blurring stage/reality boundaries, the figure of performance both represents and critiques its sociohistorical context. In this way, performance becomes a metaphor for the societal imposition of role playing and for the subversive transformation of such roles. Whether presented within a text or considered as live action, performance calls attention to the presence of an audience as well. This audience is marked by, and also shapes, the spectacle it witnesses. At the same time, performance establishes the parameters of interpretation, both for the play's implied audience and within the play itself. Diana Taylor observes that "Más que un producto dramático–sea una puesta tradicional o de performance art–performance significaría el proceso mismo de teatralización social, el acto de asumir o re-presentar o atacar un rol proviniente de nuestros limitados repertorios sociales para fines que van más allá de lo estético" ("Negotiating" 50) [More than a dramatic product–be it a traditional staging or performance art–performance is the actual process of social theatricalization, the act of assuming or re-presenting or attacking a role arising out of our limited social repertoires toward ends that reach beyond the aesthetic].

Though many performance scholars claim that performance produces free-floating, heterogeneous, playful outcomes, the Latin American context is quite different.[1] In the plays treated in this study, performance is an ambivalent and contradictory process, one that unites freedom and constraint. Moreover, within these plays, the scales have frequently been tipped far more toward coercion than rebellion. The plays thus not only raise important questions about the nature of performance, but they also shed light on many of the crucial sociopolitical issues of twentieth-century Latin America, among them economic instability, political repression, state violence, and dictatorship. In this study, a reading of performance in these plays works in two directions. It brings performance studies to bear on an analysis of the plays and opens up the texts. At the same time, it shows how the plays enact their own theorization of performance, as well as of concepts such as gender and postcoloniality.

Although they may draw from a variety of international theater currents, the playwrights I study are clearly situated within a Latin

---

[1] Diamond offers a brief summary of the ways in which views of performance have shifted over time. She writes: "Theater collectives of the 1960s were greatly influenced by Artaud and by experimentation across the arts. They and their enthusiastic theorists believed that in freeing the actor's body and eliminating aesthetic distance, they could raise political consciousness among spectators and even produce new communal structures. In performance theory of the late 1970s, the group affirmation of 'being there' tends to celebrate the self-sufficient performing instant. In performance theory of the 1980s, consciousness-raising drops away (totalizing definitions of consciousness are, after all, suspect). In line with poststructuralist claims of the death of the author, the focus in performance today has shifted from authority to effect, from text to body, to the spectator's freedom to make and transform meanings" (3). See also Marvin Carlson's *Performance: A Critical Introduction* for a helpful discussion of the many threads of performance theory.

American context, raising issues that are significant throughout contemporary Latin America. Those issues include paratheatrical performances such as religious processions and fiestas, as well as local and national history, politics, and language, and the economic inequalities that persist throughout the region. Mexican performance artist Maris Bustamante concludes that "although performance has generated its own tradition in the U.S. and Europe and is already somewhat academic, it still provides an opportunity for rupture. Performance is a way to be subversive, to directly confront the spectator" (quoted in Costantino). Although my study does not deal with performance art per se, performance is a significant concept in Latin America and an important way of understanding the texts I will examine. Plays such as *Bolívar*, by José Antonio Rial (Venezuela, 1982) directly confront the interrelations of authoritarianism and historical discourse, underscoring the theatrical manipulation of concepts such as "liberty" and "heroism" to political ends. Violence, verbal as well as physical, domestic as well as national, is a constant element, as parallels are drawn between the theatricalized (though no less real) violence of state terrorism and the attempt to represent such violence on stage.

Highly visible, enticingly adorned, yet explosive, openly contagious, the image of the blue leper brings together the wider historical context with the chief contradictions of performance. In this juxtaposition, she stands for whatever it is that remains behind, unassimilated. No matter how blurred the boundaries, something remains distinguishable: the stage is always still a stage, and the audience understands this. The residual but stubborn distinction between on stage and off underscores the possibility that offstage theatricality is a dodge, a coercive process deliberately exploited to repressive ends. To adopt theatricality outside the theater is to assume a disguise, to dissemble. For example, it becomes possible to mask a deliberate assassination with the trappings of a play, down to script and props. Political demonstrations, both oppressive and resistant, may share similar strategies. In these instances, the claim is not that the street is a stage. Rather, the spectacle demands that the audience discount the manifest transformation of street into stage and accept that the street is after all the ordinary thoroughfare its surface appearance suggests.

My analysis includes texts from a number of countries, not because all of the theaters of Latin America are the same but because questions of performance arise in similar fashion across national boundaries. Eschewing any attempt to define "a" Latin American theater, this study is an examination of the ways in which performance, coercion, and resistance are linked within a variety of plays and of the ways in which that linkage reflects broader social issues. I am interested less in the analysis of specific live-action performances, with or without prior texts, than in the implications of foregrounding a notion of performance in the analysis of playscripts and in critical discussion.

Performance as practice is provisional, contingent, "acted out," but it is not intrinsically liberating or oppositional. Indeed, the necessity of performance, and the forms performance takes, are frequently coercive. Central to this coercive representation is the physical presence of both performer and spectator. As Philip Auslander has noted, "The problematic of the performing body lies in the tension between the body's inevitably serving as a signifier while simultaneously exceeding, without transcending, that function" (8). The body of the performer represents (stands in for, mimes) the bodies of others invoked or portrayed within the spectacle, but remains an actual body, sentient and vulnerable. The mechanisms of theatricality may be manipulated with repressive intent, and performers may be trapped or violated rather than free. I use coercion in a broad sense that includes both physical force and psychological constraint. Coercion takes a variety of forms, among them social conventions, economic necessity, and physical abuse. In some instances, actors perform fictitious violence against other performers. In other cases, the performance itself is an act of violence, and performers are forced into unwanted and inescapable roles. Coercion may also occur between actor and spectator. The performer is vulnerable to the spectators' scrutiny and judgment, to their voyeuristic gaze. In addition, the audience's presence implicitly justifies even dangerous or exploitative spectacles. The audience, in turn, may be confronted with horrific images, physically threatened, or forced to grapple with its own complicity. Finally, the audience conditioned not to intervene may remain dangerously passive.

At stake in the linking of performance and coercion is the nature of social theatricality, the theatricality that takes place outside the neatly marked boundaries of the traditional—even the nontraditional—stage. The divide between stage and spectator is more membrane than wall, and as with osmosis, the *partial* permeability of that barrier is most important. The audience is drawn into the spectacle–dragged kicking and screaming onto the set, or more likely overtaken as the expanding theatrical arena absorbs spaces the spectator imagined to be hers alone. Yet the spectacle remains something separate and apart: something to observe, absorb, and then leave behind. Offstage spectacles, by contrast, may be inescapable, all-encompassing, as the audience's accustomed role as onlooker is turned against it. Taylor suggests that "theatricality is not simply what we see but a way of controlling vision, of making the invisible visible, the visible invisible" (*Theatre* 4). This widereaching theatricality–and the power to determine what is seen and by whom–is the target of my study.

My use of performance is deliberately inclusive.[2] Performance is neither a precise realization of a preordained text nor an unencumbered access to unmediated experience. Nor, despite controversy within performance studies, are theatricality and performance necessarily at odds. Where theatricality suggests an overarching quality of spectacle, of representation, performance emphasizes the deliberate realization of an action that may be compelled or freely chosen.[3] Thus the elements of performance can be seen to include role playing, repetition, improvisation, and the (partial) displacement of textual and other authority. In its most ordinary sense, to perform is to play a role, and a performance is the staging of a dramatic text, but as Henry Sayre notes, a more general performance, artistic performance, is defined in part by "its status as the single occurrence of a repeatable and preexistent text or score" (91). Sayre's conditions–single and repeatable–neatly enclose two key aspects of performance. As Herbert Blau observes, "what seems to be confirmed by the pursuit of unmediated experience through performance is that there is something in the very nature of performance which [. . .] implies *no first time*, no origin, but only recurrence and reproduction, whether improvised or ritualized," so that "a performance

---

[2] Richard Schechner writes of performance as "a very inclusive notion of action; theatre is only one node on a continuum that reaches from ritualization in animal behavior (including humans) through performances in everyday life–greetings, displays of emotion, family scenes and so on–to rites, ceremonies and performances: large-scale theatrical events" (1).

[3] Taylor writes that "the term performance, and especially the verb performing, allow for agency, which opens the way for resistance and oppositional spectacles" ("Opening" 14).

seems *written* even if there is no Text" ("Universals" 171). The singularity of performance is in turn highlighted by the understanding of performance as event. Natalie Schmitt argues that "in the increasingly widespread perception of reality as endless process, performance, not the art object, becomes primary" ("Theorizing" 231). Single and repeatable also enclose one of performance's many contradictions. The ongoing process of reality is made up of myriad, singular events; the repeatable text is never played the same way twice.

The permeable boundaries of the theater naturally highlight the importance of the stage as space, as Josette Féral contends: "With neither past nor future, performance *takes place*. It turns the stage into an event from which the subject will emerge transformed until another performance, when it can continue on its way" (177). The subject that is transformed seems to refer to the performer. For a spectator, the performance would indeed have past and future, a temporal frame mirroring the spatial frame whereby the stage is recognized as such, that is, as a space of performance. "Taking place" implies occupation as well as event, the assumption of the right to stake a claim. While Féral implies that the transformations of performance can be positive, spatial occupation can also be linked to coercion, most obviously in the sense of an army of occupation but also in the invasion of an individual's space or the violence of imprisonment, in which it is the victim who is forced to occupy a given area. The tendency to gender public spaces masculine, private spaces feminine, also creates a coercive matrix for the distribution of spatial privilege. The actual place of performance may itself be highly disputed, with access to theaters or similar venues limited by economic or other factors. The risk of appearing on stage, physically occupying a well-defined space and exposing oneself to observation or surveillance, may be substantial.

When performance as event is emphasized, the observer of the event becomes not only an objective recorder of data, but the necessary shaper of the data observed. As David George notes, in the actor-audience relationship "the spectator complements the work of the performers by the *act* of relating" so that performance functions as an axis, a process of relating rather than a relationship ("On Ambiguity" 80). Like the text, the spectator is at once a part of the performance and apart from it, isolated by a series of spatial and aesthetic conventions. Thus, Kimberly Benston argues that

"*Verfremdung* might better be understood as a performatizing of spectatorship, a shifting of performance as an active value from the stage to the auditorium of consciousness" (441). The audience distanced from the spectacle sufficiently to achieve a critical objectivity (alienation) would be similarly divided in its experience *as* audience–both spectator watching and spectator *performing* the act of watching, performing as audience.[4]

Augusto Boal's theatrical methods take the notion of the active audience a step further. Approaching the link between resistance and coercion in performance from the perspective of the audience, Boal demands that the spectators physically join (or replace) the actors on stage, taking part as performers to redirect or transform the representation. This activity, ultimately, is meant to be moved off stage, and outside the theater, into the performer-spectators' daily lives. Auslander observes that while "for Brecht, social experience should inform, and can be conveyed by, theatre, for Boal, performance is a way of exploring options which must then be tested in life" (105). Theater is not "like" the extratheatrical world; it does not resemble it so much as prepare the spectators, actively, to change it. The object of Boal's "poetics of the oppressed" is to "transformar al pueblo, 'espectador', ser pasivo en el fenómeno teatral, en sujeto, en actor, en transformador de la acción dramática" (17) [transform the public, the 'spectator,' a passive being in the theatrical phenomenon, into a subject, an actor, a transformer of dramatic action]. The interaction of actor and audience, on stage, may take a variety of forms, as the actors cooperate with or undermine the spectator's interventions. Boal's aim is that the spectator

---

[4] The theorist is performing as well. Stephen Barker observes that "'performance theory' is in its formulation (*performatio*) a redundant phrase: to theorize is to look at, consciously to view something in the spirit of an examination–already a performance" (7). Some theoretical "performances" formally mimic the traditional script, acknowledging the critic as a performer with multiple voices; one example is Gabriela Mora's "Un diálogo entre feministas hispanoamericanas" [A dialogue among Spanish American feminists]. The intermingling of the theorist's roles as critic and performer can also be seen in dramatic texts (such as Emilio Carballido's *Yo también hablo de la rosa* [Mexico, 1965] [*I Too Speak of the Rose*] and in Electa Arenal's "This life within me won't keep still," a biographical script about Sor Juana Inés de la Cruz and Anne Bradstreet, in which the critic becomes documentary playwright. That Arenal's text is offered not "strictly" as a play is suggested by both its publication and performance contexts: published in a collection of essays on U.S. and Latin American literature, performed at venues such as the MLA convention.

"se libera de su condición de 'espectador' y asume la de 'actor', en que deja de ser objeto y pasa a ser sujeto, en que de testigo se convierte en protagonista" (22) [is liberated from the condition of 'spectator' and assumes that of 'actor,' so that he or she stops being an object and becomes a subject, is converted from witness to protagonist]. Here the move is not from passive to active but from oppressed to liberated audience. Still, the audience's role need not be characterized strictly in terms of active or passive. Boal's theory presupposes that the position of onlooker is inherently oppressive for the spectator. The nonintervening bystander, however, also *facilitates* oppression, allowing torture to continue unchecked, accepting spurious "explanations" of disappearance and imprisonment.

Performance has been credited with an almost constitutive resistance to authority and hence with the wholesale displacement of the dramatic text. This in turn can lead to the devaluation of dramatic performance (what we might term "traditional" theater) for remaining dependent on such texts. Yet while dramatic performance may be viewed as secondary, a "mere" interpretation or rendition, W. B. Worthen insists that although "dramatic performance uses texts, it is hardly authorized by them: to preserve this claim is to preserve the sense of dramatic performance as a hollow, even etiolated, species of the literary" (1098). Worthen argues that, "As a citational practice, dramatic performance–like all other performance–is engaged not so much in citing texts as in reiterating its own regimes; these regimes can be understood to cite–or, perhaps subversively, to resignify–social and behavioral practices that operate outside the theater and that constitute contemporary social life" (1098). The prior texts of any performance are multiple, encompassing much more than a particular script. Moreover, the authority of any of those prior texts or practices remains negotiable.

In performance, any preexisting text is necessarily decentered through the multiple interpretations of actors, directors, set designers, and spectators. Within a dramatic text, an emphasis on performance may function as a means of questioning that text, displacing its authority and highlighting the manner of its construction. Performance may be evoked, in ways often similar to the play within the play of self-referential theater, as a site of negotiation between dramatic text and social context or as a means of questioning the viability of the theater itself. Yet the foregrounding of performance within dramatic texts suggests that the divide between performance and text is by no means absolute. Textual authority is questioned, but the imperative to perform remains in force.[5]

Similarly, the constitution of self or society as performance is both a reclaiming (through restaging) of earlier models to serve new ends and a repetition of the original forms. Awareness of performance does not eliminate its force. As Diamond observes, "Critique of performance (and the performance of critique) can remind us of the unstable improvisations within our deep cultural performances; it can expose the fissures, ruptures, and revisions that have settled into continuous reenactment" (2). Elizabeth Burns's assertion that "the understanding of theatricality depends on the perception of the two-way process whereby drama in performance is both formed by and helps to re-form and so conserve or change the values and norms of the society which supports it" (3-4) aptly describes the interrelations of on and offstage theatricality depicted in the plays under consideration.

Griselda Gambaro maintains that "ningún texto dramático está concebido para ser respetado ni ilustrado. El respeto es la incapacidad para un acercamiento más cálido y profundo, la ilustración es un modo subalterno que congela el arte" ("Voracidad" 62) [no dramatic text is conceived to be respected or "illustrated". Respect is the incapacity for a more personal and profound approach, "illustration" is a subaltern mode that freezes art]. Although, in its appropriation by the director, the dramatic text "trasciende su propio destino de literatura dramática" [transcends its own destiny as dramatic literature], Gambaro does not give the director free rein. She writes:

> La apropiación no es tabla rasa, es un canibalismo amoroso. Si el director no consume este canibalismo amoroso sólo ejecuta un simple acto de voracidad o soberbia. El texto dramático desaparece. Desaparece el signo. La palabra, esa gran despreciada de nuestro teatro porque se la entiende desprovista de su carga

---

[5] The ever-receding horizon of displaced authority is a fundamental, and perhaps insuperable, problem of performance theorizing, a reflection of Blau's contention that "there is nothing more illusory in performance than the illusion of the unmediated" ("Universals" 164). As Keir Elam suggests, "the written text/performance text relationship is not one of simple priority but a complex of reciprocal constraints constituting a powerful *intertextuality*. [. . .] [T]his intertextual relationship is problematic rather than axiomatic and symmetrical" (209).

dramática y se la subestima como en la vida real, es la primera afectada en este proceso. Del respeto absurdo por el autor, hemos pasado a la convicción de que el autor proporciona un pretexto para la puesta en escena. Pero el autor no proporciona un pretexto, proporciona una visión y una filosofía sobre el mundo. ("Voracidad" 62-63)

[Appropriation does not produce a blank slate, it is a loving cannibalism. If the director does not consummate this loving cannibalism, s/he executes a simple act of voraciousness or pride. The dramatic text disappears. The sign disappears. The word, a disdained element of our theater because it is understood as devoid of dramatic weight and is undervalued as in real life, is the first to be affected in this process. From an absurd respect for the author, we have moved to the conviction that the author provides a pretext for the staging. But the author does not provide a pretext, but a vision and a philosophy about the world.]

The seemingly incompatible linkages suggested by a loving cannibalism evoke once again the multiple nature of performance, ludic yet constrained, disruptive yet repetitious. Gambaro's specificity –appropriation is not a free-for-all; the text is not mere pretext–cautions against an overenthusiastic embrace of multiplicity that would lose the concrete possibilities of performance as a destabilizing force in an unexamined rejection of the text. Still, the text as "pretext" may be given a different cast. Enrique Buenaventura describes a censor-passing text which can differ in performance, transmitting a coded message to the audience by way of the performance's nonverbal texts. Verbal codes are also capable of such evasion. The use of dramatic text as pretext in this sense–that is, as cover–brings a distinctly political dimension to the text/performance debate.

In his essay "Performance as Metaphor," Bert States issues a caution about what he terms the "versatile, if not insatiable" terminology of performance (5). The limit problem outlined by States–in which the observer is always part of the field under examination– produces the danger of circular argument: social theatricality resembles the stage, which already necessarily resembles the offstage world.[6] What I want here to emphasize is the interplay of self-con-

---

[6] States writes: "*anything the theatre knows was taught to it by reality*. Maybe people deliberately 'theatricalize' themselves in dress, manner, or life-style according to popular theatre stereotypes (James Dean, Madonna), but where did the stereotypes originate?" (26).

scious and socially constrained performance, so that, for instance, as represented on stage, gender becomes a performance both obligatory and chosen, one that is inescapable yet vulnerable to aesthetic or playful manipulation. States describes "what we might call the kernel or gene of performativity from which all divided forms of artistic performance spring: the collapse of means and ends into each other, the simultaneity of producing something and responding to it in the same behavioral act. All artistic performance is grounded in this pleasure" (25). Thus, the problem of limits is also part of the inherent pleasure of performance. States suggests that "we think of performance as *a way of seeing*–not, that is, the thing seen or performed (from ritual to parade to play to photograph) but seeing that involves certain collaborative and contextual functions (between work and spectator) which are highly elastic" (13). Not only are these functions elastic, they are highly interdependent. The ways in which the playwrights I will discuss highlight, on stage, the apparent theatricality of, for example, offstage relations of gender performance or historical discourse, emphasize the importance of the theatrical space to those relations as well. In other words, this particular critique can take place only within a deliberately theatrical space. On and offstage theatricality are mutually reinforcing.

In its mirroring, however distorted, of offstage reality, theatrical representation translates that reality. This translation is a spatial one, a shifting across lines in the sense of a geometric transformation. Translation, of course, is also a form of mediation. Translation may be a trope of coercion as well, as in the reconsideration of the role of La Malinche in Sabina Berman's *Águila o sol* (Mexico, 1984) [Eagle or sun]. The issue of translation is especially pertinent in light of the question of how to translate the term "performance" into Spanish. *Representación*, the standard dictionary equivalent of "performance," loses certain implications of the English word while adding nuances of its own. Like *historia*, story and history, *representación* is both performance and representation, underscoring, perhaps, the ultimate inseparability of the two. *Representación*–re-presentation–also highlights the repetition, the "no first time" quality of performance already discussed. At the same time, Latin American performance artists and other less traditional theater practitioners often turn to distinct terms. Rosa Luisa Márquez favors "performance."[7] Guillermo Gómez-Peña offers the term "ac-

---

[7] Personal communication, February 1993.

ciones."[8] Writers like Boal, Buenaventura, and Santiago García often use *espectáculo* and *presentación* interchangeably with *representación*. The search for a term other than *representación* echoes the problems with "representation" raised by many performance theorists, while also pointing to other inadequacies in the standard word to designate something new or different. Yet I would agree with Taylor who, after acknowledging the contradictory definitions of "performance" in English and the lack of an equivalent term in Spanish, asserts that "aunque nos falte el vocabulario, el fenómeno mismo tiene una larga y rica tradición en nuestras culturas que, simplemente, no se ha teorizado" ("Negotiating" 49) [although we lack the vocabulary, the phenomenon itself has a long and rich tradition in our cultures that simply has not been theorized]. Mexican theater artist and entrepreneur Jesusa Rodríguez reaches a similar conclusion. Roselyn Costantino writes that according to Rodríguez, performance "is a *gabacho* [gringo] term that, nonetheless, is useful in describing forms and structures whose origins can be found in pre-Columbian society."[9] Despite its difficulty of translation, "performance" serves as the most economical term for the theatricalities evoked in the plays under discussion.

The following chapters trace the expanding parameters of performance as addressed within a variety of dramatic texts. My aim is not an overview of Latin American theater, but instead an examination of the ways in which a select group of plays foreground issues of performance, as well as the issues foregrounded *by* performance. The geographical distribution of plays is therefore uneven, and the selection is not meant to be representative. The plays I will analyze date from 1967 to 1990 and a majority come from Mexico and Argentina. Although many of the plays were written and premiered in the 1970s, the selection does not entirely correspond to the period (1965-70) that Taylor defines as "theater of crisis" in her important study of the same name. My selection is not based on strict chrono-

---

[8] "Groups such as Proceso Pentagono, Suma and Peyote y la Compañia [sic], among others, produced irreverent *acciones* (performances), installations, and *pintas* (impromptu murals) inspired by urban pop culture and oppositional politics" (Gómez-Peña 28).

[9] My thanks to Roselyn Costantino for permission to quote from her forthcoming essay, which draws on her personal interviews with a number of performance artists in Mexico.

logical criteria but rather informed by the presence of distinct and unsettling representations of performance within the plays themselves. That said, all of the plays reflect, to greater or lesser degrees, elements of the crisis Taylor outlines as "a suspension, a rupture between two states" (*Theatre* 20).

Latin American theater, while regionally specific, is also shaped by–and contributes to–the aesthetic and critical currents that affect theater in other parts of the world. For this reason, I have included English translations for all citations of Spanish texts. In a few instances, published translations of the plays are available, and I have modified those translations only when necessary to highlight a particular passage. In most cases, however, the translations are my own. Where plays are divided into numbered acts, scenes, or parts, I have included that information parenthetically as well.

Chapter 1 examines texts in which history is reenacted not only *through* but *as* performance: the events recreated are portrayed as unstable, even arbitrary in their original, "factual" occurrence, and all historical accounts are revealed as inherently contingent. In the play about historical events, there is a double (pre)texting: the playscript and the historical record's script. The foregrounding of performance ultimately destabilizes all historical authority, so that the alternative versions proposed are no more reliable than the official stories they displace. The plays discussed are Vicente Leñero's *Martirio de Morelos* (Mexico, 1981) [Martyrdom of Morelos], José Antonio Rial's *Bolívar*, Sabina Berman's *Águila o sol*, and Miguel Sabido's *Falsa crónica de Juana la Loca* (Mexico, 1985) [False chronicle of Juana the Mad].

Chapter 2 shifts to violent games and the problem of passivity as a strategy of resistance. The games rehearsed and reenacted in Mariela Romero's *El juego* (Venezuela, 1976) [*The Game*] are not uncomplicated, childlike entertainments but instead contain a high degree of violence and real danger. Again, there is no privileged alternative version–the women's mutual abuse works against an interpretation of feigned paralysis and the performance it entails as liberating. Also discussed are Maruxa Vilalta's *Pequeña historia de horror (y de amor desenfrenado)* (Mexico, 1985) [*A Little Tale of Horror (And Unbridled Love)*] and Esteban Navajas's *La agonía del difunto* (Colombia, 1977) [The agony of the deceased].

Chapter 3 turns to the examination of gender itself as performance. The uneasy implications of feigned paralysis and the woman's role in ritual violence and interpretation in *El juego* carry over into the equally, if not more, playful exploration of the construction of a "feminine" identity in Rosario Castellanos's *El eterno femenino*, which traces the multiple performances inherent in "being" feminine. Sabina Berman's *El suplicio del placer* and Susana Torres Molina's . . .*Y a otra cosa mariposa* (Argentina, 1981) [And that's enough of that] destabilize the overall notion of gender. Through its interpretation and enforcement of gender, the audience is once again implicated in the performance.

The audience's importance as enabling witness is still clearer in plays depicting torture and terrorism. Chapter 4 concerns the interwoven nature of horror and spectacle in four plays that deal with physical torment and the effects of theatricalized politics: Mario Benedetti's *Pedro y el Capitán* (Uruguay, 1979) [*Pedro and the Captain*], Eduardo Pavlovsky's *El señor Galíndez* (Argentina, 1973) [*Mr. Galíndez*], Griselda Gambaro's *El campo* (Argentina, 1967) [*The Camp*], and Ariel Dorfman's *La Muerte y la Doncella* (Chile, 1990) [*Death and the Maiden*]. In a consideration of the interplay between theatrical depictions of torture and the use of theatrical imagery in extratheatrical descriptions of torture and terrorism, the question of the text-performance relation arises yet again as a question of the extent to which torture scenes are "scripted."

Finally, Chapter 5 explores the ways in which performance itself–not just the material performed–may be coercive, impossible to realize yet impossible to avoid. Individual characters are the focus not only of a coercive textual authority but of inescapable, exterior demands that they perform. The plays discussed are Isaac Chocrón's *La revolución* (Venezuela, 1971), Gambaro's *Información para extranjeros* (Argentina, 1973) [*Information for Foreigners*] and *El despojamiento* (Argentina, 1974) [The striptease], Berman's *Esta no es una obra de teatro* (1975) [This is not a work of theater], and José Ignacio Cabrujas's *Acto cultural* (Venezuela, 1976) [Cultural ceremony]. Plays centering on nonperformance enact the "emptying out" of the ritual games and the extension of the difficulty (or impossibility) of performing certain types of action to the impossibility of performing at all. At the same time, it is not always the dominance of a preordained *text* that is at issue. In Berman's monologue *Esta no es una obra de teatro*, for instance, an acting student's final exam becomes tortuous because of the *lack* of a text to represent.

Even as performance becomes the vehicle for revisions of history or a critique of culturally imposed gender roles, there are within the model, perhaps unexamined, potentially conservative or coercive implications. If everyone is already a rebel, enjoying the displaced authority of antinarrative, unmediated performance, transformative political action becomes unnecessary. Theatricality offers seductive traps for the interpreter as well. Mária Brewer's caution about the unexamined model of theater underlying theatrical metaphors in theoretical discourse suggests a parallel questioning of the models of performance privileged within dramatic texts.[10] As Taylor argues, "the theatricality of torture and terrorism tempts us to rethink our world, to somehow accept or make room for these performative acts within our canon of the admissible" (*Theatre* 143). The plays I examine highlight the coercive properties of performance along with its potentially liberating contingency. In so doing, they retain performance as a transformative mechanism while acknowledging the degree to which performance is implicated as much in oppressive structures as in liberation. Performance is both space and process of negotiation. As space, performance represents the arena of dispute, the shifting ground of improvisation. As process, performance establishes an ambiguous axis of relating that at any moment might go either way, toward greater freedom or more pronounced coercion. The tension between freedom and compulsion inherent in performance remains constant. Performance is not so much the sign of a universal resistance to a dominant authority as a paradoxical figure which demands compliance even as it draws out a suggestion of rebellion. And the blue leper is that which remains impossible to pin down, of the representation yet apart: the unasked question, the unmet applause, the silent ambivalence of the spectator both lured and repelled by the stage.

---

[10] Brewer argues that the implicit model of the theater underlying theoretical metaphors often goes unexamined, as if there were only one possible–or relevant–theater. Furthermore, Brewer asserts, "theatricalization also possesses a conservative power" largely because of the model of theater uncritically brought into play, "a surprisingly conventional and unproblematic one of textual self-representation that is at odds with the challenge to narrative representation in contemporary writing" (15). She concludes that "because the modes of theatricality that pervade the rhetoric of theory's performance are precisely those that deal with the *parameters* of interpretation and/as performance, they provide an especially relevant opening onto historical and contextual questions" (30).

Chapter 1

PERFORMANCE, TEXTUALITY, AND THE NARRATION OF HISTORY

IN plays in which historical material is reenacted, the performance becomes an acted-out narration for the audience, while "history itself," the recorded events that form the basis of the presentation, is revealed or constructed as a series of provisional, partial, and highly problematic live representations which later become "fact." Reconsiderations of history are a recurrent theme in Latin American theater, perhaps most prominently in Mexico. Examples of plays with historical themes include Rodolfo Usigli's *El gesticulador* (Mexico, 1947) [The gesticulator], René Marqués's *Los soles truncos* (Puerto Rico, 1958) [*The Fanlights*], and Carlos Fuentes's *Todos los gatos son pardos* (Mexico, 1971) [All cats are gray], as well as many other Mexican plays that focus on the figure of La Malinche. Not all such plays necessarily produce revisionist readings of the past. Rather than rewrite the history of the revolution, for example, *El gesticulador* explores the power inherent in the monopolization of historical knowledge (César Rubio boasts, "no hay un solo hombre en México que sepa todo lo que yo sé de la revolución" [there is not a single man in Mexico who knows all that I do about the revolution]) and the seductions of self-dramatization (12; 1.1). In this chapter, I will focus on four plays: Vicente Leñero's *Martirio de Morelos* (Mexico, 1981) [Martyrdom of Morelos], José Antonio Rial's *Bolívar* (Venezuela, 1982), Sabina Berman's *Águila o sol* (Mexico, 1984) [Eagle or sun], and Miguel Sabido's *Falsa crónica de Juana la Loca* (Mexico, 1985) [False chronicle of Juana the Mad].[1] All four texts reflect the interplay of performance and his-

---

[1] No selection of plays here could hope to be exhaustive. The plays under dis-

torical material, presenting both the reinscription of history *through* performance and the reinscription of history *as* performance.[2]

A construction of history as performance (as opposed to the performance of history) encompasses two aspects. First, the history (events, facts) may be presented as performance; for example, the miracle in Rodolfo Usigli's *Corona de luz* (Mexico, 1963) [*Crown of Lights*] is presented as being at some level, though not unambiguously, staged. Secondly, the writing, interpretation, and recording of history may be construed as performance. The performance of historical material may dominate its interpretation, as in *Bolívar*; in *Martirio*, the voice of history is presented in the reading (performance) of El Lector [The Reader].

My argument centers not simply on plays set in the past but on plays in which the historical material is specifically foregrounded and reexamined. The reworking of history in the play creates the possibility of understanding the play itself as history, as the versions of historical events constructed in the plays are placed beside more traditional renderings. In any history play, the playwright's text is necessarily a rewriting of prior historical texts. Although performance is not strictly writing, or rewriting, issues of text and recording are highly important as the written record is reexamined (or performed). Text/script issues are particularly relevant in *Bolívar*, in which the script of the play within the play is frequently challenged on historical as well as aesthetic grounds by the authorities overseeing the production.

The historical play presents a set of events already framed and recognizable for the audience. One aim of self-reflexive, historical drama is to foreground the means through which the framed events reexamined in the play were originally constituted as "history." Sharon Magnarelli defines the history play thus: "historical theatre

---

cussion provide useful contrasts while illustrating a variety of performance strategies. Other plays in which history is represented in terms of performance include Jorge Enrique Adoum's *El sol bajo las patas de los caballos* (Ecuador, 1972) [The sun beneath the horses hooves]; Luis Alberto García's *I Took Panamá* (Colombia, 1974); Guillermo Schmidhuber's *Por las tierras de Colón* (Mexico, 1986) [In the lands of Columbus]; and Raúl Arias and Iván Toledo's *Luces y espejos en la oscuridad* (Ecuador, 1990) [Lights and mirrors in the darkness].

[2] This corresponds to what Hayden White calls the "performance model of discourse," according to which "a discourse is regarded as an apparatus for the production of meaning rather than as only a vehicle for the transmission of information about an extrinsic referent" (*Content* 42).

centers on a specific time, place, and events, already recorded, as opposed to other theatrical forms which derive their universality from their nonspecificity. In this regard, historical theatre is always a rewriting or rereading of prior discourse" ("Dramatic" 55). Herbert Lindenberger notes that "our first notion in reflecting about a history play is not to view it as an imaginative structure in its own right but to ask how it deals with its historical materials" (3). For this reason, the preexisting, contextual frame may dominate reception of the play. The existence of prior audience frameworks is by no means unique to the history play. Barbara Foley observes that "there are no innocent perceptions: if perception is to produce cognition, it must invoke a framework of prior assumptions about what is being seen" (36). This is perhaps doubly true of the history play, especially the play designed to question those prior assumptions.

At the same time, as Hayden White points out, "the presumed concreteness and accessibility of historical milieux, these contexts of the texts that literary scholars study, are themselves products of the fictive capability of the historians who have studied those contexts" (*Tropics* 89). Jacqueline Bixler stresses the "ambiguity contained within the word 'history' itself, which at once signifies the events as they purportedly occurred at a given time and place and the subsequent written narrative of those same episodes" ("Historical" 90). The ambiguity is extended in Spanish as *historia* alludes as well to a fictional narrative, a convergence supported by White's analysis of the similarity of historical to fictive discourse.[3] Facts are not givens, but become facts only through interpretation, and no single prior text of the history play can be privileged as unambiguously accurate. Each must be understood as a partial, contingent account.

The problematic temporality of performance relates to the equally problematic temporality of the history play, in which tem-

---

[3] White contends that "events are *made* into a story by the suppression or subordination of certain of them and the highlighting of others, by characterization, motific repetition, variation of tone and point of view, alternative descriptive strategies, and the like–in short, all of the techniques that we would normally expect to find in the emplotment of a novel or a play" (*Tropics* 84). In a similar vein, Linda Hutcheon discusses "historiographic metafiction" in which "the text's self-reflexivity points in two directions at once, toward the events being represented in the narrative and toward the act of narration itself. This is precisely the same doubleness that characterizes all historical narrative. Neither form of representation can separate 'facts' from the acts of interpretation and narration that constitute them, for facts (though not events) are created in and by those acts" (76).

poral boundaries are blurred (within recognizable stage conventions) as in the encounters between the characters of Morelos and El Lector in *Martirio*. Performance highlights the framing inherent in the use of historical material in order to examine both the historical context and its distortions. Through the use of foregrounded performance, these playwrights address both the aesthetic and political manifestations of what Diana Taylor has called social theatricalization. It is important to recognize that "performance" may carry its own ideological baggage, a problem treated in Mária Brewer's discussion of performance theory. In these plays, performance is constructed as a destabilizing practice. Taylor argues that "la teatralización social no es antitética ni al teatro ni al performance art sino que sería el elemento deconstructivo capaz de cuestionar la ideología subyacente de todo sistema cultural de representación" ("Negotiating" 50) [social theatricalization is antithetical to neither theater nor performance art but rather it would be the deconstructive element capable of questioning the underlying ideology of any cultural system of representation]. In the history play, multiple, interrelated systems of representation become operative, including those concerned with factual events, fictional narrative, and national mythologizing. In the plays under consideration, the use and representation of performance within the texts calls all of these into question.

The four plays discussed here deal with historical moments of violence, one explicitly within a contemporary (and frame play) context of terror. The oppression and violence within the plays is tied to the conceptual violence of the official histories they contest. Taylor describes a "theatre of crisis" in which "the moment of crisis is one of rupture, of critical irresolution, the 'in between' of life and death, order and chaos. And because these plays combine feelings of decomposition with the threat of imminent extinction, they often reflect the moment of annihilation and/or terror. The characters, locked in a dreadful present, perceive time as a contradiction. The historical moment is lived as ahistorical" (*Theatre* 56). Although the plays I will examine do not correspond entirely to Taylor's theater of crisis, the temporal contradictions she describes are relevant. The interplay of the contradictory time of the ahistorical moment of terror and the attempt to recuperate time through historical representation is particularly evident in *Bolívar*, in which the prison camp inmates staging the historical drama are subjected to offstage physical torture in the space between interior play and extratheatrical reality. In all four plays the temporal dislocations produced by performance as well as by the historical material itself are compounded by the tension between the atemporal moment of terror and the temporality of its reproduction.

Vicente Leñero's documentary play *Martirio de Morelos* centers on the trials and execution of José María Morelos, hero of Mexican independence. The play is divided into two parts, each in turn subdivided into numbered segments. Performance is tied to the representation of history through the performance of the historical record, realized in this play as both reading aloud and acting out. History as text appears in two senses: history can be read (interpreted) as a text; history is that which is contained in a book. At issue, too, is the disjunction between Morelos's interpretation of events and that offered in the permanent record; hence his concern as to whether El Lector's book has pardoned him and his need to recognize himself in the (written) history. It is from this lack of recognition that Morelos pulls back, remembering his last days not as a heroic martyrdom but as a desperate, earth-shattering collapse.

The exchanges between El Lector and Morelos comprise the openly fabricated portion of the play. As such, the construction of Morelos as a character might be especially vulnerable to historically based (or mythically based) criticisms. The relations between Morelos and El Lector contain a tension, as El Lector struggles to retain his preconceptions and Morelos worries about his reception. Morelos's contact with El Lector is also mediated by other characters, as when a priest interrupts El Lector to say that the prisoner must remain incommunicado. Morelos's encounters with El Lector tend to raise questions of reception and to highlight the interpretive role of the audience.

Although Leñero's play relies on documentary material, it diverges in several ways from accepted definitions of documentary drama. Peter Weiss suggests that "Documentary Theatre is a reflection of life as we witness it through the mass media, re-defined by asking various critical questions," which is a definition that implies contemporary subject matter (41). However, the division between historical drama and a necessarily contemporary documentary drama is not hard and fast. Pedro Bravo-Elizondo proposes that the selection of historical moments for documentary theater produces its own set of questions that must be resolved: "por qué un personaje histórico, un período, una época, son sepultados en el olvido; quiénes se benefician con esta omisión" (204) [why a historical character, a time period, an era, are buried in oblivion; who benefits from this omission].[4] In addition to fictional and historical characters, past and present moments, *Martirio* combines a variety of "documents," so that a poem by Carlos Pellicer is placed alongside the judicial proceedings. Leñero's choice of subject is not a forgotten man so much as one excessively yet inadequately remembered, part history, part myth, and his text is thus both contemporary and historical, a partially documentary play.

Priscilla Meléndez describes "the disruption between the expected theatricality of performance and the absence of overt dramatic action in *Martirio de Morelos*," arguing that "few things might seem less dramatic than reading on stage from a history book to an audience that normally would not tolerate the absence or minimization of theatrical action" ("On Leñero's" 53). One might add that this action is particularly nondramatic to the extent that "drama" is believed to contain some inherent suspense or unknown, an unresolved tension, while the history El Lector reads is the widely accepted history known to the audience. Magnarelli proposes in her discussion of *Falsa crónica*, "if we begin by defining historical theatre as those dramatic works which center on a familiar figure or incident from history, then by definition such theatre is predicated on dramatic irony, since the events and their conclusions are already known to the spectator but not to the characters themselves" ("Dramatic" 47). Although the audience's familiarity with the events portrayed does not necessarily undermine the play's theatricality, this prior knowledge is implicated in the process of foregrounded yet undermined (historical) textuality that Leñero's play presents.

---

[4] Similarly, Leñero argues that the difference between historical and documentary drama is one of intention: "El drama histórico normalmente no se preocupa por el presente y es más como un escape hacia el pasado. Y el drama documental, un poco como lo entendían Peter Weiss y Piscator, es tomar el pasado pero para reflejar nuestro presente. Claro, en un continente como Latinoamérica, donde todo está por escribirse, todo es documental, todo nos está hablando de nuestro presente" (Nigro, "Entrevista" 80-81) [Historical drama normally does not concern itself with the present and is more an escape to the past. And documentary drama, as understood by Peter Weiss and Piscator, uses the past to reflect our present. Of course, in a continent like Latin America, where everything is yet to be written, everything is documentary, everything is talking to us about our present].

The character's lack of knowledge is complicated. The events of his last days are well known to the character Morelos; he never asks El Lector, How did I die? Instead, it is the reception of those days as historical text that worries him. Lindenberger points out that statements that take advantage of hindsight, as when a character in a historical drama confidently predicts the future, "provide an easy means of asserting the historical reality of what is happening on stage, but in another sense they serve as a way of breaking the illusion, at least to the extent that we see the events on stage spilling over into a historical continuum." Moreover, "such statements also increase our participation in the play, for through our hindsight about how things eventually worked themselves out in history, we flatter ourselves that we, in effect, can sit like demigods presiding omnisciently over the action" (6). An explanation for the outrage often caused by revisionist histories may lie in part in the violation of the audience's omniscience, the deliberate denial of the audience's privileged hindsight. Morelos's concern with his reception layers yet another audience between Morelos the character, interpreted in such and such a way in a specific book, and the theatrical audience reading the stage performance against its prior knowledge of the hero.

Issues of sources and of textuality are central to *Martirio*, not only through the use of documentary records, but in the exchanges between characters. Many historical plays acknowledge or list their sources of information. Leñero is particularly detailed in his catalogue, noting which texts served as base material for which segments of his play and describing departures from the record. However, this apparent precision may be misleading. As Bixler makes clear, "instead of reinforcing the credibility of the documents contained within the text, Leñero consciously undermines the authority of these same documents and of historical writing in general by presenting in one work contradictory versions of the same historical phenomena" ("Historical" 88). The play sets up a tension between document or raw materials–such as court papers or historical accounts–and the performance of those documents, with performance encompassing reading aloud or acting out as well as the process of interpretation. It is in the moment of performance that slippage occurs and all prior versions of the history represented are called into question. The shift between document and performance occurs at multiple levels: between Leñero and the reader (as in the

"Advertencias"), between play and theater audience, and between characters within the play. The play of textual accuracy, at any given level, may be double edged. Bixler notes that "the heading, 'advertencias,' suggests some form of warning, yet rather than prepare the audience for a character portrayal in complete disaccord with popular history, Leñero merely acknowledges minor stylistic revisions in the court transcripts and other legal documents" ("Historical" 91). The exactness with which Leñero cites his authorizing historical sources suggests that his relation to these sources, his position vis-à-vis the official record, is not so much antagonistic as intended to modify. A further possibility is that the mere fact of reading aloud and acting out–performing–changes the meaning of the official documents, or at least their tone, so that few adjustments are necessary.

In the prologue, Morelos approaches, with exaggerated casualness, a book lying open on a lectern. Interrupted in his reading by El Lector, Morelos asks whether he appears in the book, eliciting El Lector's first recitation of the official record. Morelos's physical confrontation with history in the tangible form of the book is repeated in the fourth section of Part One. When El Lector leaves the stage, Morelos "Al cerciorarse de su ausencia adopta un aire de abandono. Reacciona. Se aproxima al libro y se pone a hojearlo y a leer con cierta febrilidad" (73; pt. 1, sc. 4) [adopts an air of abandonment upon ascertaining his absence. He reacts. He approaches the book and starts to leaf through it and to read with a certain feverishness]. What Meléndez has called the nondramatic action of reading on stage applies not only to El Lector but to Morelos as well. Yet despite Morelos's desire to ascertain what history says about him, he also questions the book's accuracy. Early in the play, when El Lector reads: "Sus jueces lo trataron como a un endemoniado. Fue un mártir" [His judges treated him like one possessed by the devil. He was a martyr], Morelos asks: "¿Emplea el libro la palabra mártir?, ¿textualmente?" (19; pt. 1, sc. 1) [Does the book use the word martyr? Textually?]. Discounting his martyrdom as "un martirio que no resistió" [a martyrdom that he did not resist], Morelos overrides El Lector's assertion that "históricamente hablando es imposible determinarlo" (19; pt. 1, sc. 1) [historically speaking it is impossible to determine]. He insists: "El fin se precipitó de golpe como un terremoto. Fue demasiado para su ánimo herido" (19; pt. 1, sc. 1) [The end came suddenly like an earthquake. It was too much for his wounded spirit]. Morelos refers to himself in the third person, his voice that of yet another historian. Although El Lector tries once more–"El libro dice . . ." [The book says . . .]–the Prologue closes with Morelos's assertion: "El libro no sabe lo que fueron esos últimos días" (19; pt. 1, sc. 1) [The book does not know what those last days were like]. Hearing the contents of the book, receiving history's pardon, is necessary, but it is not enough.

The issue of textual exactness, both in Leñero's prefatory "Advertencias" and in Morelos's concern as to whether the book actually uses the word martyr, is tied to the question of performance. There is a need, at one level, to make certain of what is performed, what constitutes the base material, so that in a sense Leñero's "performance" of his own prior reading, in the form of his play, must be properly grounded. At the same time, the supposed split between text and performance is continually called into question. In part this subversion of the text/performance split is inherent in the documentary genre. The text/performance division generally refers to the distinction between a playscript and a performance of (or based on) that script. Here, the performance is not only *of* the text, it is *about* the text. *Martirio de Morelos* questions the fixity of the historical record, attempting, through performance, to restore some of the complexity that inhered in the original, replaced by sententious aphorisms about Morelos's heroism and martyrdom. The texts of history become as unstable as performance itself, as improvisational and unfixed.

In *La ruta crítica de "Martirio de Morelos,"* Leñero reprints a selection of critical responses to the play, along with a narrative of its initial production and the text of the play itself. The narrative, "Crónica," includes the transcribed texts of letters and telegrams written to protest the threatened prohibition of the play's opening and can be read as its own documentary performance. Leñero's stated intention was to humanize the hero: "estaba convencido [. . .] que los amargos episodios de su triple proceso antes que infamar al siervo de la nación lo exaltan, porque lo humanizan" (*La ruta* 19) [I was convinced {. . .} that the bitter episodes of his triple trial exalt the "slave of the nation" rather than slander him, because they make him human]. Taken with received history, Leñero implies, *Martirio* ought to have provided a more complex vision of Morelos, although this total portrayal would of necessity be highly dependent on the context of interpretation. (A non-Mexican audience, lacking prior knowledge of the hero's stature, would receive a substantially different impression.) A frequent objection to Leñero's play was precisely this presentation of Morelos, hero, as weak, broken martyr. Leñero's choice was read not as an expansion or complication of the image of the hero but as a highlighting of the *wrong* facet, a loss of complexity.[5] The critics variously take Leñero to task for historical inaccuracy, for highlighting that which, though true, was best forgotten, and for sullying a national hero. The argument was not always with the objective "truth" of Leñero's sources but with his project of bringing them to light, that is, the performance of the objectionable documents. Julio Figueroa's article cites a letter published in *Unomásuno* which argued: "hay 'verdades' que deben guardarse pudorosamente en el cubículo más sagrado de la Academia de la historia" (148) [there are truths that should be kept chastely in the most sacred cubicle of the Academy of history]. Yet given the well-known character of Morelos the hero, his antiheroic portrayal in Leñero's play necessarily stands in contrast, or in complement, to that standard version; whether or not Leñero's play depicts the heroic aspect of Morelos, that image is intertextually evoked.

El Lector, the play's designated Reader, is not the only one who reads aloud. The "relación" El Militar offers to El Virrey provides an extended narration much like a read document. Following a lengthy description of the battle, the stage direction reads: "Se escenifica la batalla" (24; pt. 1, sc. 2) [The battle is staged]. El Militar continues: "Luego, en una cañada, tomamos prisionero a Morelos que se entregó sin mayor resistencia" (24; pt. 1, sc. 2) [Then, in a gully, we took Morelos prisoner and he surrendered without resis-

---

[5] Leñero's reconsiderations of Morelos take place within a highly charged political context, coinciding with the Morelos-invoking presidential campaign of Miguel de la Madrid. Alan Riding observes that, "In view of De la Madrid's fascination with Morelos, the presentation was presumed to be simple cultural opportunism." However, once the nature of the play became clear, "university authorities intervened to suspend rehearsals, worried not only about offending the President but also about denigrating an immaculate hero. Assorted civic associations then mobilized to defend 'the honor and glory' of Morelos, a leading politician devoted an entire speech to praising the 'founder of the nation' and excoriating his critics, a controversial actor playing the part of Morelos was replaced and the producers took precautions against violent protests when the play was eventually opened to the public" (22-23).

tance]. Breaking from his role as narrator, El Militar approaches Morelos, now surrounded by royalist soldiers, and takes him prisoner. The character as narrator both describes and participates in the action. The destabilizing effect of this foregrounding is related to the questioning of historical documentation throughout Leñero's play. Just as the fluidity of time and context achieved by the character/narrator undermines narrative coherence, the interpenetration of reading, text, and reenactment undermines the coherence of the historical record.

During "La aprehensión" (part 1, scene 2), the First Inquisitor takes out his papers and describes the document he proposes to read: "El promotor fiscal del Santo Oficio se ha tomado la molestia de redactar un pedimento en donde demuestra que el perverso cabecilla Morelos [. . .] incurrió en las excomuniones fulminadas por algunos obispos" (30) [The prosecuting magistrate of the Inquisition has taken the trouble to compose a petition that shows that the perverse hotheaded Morelos {. . .} became a victim of the excommunications fulminated by certain bishops]. Faced with the mounting impatience of El Virrey and El Militar, El Lector steps in to read the notice of excommunication the First Inquisitor has been unable to find. While this substitution suggests the ineptitude (or worse) of the Inquisition, it also presents a seamlessness between Inquisitor and Historian. Accentuating the slippage between Lector and Inquisidor, Inquisidor 1, turning again to El Virrey, closes the reading of the document: "Edicto reafirmado el veintiséis de enero de 1811" (31) [Edict reaffirmed the twenty-sixth of January 1811]. That the historian must fill in the gaps in the reenactment, albeit with ostensibly contemporaneous documentation, implies a lack of clarity in the event, a degree to which the absoluteness of the historical record not only supplements but distorts the original confusion. That El Inquisidor speaks *around* his proofs in this instance–that is, describes the papers he is unable to locate, stalling for time but also contributing to the accumulating condemnations of the prisoner–while the historian offers chapter and verse without missing a beat, presents a certain reversal of roles. The self-serving metadiscourse about the various edicts (the prosecutor has gone to some trouble) occurs even before the edict is read out, whereas the historian, speaking through El Lector, simply gives the "facts." The historian, rather than the contemporary witness, provides the detail in this instance, while the Inquisitor offers only the frame. In this case, it would seem that the history book is less biased than the contemporary account.

The issue of documentary authority also arises within the historical reenactments. Questioned by El Auditor as to whether he has read the official notices in which Fernando VII's return to the throne is established, Morelos replies: "sí se leen las gacetas oficiales pero no se les da mucho crédito" (38; pt. 1, sc. 3) [yes, the official journals are read but they are not given much credence]. Still, it must be remembered that the entire play is dependent on historical documentation or must be imagined anew, as all of the events portrayed occur well before living memory. El Inquisidor's version appears less reliable than the text read out by El Lector. In addition, because El Lector has his script quickly to hand, his treatment of that script may be seen as more reliable than that of El Inquisidor. Yet El Lector is performing as well, and his performance, too, calls historical authority into question.[6] El Lector is at once of the action and apart from it, a distanced witness, present for the reenactments but unable, or unwilling, to comment. During a pause in the third segment of the first part, "Proceso de la jurisdicción unida," [Proceedings of the united jurisdiction] Morelos approaches El Lector, whose first words present yet another instance of onstage reading:

> LECTOR: No lo amedrentaron las acusaciones de sus jueces. Enfrentó los cargos con respuestas serenas, sencillas, francas.
> MORELOS: ¿Ésa fue su impresión? ¿Le parece entonces que estuve?
> LECTOR (*interrumpiendo*): Eso dice el libro.
> MORELOS: ¿Pero usted cómo vio el interrogatorio? Traté de ser convincente. Dije la verdad, solamente la verdad . . . ¿O qué piensa?, dígame.
> LECTOR: Es muy poco lo que puedo decir.
> MORELOS: Usted fue testigo. Tendrá una opinión personal.
> LECTOR: Yo no tengo opiniones personales, me limito a escuchar lo que escucho.

---

[6] In Luis de Tavira's production of *Martirio de Morelos*, El Lector was replaced by a history seminar, making the "voice of history" initially represented by El Lector multivocal from the outset (Leñero, *La ruta* 25). The performance history of the play is clearly important. At the same time, the interplay of text and performance in the published version of the play remains striking, and will be the focus of my analysis here.

MORELOS: ¿Me vio temeroso?
LECTOR: El libro dice que estuvo sereno, impávido, valiente, inalterable.
MORELOS: Pero qué dice usted. Usted que se hallaba aquí. Usted que me vio, que me escuchó hablar.
LECTOR: Yo no sé más de lo que se encuentra escrito en el libro. (47-48; pt. 1, sc. 3)

[LECTOR: The accusations of the judges didn't intimidate him. He rebutted the charges with calm, simple, frank answers.
MORELOS: Was that your impression? Do you think I was . . .?
LECTOR (*interrupting*): That's what the book says.
MORELOS: But how did you see the interrogation? I tried to be convincing. I told the truth, only the truth . . . Or what do you think? Tell me.
LECTOR: I can't tell you much.
MORELOS: You were a witness. You must have a personal opinion.
LECTOR: I don't have personal opinions, I only listen to what I hear.
MORELOS: Did you think I was timid?
LECTOR: The book says you were calm, brave, valiant, unalterable.
MORELOS: But what do you say. You were here. You saw me, you heard me speak.
LECTOR: I don't know more than what's written in the book.]

Morelos is concerned about his performance in fairly traditional terms: Did I do well? Was I convincing? Appealing to the Lector's presence at the trial as the basis for a reaction, he brings in the issue of the witness (an issue that will become salient in *Bolívar* as well). An additional problem for Morelos, resuscitated for this portrayal of his life, is the impersonal quality of the record. History may laud him as hero and martyr, but no single person can tell him how he did. The physical presence of Morelos as an individual disrupts the historical discourse that presence is meant to illuminate. Morelos is, in effect, the blue leper, the figure whose presence on stage disrupts all prior or provisional interpretations.

El Lector can read at length from the book occupying the lectern, answering Morelos's questions, but he cannot speak for himself or judge the passages he reads. His position coincides with the presumed "objectivity" of the modern historian. However, such objectivity is framed as a deliberate self-silencing, a turning away from available evidence. Bixler argues that "the Lector's reluctance to discredit the book and to concede authority to the mounting evidence of betrayal will likely be shared by the audience, whose growing identification with the Lector owes in large part to his status as the only present-day, non-historical character and to his anonymity" ("Historical" 92). El Lector's unwillingness to discredit the book also reflects his role as reader of official history. The anonymous scholar unwilling to doubt his hero becomes a stand-in for the audience's reluctance to question the received account of Morelos's life. (Again, the effect may be mitigated for a non-Mexican audience less familiar with the heroic rendering of Morelos.) The suggestion that El Lector's self-silencing "objectivity" is in fact a deliberate distortion comes into conflict with the audience's own desire to resist the revised version that the character of Morelos represents. The status of the audience with all the answers that Lindenberger describes is challenged. In this case, the play contains as well a confrontation with the audience, not only in the subject matter–the perceived reconsideration of a national hero–but in the organization of the play.

It is also possible to read this passage as an indication of the historian's frustration at his limitations. Much as El Lector might wish to go beyond what he reads, he has no other information. In this way, Morelos might function as a projection of El Lector's imagination, a prodding figment that questions the firmly established boundaries of his knowledge without providing additional material. When he witnesses the reenactments, El Lector finds himself in a position contemporaneous to the events he describes, yet his ability to judge derives from his retrospective knowledge. His inability to intervene corresponds to the limits of his vision, to the fact that the authority of anything he might learn about Morelos, whether contained in the lectern's giant book or in the framed reenactments, is suspect. From a metatheatrical perspective, this scene shows Morelos *unable* to recognize his position in a script and unwilling to accept El Lector as distant audience rather than controlling playwright–that is, as receiving (reading) information rather than producing (writing) his own judgment.

El Lector becomes less noncommittal later in the play. When El Militar, reading Morelos's sentence, describes Morelos's offer to "escribir en lo general y en lo particular a los rebeldes para retraerlos de su errado sistema," [write generally and particularly to the rebels to dissuade them from their mistaken system], El Lector interrupts: "De eso nunca se habló aquí. Es mentira. Morelos nunca ofreció" (126; pt. 2, sc. 7) [That was never talked about here. It's a lie. Morelos never offered]. At this moment, El Lector steps down from his lectern as the unimaginable charge leads him to doubt. El Lector, representative of the historical record as it has been passed down to succeeding generations, begins to question his sources. Although he quickly returns to the podium, the move away from the book allows him to discuss what is *not* written in it. Physical distance from the book allows mental distance as well, providing the necessary space, at least briefly, in which to doubt.

In the final scene, El Lector's elegiac assertion that Morelos's existence "como héroe, como estadista, como caudillo, como ejemplo, continúa vivo en las sagradas páginas de la historia de su grandiosa epopeya" [as a hero, as a statesman, as leader, as an example, continues to live in the sacred pages of the history of his great epic] is challenged by El Virrey, who accuses him of lying and insists that he is covering up Morelos's retraction (130; pt. 2, sc. 7). Arguing that his book acknowledges the existence of the retraction but considers it spurious, El Lector quotes directly: "En 1851, Lucas Alamán escribió: (*Leyendo*) 'Una retractación que con la firma de Morelos se publicó por el gobierno después de la ejecución, y que llevaba la fecha diez de diciembre, no hay apariencia alguna de que fuese suya pues es enteramente ajena a su estilo . . .'" (131; pt. 2, sc. 7) [In 1851, Lucas Alamán wrote: (*Reading*) "A retraction that was published with Morelos's signature by the government after the execution, and that was dated the tenth of December, does not appear to be his since it is entirely foreign to his style . . ."]. El Lector's ongoing reliance on his sources is emphasized. The reading of the retraction does not appear in the revised version of the play published in *La ruta crítica de "Martirio de Morelos."* Yet whether or not the retraction is included, the play has already demonstrated that Morelos's last days were not unquestionably heroic but that this reality has not diminished his portrayal in history as myth. The retraction itself becomes redundant, although its placement at the end of the play gives it additional weight in the face of El Lector's–and other historians'–objections.

The discussion between El Lector and El Virrey over whether to include the retraction is illustrative of the historian's role. Privileging the objective "witness" to past events (or the documents left by such witnesses), El Virrey counters El Lector's refusal to read "un documento amañado" [a fake document] with the assertion: "A usted no le toca juzgarlo" (132; pt. 2, sc. 7) [It's not for you to judge]. El Lector's rejection of the retraction contradicts his earlier refusal to pass judgment, a refusal that may be as self-protecting as it is "objective." He resists the inclusion of the retraction in his reading because "esto ya terminó. [. . .] Morelos está muerto," [this already finished. {. . .} Morelos is dead] an obviously moot point as Morelos has been dead since before the play began (132; pt. 2, sc. 7). Meléndez comments that this final scene "is extremely effective in its antagonism with conventional structures of representation, and it clearly serves as a *dramatic* strategy to underline the complex, ambiguous and even contradictory nature of documentary drama" ("On Leñero's" 54). El Lector's deliberate selection of the text he will include dramatizes the constitution of both historical and theatrical texts in performance and underscores the authority performance can confer.

The historian's role as editor, condensing the "raw data," is illustrated in section 6, "Proceso de la Jurisdicción Militar" [Proceedings of the Military Jurisdiction]. As Morelos mimes his own speech, El Lector reads it in abbreviated form; the stage direction requires that "Morelos habla ante el tribunal pero su voz resulta ahora inaudible. Sustituye a su relato, lo abrevia, el parlamento del Lector" (106; pt. 2, sc. 6) [Morelos speaks before the tribunal but his voice now becomes inaudible. The Lector's speech replaces his story and cuts it short].[7] The read voice of "history" overwhelms (in this case replaces) the voice of the past as heard in the past. At the same time, it is evident that history, as discourse, alters or edits the past rather than offering a verbatim account, if that were possible, of events as they occurred.[8] When El Lector begins to read, his account is a description, rather than a quotation, of what Morelos said; he offers a narrative about the trial rather than a transcript:

---

[7] At other times, Morelos is the one speaking another's lines. In the "Auto de fe" that opens the second part of the play, "un miembro encapuchado de la Inquisición le va dictando en voz baja las frases que Morelos repite en voz alta" (91; pt. 2, sc. 5) [a hooded member of the Inquisition dictates softly the phrases that Morelos repeats aloud].

[8] White stresses the degree to which the "commonplace" that "historical discourse does not represent a perfect equivalent of the phenomenal field it purports to describe [. . .] is usually construed as a simple *reduction* by selection, rather than as the *distortion* which it truly is" (*Tropics* 111).

"Amplia, prolijamente, Morelos describió ante la Jurisdicción Militar sus campañas guerreras. Cómo salió de Carácuaro con sólo veinticinco hombres y llegó al Aguacatillo [. . .]. Cómo libró su primera acción militar en el Veladero el trece de noviembre de 1810" (106; pt. 2, sc. 6) [Long-windedly and in great detail, Morelos described his military campaigns before the Military Jurisdiction. How he left Carácuaro with only twenty-five men and arrived at Aguacatillo {. . .}. How he fought his first military action in the Veladero on the thirteenth of November 1810]. El Lector's summary eliminates the detail that is at the heart of the Jurisdicción Militar's interest: El Lector informs the audience that Morelos told the court how he did such and such a thing; he does not, however, tell *us* how. The scene echoes El Inquisidor's earlier description of the document he meant to read but was unable to find. Again, the historical voice must be provided by El Lector. At the same time, the open acknowledgment of abridgment cannot but undermine, at least partially, the authority of El Lector's ostensibly complete text. The experience offered by El Lector is clearly one of reading: not only is he reading, but the way he reads recalls other instances of reading. The inviolable authority of all historical texts is continually questioned.

Meléndez notes that "the realization that *Martirio de Morelos* is for [the] most part a text to be read and not necessarily to be transformed into a performance act, suggests Leñero's evident awareness of the anti-dramatic nature of his 'play'" ("On Leñero's" 57). I would argue that the play's strength lies precisely in the tension between reading and performance that Meléndez underscores. As Meléndez observes in a footnote, there are "important parallelisms between the act of selecting and interpreting documents and the act of staging a documentary play, since they both represent subjective acts of interpretation" ("On Leñero's" 63). It is the reading-as-performance which ultimately produces both the questioning of historical authority, as the documents of both official and alternative versions are given voice, and the recreation of Morelos as less mythified entity.

El Lector's performance is not so much a direct presentation of Morelos's testimony as it is a historian's narrative rendering of that testimony, a testimony that undermines both the original event (by cutting off any direct audience contact with it) and a textual rendition clearly at odds with its origins. The distortion of this material may not be deliberate, but the lack of fit is inevitable, given the necessarily mediating position of the historical narrative. The role of El Lector demonstrates that when the material read is called into question, what remains (or rather, replaces it as authoritative version) is not necessarily either the reading or the performance. Based as it is on a questionable script, El Lector's reading is no more reliable than Morelos's desperate attempts to appear convincing to his judges. Morelos's self-consciousness, his awareness that he is performing a role, is evident in his concern as to whether he was successful. Yet as El Lector's text replaces Morelos's performance for the jury, El Lector's voice replaces Morelos through a text, but as a performance. As he stresses repeatedly, El Lector is not creating his text but reading it, much like an actor closely following a script. Nevertheless, while El Lector's voice supersedes that of Morelos, the silent reenactment by Morelos upstages El Lector's narrative. The opening stage direction of "La aprehensión" describes a scene in which "en el fondo del escenario, Morelos se reúne con un grupo de insurgentes armados [. . .]. A la derecha, en el proscenio, el Virrey se encuentra con el Militar. A la izquierda, el Lector frente al atril" (23; pt. 1, sc. 2) [at the back of the stage, Morelos meets with a group of armed insurgents {. . .}. To the right, in the proscenium, the Virrey meets with the Militar. To the left, the Lector stands in front of the lectern]. This upstage/downstage division of reenactment and narration is visible later in the scene when "la persecución dentro del foro se lleva a cabo mientras el Militar profiere su relación al Virrey" (24; pt. 1, sc. 2) [the pursuit in the upstage area is carried out while the Militar makes his report to the Viceroy]. The stage positioning presents a visual representation of the displacement of both official history and textual authority.

While the reenactment of historical events is not eliminated from Leñero's play, there is a shift in emphasis, so that what is stressed is the performance of the history text, the reading (performance) of the enormous book that dominates the lectern. This foregrounding carries with it a comment on the extratheatrical privileging of the official, popular version of Morelos's death, a version which cannot, it seems, be fully displaced even within a questioning play. Morelos "himself" (i.e., the actor playing Morelos) is pushed to the background.[9] Again, as Bixler points out, Leñero's play does

---

[9] A further doubling of visual representation and historical narration occurs at the beginning of the military trial. El Virrey, posed rigidly for the court painter

not privilege a particular version.[10] Yet the act of highlighting (or simply presenting) elements of the story ordinarily deemphasized or glossed over–the duality of Morelos, his humanity, his possible retraction–by default becomes an alternative version, although not necessarily an authoritative version. Historical discourse mediates past and present, but here only through the performance–the literal reading aloud–of historical texts. The "facts" presented are then doubly mediated, first through the textual account, then through the performance of that account. The use of performance within the play is instrumental in the questioning of both received and alternative histories.

Like *Martirio de Morelos*, Rial's *Bolívar* presents the performance of a portion of the historical record. Here, however, it is not the record as such that is performed but an interior drama based on historical events. The text is divided into eighteen numbered segments, many quite short, rather than acts and scenes. The play takes place in a concentration camp, in which the prisoners are to perform a play based on the last days of Simón Bolívar in Santa Marta, a coerced performance which, ultimately, never moves beyond rehearsal.[11] The final cancellation of the performance is prefigured in El Funcionario's violent command "¡Calle!" [Quiet!] which initiates the rehearsal (28; sc. 2). El Poeta, author of the script for the

---

composing his portrait, listens attentively as El Lector provides an extended verbal description, encompassing the viceroy's family background, refined manners, and military exploits (99; pt. 2, sc. 6). The painted portrait, still in progress, is supplemented by El Lector's copious documentation. Again, the latter-day, historical record supersedes the reenactment of earlier events. In their flattery of the viceroy, the two portraits may be functionally equivalent. However, the historical record is given voice, in a manner similar to the scene in which Morelos gestures mutely in the background while El Lector at the podium provides the information.

[10] This interpretation immediately comes into conflict with the generic expectations of documentary theater. As Judith Bissett puts it, "segments of life–documents–are organized in the most effective manner for presentation, placed on stage and become, not counterfactual occurrences, but alternative views of factual events" (71). Leñero's transgression of genre expectations is discussed more fully in Meléndez's study of *Martirio*.

[11] The forced performance within a concentration camp recalls Gambaro's *El campo*. The fact that the play is never officially performed, or never performed start to finish without breaks, places it with the unrealized performances, or nonperformances, discussed in chapter 5. The performance as rehearsal is also part of the nonperformance structure. *Bolívar* is discussed here, rather than in the later chapter, because of its use of historical material, explicitly in terms of performance. Unless otherwise noted, all citations refer to the Monte Avila edition of the play.

play within the play written under El Funcionario's strict vigilance, "ha logrado intercalar hechos o argumentos heterodoxos, prohibidos" (25) [has managed to intertwine heterodoxical and prohibited arguments]. History, performance, and contemporary reality are linked in *Bolívar*. Rial argues in his preface to the play: "Respecto a si en un campo de concentración se podría intentar una representación teatral con presos, en homenaje a Bolívar, es más que verosímil, por más que la verosimilitud en arte no nos preocupa demasiado. No es casualidad que los dictadores y sus ministros en esta América sean todos 'bolivarianos.' No pierden fecha –es lo único que no pierden–, propicia para elogiar a su ídolo de bronce o piedra. Y como en los países de dictadura casi todos los artistas están presos o en exilio, no hay nada extraño en que con actores 'de verdad cautivos', haya que montar un 'Bolívar' de teatro" (20) [To attempt a theatrical performance in homage to Bolivar with prisoners in a concentration camp is more than credible, although the credibility of art does not worry us too much. It is no accident that the dictators and their ministers in this America are all 'Bolivarians'. They do not miss a propitious date –that is the only thing they do not miss–, to elegize their idol of bronze or stone. And since in the countries under dictatorships almost all of the artists are in prison or exile, there is nothing strange in having actors who are 'really captives' present a theatrical presentation of 'Bolívar'].[12] The opening stage direction reiterates the point: the play will be presented by "presos, entre los cuales hay actores" (25) [prisoners, among whom there are actors]. Ironically, the artists often singled out for repression are, once imprisoned, obliged to exercise their arts. In keeping with the need for practice that the rehearsals represent, as well as with the unwillingness of many of the performers, there are frequent instances of forgotten lines, missed cues, and a general inability to perform. These performance difficulties are compounded by the instability of the script, frequently attacked by prison censors. The rehearsals establish a constant tension between the text as written by El Poeta and as edited by El Funcionario. Yet neither El

---

[12] Among the exiled artists is Rial, himself a Spanish exile in Venezuela. The myriad reverent portrayals of Bolívar in Latin American literature form an implicit context of Rial's play. Examples might include José Joaquín de Olmedo's "Canto a Junín" or commemorative collections such as Tiello's *Los poetas a Bolívar* or Castañón's *Bolívar y los poetas*.

Poeta's nor El Funcionario's text will ultimately be performed; the performance is limited to the rehearsals.

The ironies of the manipulation of the Bolívar figure, on and off stage, are multiple. Despite the clear linkage of acting or performance and coercion, the rehearsals may also be curiously liberating. The prisoner playing Bolívar, a "dangerous criminal" brought in wearing handcuffs, is uncuffed during his performance (31; sc. 5). The name, "El Preso Bolívar," stresses the actor's two roles, Prisoner and Bolívar, while offering as a secondary meaning "Bolívar imprisoned," his legacy reduced to high-sounding oratory within a fascist camp. As Kirsten Nigro explains, "the distinction Bolívar/prisoner, character/actor is always clear; at the same time, an insinuat[ion] is that Bolívar, like his interpreter, is also a prisoner–a prisoner of official history" ("History" 39). Yet Bolívar is not an unambiguous figure of liberation. Accused of Napoleonic tendencies by many of his contemporaries, he was himself something of a dictator. Rial also addresses the issue of "irreverence" in his treatment of Bolívar, both in the overall presentation and in the use of a ragged prisoner to play the hero (17-18). A key effort in both *Bolívar* and *Martirio de Morelos* is to undercut the reverence of the mythified versions that have usurped the heroes' names, striving rather to humanize the revolutionary figures.[13]

Like spectators taking their places, as the second scene opens, "El Funcionario y sus guardianes avanzan y vigilan" (27; sc. 2) [The Funcionario and his wardens advance and watch]. Their vigilance parallels that of the theatrical audience. The presence of this ominous, in no way disinterested, audience also addresses the theatrical audience's willingness to observe, even participate in, heroic anniversary pageants, no matter how they are produced. By extension, the prison guards, silently vigilant, implicate the audience's nonintervention in the many real prison camps the play is meant to evoke. The use of a figure commemorated, as Rial stresses, by a variety of authoritarian regimes, establishes an overlap between the theatrical audience of *Bolívar* and that same audience's witness, if not support, of the Bolívar pageants realized offstage, in the streets

---

[13] Irreverence plays a rather different role in *Águila o sol*, with its obscene games and street theater conventions. Juana la Loca, in turn, is hardly a figure obscured by self-interested reverence but more properly the reverse, relegated in her treatment, marked by the tag Loca, to a clichéd historical scorn.

of the "países bolivarianos" [Bolivarian countries] that *Bolívar's* camp represents. The question of the visible, and hence of performance as something to be seen, and the tension between safety and danger in being observed are evident as well.[14] History is again treated in terms of vigilance when the character Bolívar observes: "No se trata de confesar o de no confesar. No es cuestión de forcejeo con la Iglesia o con el obispo. Es esta Historia vigilante y son estos hombres acuciosos, desalmados en su oficio, quienes estudiarán con lupa cada papel que escribí, febrilmente, a amigos y rivales" (45; sc. 12) [It has nothing to do with confessing or not confessing. It is not a question of violent struggles with the Church or the bishop. It is this vigilant History and these zealous men, heartless in their work, who will study with a magnifying glass each paper I feverishly wrote to friends and rivals]. Given the emphasis on watching, the action (along with listening) most identified with the spectator, the vigilance of the historian is again that of the audience.

The idea of history in or as book, already treated in *Martirio*, is significant in Rial's play as well. Bolívar refers to "la Historia, ese terrible libro," [History, that terrible book] and laments, "No me recordarán por mis ideas. ¿Quién me habrá leído?" (49; sc. 13) [They will not remember me for my ideas. Who will have read me?].[15] As in *Martirio*, official history is represented by a scholar at a lectern. El Erudito, described by El Funcionario as "erudito, filósofo, investigador y especialista en próceres," [erudite, philosopher, investigator and specialist in heroes] presents himself as the owner of knowledge, and his mere entrance on stage strikes terror among

---

[14] Michel Foucault writes of the development of discipline in the seventeenth century, "The exercise of discipline presupposes a mechanism that coerces by means of observation; an apparatus in which the techniques that make it possible to see induce effects of power, and in which, conversely, the means of coercion make those on whom they are applied clearly visible" (170-71).

[15] The quotation, elaborating on the dangers of the dreaded book, continues: "La Historia, ese terrible libro, puede presentarme como un ambicioso, como un pretoriano, como un abyecto ávido de gloria. Y errar hasta cuando me elogie. [. . .] Fui un ser de pasiones, en una época de ferocidad, pero no me batí por mi fama, como piensan, sino por esta obra que concebí inmensa y que se está derrumbando ante mis ojos de moribundo" (49; sc. 13) [History, that terrible book, can present me as ambitious, as praetorian, as an abject person eager for glory. And be mistaken even as it praises me. {. . .} I was a passionate being in a ferocious era. But I didn't sacrifice myself for fame, as they think, but rather for that immense work that I conceived and that is being demolished before my dying eyes].

the prisoners (38; sc. 9). El Erudito also plays the bishop urging Bolívar to make confession, implying a complicity between the church and official history. Such complicity, already treated in *Martirio*, is salient in *Águila o sol* and *Falsa crónica* as well. By playing the bishop, El Erudito presents a further blurring of roles: not only the prisoners are doubly cast. The interior/exterior split between camp and freedom is challenged as the interior play to be performed by the inmates is joined by an actor from outside the prison space.

The interplay of visibility or observation and historical discourse is extended through the image of the reporter. A number of historical plays employ the image of a present-day reporter interrogating a historical figure. "Interrogate" is a loaded word in any event but certainly in the discussion of a play situated within a concentration camp.[16] The term is appropriate, however, because of the pressing nature of the questions posed by the prisoner/reporters. The interview format places historical figures on a level with those who learn about them later. As the interrogation continues, the leveling process may even subordinate the hero, a subordination necessary in order to undo prior mythifications. The reporters' interrogation occurs in scene 12, "El juicio," with its double implication of trial and judgment: "Los presos son ahora la historia e interrogan al Preso Bolívar. Se sugiere que estos presos podrían ser periodistas siglo XX" (44) [The prisoners are now history and they interrogate the Prisoner Bolívar. It is suggested that these prisoners be journalists of the twentieth century]. Bolívar's response is contradictory. After the first round of questions ("¿por qué hizo detener a Miranda?" [why did you have Miranda detained?]), Bolívar responds angrily: "Ustedes son la Historia. ¡Escriban!" (44-45) [You are History. Write!]. Preso 1 then attempts to "write," stating rather than asking: "Miranda se había rendido. Huía" (45) [Miranda had surrendered. He was fleeing]. Whether or not Preso 1 is prodding (criticizing Bolívar for seizing a man who had already surrendered), the act of making a statement is more or less in keeping with Bolívar's demand that he write. Yet the character of Bolívar

---

[16] The use of interrogation here differs from the dynamic of interrogation in plays concerning torture both in its greater narrative purpose–it provides the audience with necessary information–and in the absence of immediate physical violence between questioner and questioned. The issue of interrogation will be explored more fully in chapter 4.

privileges the witness over the historian when he answers: "Los juicios de la historia deberían hacerse en el campo de batalla. En la furia del ataque y la defensa. Cuando se busca el camino de la libertad y todo lo que estorba es derribado. No en frío. (*Retador*): ¿Estaban ustedes allí?" (45) [The judgment of history should be made on the battlefield. In the fury of attack and defense. When one looks for the road to liberty and everything that interferes is knocked down. Not coldly, without the experience. (*Defiant*): Were you there?].[17] One significance of the reporter figure might be an attempt to bridge this divide, as the reporter is supposed to offer a live dispatch. Still, the prisoner/reporters in this scene are writing after the fact, asking Bolívar to justify earlier actions. At the same time, Bolívar expresses concern for what history will say about him. This concern may not be at all contradictory but reflect rather a worry as to how history, inappropriately written "en frío," will distort him.[18]

Distortion in the play is not limited to history texts. El Poeta employs the image of a concave mirror to describe the distortion of everything within the prison. He tells El Erudito: "Se habrá visto en el espejo cóncavo, a la entrada. Alarga mucho las figuras. Incluso las ideas" (38; sc. 9) [You must have seen the concave mirror at the entrance. It stretches figures out a lot. Including ideas]. El Erudito, however, has his answer ready:

> Las ideas, la Historia, los espejos. Todo nos pertenece. ¿No lo sabe? Deberá aprenderlo. ¡El orden! Estáis convencidos de que

---

[17] A similar use of reporter/historian occurs in Luis Alberto García's *I Took Panamá*. In this case, El Actor himself identifies the role of "reportero de la historia" (136) [history's reporter]. Initially, El Reportero limits himself to announcing dates and locations, in the manner of a newspaper dateline. Later he confronts Marroquín directly. The reporter takes on the role of historian, speaking not for posterity but from hindsight. The emphasis on his role as actor underscores again the performance of history, not just as it is reenacted on stage, in a play such as *Bolívar* or *I Took Panamá*, but in the initial writing or recording of events, and in the construction or realization of the events themselves. By speaking directly to the audience, El Actor also effects the connection of audience to historical figure, himself acting as bridge.

[18] The tension expressed here between Bolívar and those who would portray him has its extratheatrical analogue as well. The playwright Carlos José Reyes notes: "también Bolívar en su tiempo protestaba por la desfiguración que de él había hecho la literatura" [in his time, Bolívar also protested the disfiguration that literature had made of him], a protest illustrated in Reyes's essay through an exchange of letters between Olmedo and Bolívar (151).

sabemos guardar el orden. Nada de pensar en espejos, ni convexos, ni cóncavos, ni curvos. La historia es la historia, como los próceres son los próceres, sin refracción posible. Los modelos son arquetipos. Pero los arquetipos son nuestros. Arquetipo de caudillo a caballo: Jefe. Ustedes están aquí para repetir, imitar, copiar, multiplicarse en la obediencia. (38; sc. 9)

[Ideas, History, mirrors. Everything belongs to us. Don't you know that? You should learn. Order! Be convinced that we know how to maintain order. Don't think about mirrors, either convex, concave or curved. History is history, like the heroes are heroes, without any possible refraction. Models are archetypes. But the archetypes are ours. Archetype of the leader on horseback: Chief. You are here to repeat, imitate, copy, multiply yourselves in obedience.]

Under El Erudito's control, no distortion will be allowed, a cutting-off of possibility accomplished when the performance goes unrealized. Only by prohibiting the performance can distortion be effectively evaded. Nevertheless, although the full performance is cut off, the theatrical audience of *Bolívar* is privy to a sufficient portion of the script (as presented in rehearsals) to recognize the alternative vision El Poeta proposes. All of the terms El Erudito offers–imitate, copy, repeat, multiply–are frequently related to performance, at least to a particular kind of "realistic" performance defined as reproduction. It is precisely this mimetic (by his standards), slavishly imitative performance El Erudito demands. Yet the processes of repetition and multiplication underlie performance's instability both for description and as a process in itself. It is the endless multiplication–multiplication in repetition–that characterizes the slipperiness of a performance that cannot be reliably pinned down. The medium the prison rulers have selected for their homage to Bolívar, no matter how carefully they edit the poet's script, will necessarily slip beyond their control.

El Erudito categorically rejects the mirror reference: "He dicho que nada de espejos. Historia es lejanía y abruma frente al glorioso presente. La corona es símbolo decrépito contra nuestra gloriosa República. Como el jefe, opino que la historia la hacemos hoy. El presente exige una corrección de los sucesos pasados. Hay que quemar libros inútiles. Soy especialista en tachar en las páginas los hechos que no debieron suceder" (43; sc. 10) [I said no talk of mirrors. History is remoteness and it clouds over before the glorious present. The crown is a decrepit symbol against our glorious Republic. Like the boss, I think that we make history today. The present demands a correction of past incidents. We must burn useless books. I am a specialist in erasing from the pages facts that shouldn't have happened]. This is the second time El Erudito is identified as "especialista," and the implication is that "próceres" are in some way equivalent to censorship, or at least created through the strategic obliteration of inconvenient "hechos." El Erudito may simply be acknowledging openly his own manipulations of the distortion inevitable in historical writing. As Linda Hutcheon points out, "all past 'events' are potential historical 'facts,' but the ones that become facts are those that are chosen to be narrated" (75). Yet the common acceptance of "fact" as something true gives El Erudito's explanation a particularly sinister cast, as his specialty becomes the crossing out of things he knows to be true.

Bolívar ultimately demands to be removed from El Erudito's history: "Táchame en tu contrahecha historia de bandidos" (62; sc. 17) [Erase me from your forged history of bandits]. Several fictional and historical levels are evident here. The Bolívar who demands to be removed is not Bolívar at all, even within the stage fiction, but a dangerous criminal rehearsing a theatrical role. El Erudito, representing official history (and himself a fictional character), is face to face with an actor speaking as a real historical person. Unlike *Martirio* in which, Bixler argued, the audience would tend to identify with the present-day Lector rather than the historically based characters, all of the historical characters in *Bolívar* are doubled, both prisoner and actor, contemporary and historical, so that the potential for audience identification is filtered through multiple roles.

There is a parallel between the names of enemies Manuela recites and the "enemy names" listed by El Funcionario: "Simón Bolívar, prócer de la Independencia. Simón Bolívar, juramento del Monte Sacro, émulo de Alejandro, émulo de César, émulo de Napoleón, primer caudillo de América," [Simon Bolívar, leader of Independence. Simón Bolívar, oath of Monte Sacro, rival of Alexander, rival of Caesar, rival of Napoleon, first leader of America] and so on in a deafening catalogue that imposes El Funcionario's agenda on Bolívar (or his memory) as surely as any of his competitors might have done (49; sc. 13).[19] The list of enemy labels

---

[19] Bolívar's surfeit of names contrasts with the numbers assigned the prisoners

demonstrates the degree to which Manuela, among others, failed Bolívar's charge: "No permitirás que me transformen en un mito" (48; sc. 13) [Don't allow them to transform me into a myth]. Of course, Bolívar himself (the character) realizes the question is out of Manuela's hands: "será más tarde, después de mi muerte y de la tuya. [. . .] Seré un ídolo, acaso, y sólo quiero ser, en el recuerdo, un hombre" (48; sc. 13) [it will be later, after my death and yours. {. . .} I will be an idol, maybe, and I only want to be, in memory, a man]. Bolívar's words, too, may be disingenuous, producing ironic echoes with both nineteenth-century and more recent criticism of the Liberator's own authoritarian tendencies. The appropriation of Bolívar by the prison officials represents the authoritarian adoption of a leader ostensibly identified with freedom whose degree of egalitarianism nevertheless remains in question. Bolívar's explanation comes after a long pause and El Funcionario's repetition of the cue, originally delivered by Manuela. That this performance gap occurs around the discussion of his historical memory indicates a bleeding between categories, El Preso Bolívar become the dying hero and so unable to follow the rhythm of the previously established script. The dramatic irony Magnarelli discusses as central to historical drama is particularly evident at moments such as this, in which the prisoner, in character as Bolívar, describes precisely the rite of mythification of which his acting as Bolívar forms a part. Yet Bolívar the character also participates in mythification, offering his own idealized vision of Sucre who, in his turn, describes his relation to Bolívar in almost theatrical terms–"me dejó ser el bueno" [he left me to be the good one]–as though that were the role left him once the traitors had been cast (61; sc. 17). If, however, heroism is itself a performance, a quasi-spontaneous, at least unstable, improvisation, the myth is already undermined in its creation.

The concave mirror also recalls Valle-Inclán's *Luces de bohemia* [*Bohemian Lights*] and the poet Máximo Estrella's definition of the *esperpento*: "Los héroes clásicos reflejados en los espejos cóncavos

---

and the subsequently unstable understanding of "name." In response to El Erudito's repeated demand "¡Dígame su nombre!" [Tell me your name!], El Preso Robinson first responds "Samuel Robinson" and then, under further pressure, "El preso 5059" (38-39; sc. 9) [Prisoner 5059]. This scene is inverted in an exchange between La Presa Manuela, El Preso Bolívar, El Preso Robinson, and El Poeta, when Manuela's initial response to the prompt, "tu nombre" [your name], "52. . .," is cut off by El Preso Bolívar's more insistent "¡¡Tu nombre!!" (43-44; sc. 11).

dan el Esperpento" (168; sc. 12) ["Classical heroes reflected in concave mirrors yield the Grotesque" (183)]. In the preface to his play published in *Conjunto*, Rial describes it as "concebida en ese campo de concentración que es hoy algún país bolivariano caído en el nazi-fascismo, y procura contrastar, hasta esperpentalmente, la idea bolivariana de unidad Gran-Colombiana en la libertad, con la realidad presente de los estadios, las plazas de toros, teatros y hasta templos convertidos en prisiones" (12) [conceived in that concentration camp that today is any Bolivarian country fallen into nazi-fascism, and it attempts to contrast, frighteningly, the Bolivarian idea of Grand-Colombian unity in freedom, with the present reality of the stadiums, bullrings, theaters, and even temples converted into prisons].[20] That El Poeta is the one to employ the image of the mirror continues the allusion to Max Estrella. El Poeta's reference to the mirror intimates that in entering the prison–and, by implication, the cultural space El Funcionario and his ilk control–all is distorted. The hero is distorted by the mirror of the concentration camp into a barely recognizable grotesque, usurping his historical "reality" in the interests of control and domination. El Erudito's order can spring only from the disorder of the distorting mirror, so that the refraction he rejects has already occurred.

El Poeta's script has already been censored. El Funcionario is not spontaneously objecting to a portion of the work but referring to the marked-up text in his hand when he announces: "Aquí está tachado todo eso" (33; sc. 6) [Here all that is erased]. However, not all censorship occurs before the rehearsal. The instability of the script is evident in El Poeta's remark: "ese fusilamiento de antes, si es que va, tendrán que . . ." [that shooting before, if it happens, they will have to . . .], to which El Preso Robinson replies: "hasta ahora, dicen que todo va" (30; sc. 4) [up to now, they say everything's in]. The penalty for altering one's lines is harsh. El Erudito orders the guards to seize Bolívar and Robinson; in the next scene, "los guardias hacen entrar al Preso Bolívar, que ha sido torturado" (57; sc. 16) [the wardens make the prisoner Bolívar enter. He has been tortured]. Torture occurs off stage, unseen but alluded to. El Poeta, author of the problematic script, is threatened more than

---

[20] I have argued elsewhere that the concave mirror is misleading as a definition of Valle-Inclán's "esperpento," but the aptness of the allusion is not diminished here.

once. El Funcionario accuses him of feigning madness and warns: "después de la representación lo enviaré a la enfermería" (30; sc. 4) [after the performance I will send him to the infirmary]. The representation of madness leads to a very real cell, once again obscured by a bureaucratic feigning. As El Poeta recognizes, "todo aquí adentro es muy eufemístico" (34; sc. 6) [everything in here is very euphemistic]. When El Erudito directs the guards to take Bolívar and Robinson, it is to the "infirmary."

The tie between theatricality and state control is underscored throughout the play. The prisoners are forced to reenact the story of Bolívar, a story so thoroughly transformed into myth that a symbol of freedom becomes the instrument of oppression. Nigro argues that Rial's text points "to the complicity of *theatrical* discourse in the process, for it is the languages of the stage–props, pomp and illusionistic tricks–that are being particularly used and abused in the rituals and mythification Rial depicts" ("History" 41).[21] Yet the performative process remains a destabilizing force, as El Poeta's subversion of the official script makes clear. El Funcionario's final instructions call for yet another performance: "Por orden superior, ustedes cantarán los coros de las ceremonias religiosas así como nuestro vibrante himno penitenciario, en las Fiestas Patrias. Vestirán esos trajes de teatro para dar brillo a la celebración" (63; sc. 18) [By superior order you will sing the choruses of the religious ceremonies as well as our vibrant penitentiary hymn in the Patriotic Festivities. You will wear those theatrical costumes in order to give brilliance to the celebration]. While the prisoners' formal presentation is never realized, El Preso Bolívar resists El Funcionario's charge, killing El Knaben Sopranen in the final moments of the play. Still, the Chorus, singing "Sic transit gloria mundi," has the last word.

The role of the historian, the suspicion of written history, the constant vigilance of outside observers, and the need to humanize the hero's myth are bound together. The unperformed play in *Bolívar* presents a suspicion of history written long after the fact, and the uses to which it can be put, even as the overall play represents

---

[21] The overlapping layers of performance continue within the prison's "teatrino" as well. The Knaben Sopranen, brought in for the "ritual nazi" of "El Funeral" (51), "sings in his eunuch voice a patriotic Venezuelan song, 'República de los hombres sin sombra'" (Nigro, "History" 40).

an attempt at reclaiming history. The multiplication of observers, in the form of guards, functionaries, and theatrical spectators, underscores the need for vigilance by the audience, not so as to keep the imprisoned actors in their places but in order to observe the manipulations underway. The play offers as well a serious consideration of the text/performance relation, as both enable each other and as both suffer mutilations. El Poeta is tortured; the prisoner playing the hero handcuffed. The text is mutilated by El Funcionario, literally crossed out or erased, an alteration that leaves a mark in the same way the partially performed tribute to Bolívar marks both prisoner and audience. Multiple layerings of simultaneous time are interwoven. The ahistorical moment of terror is presented within an explicitly historical play, the performance of which is necessarily implicated in the multiple temporality of the performance process.[22] The interior history play presents divergent moments as well, collapsing years of Bolívar's life into the hallucinatory memories of his death bed and mixing twentieth-century reporters with nineteenth-century generals. Yet as the play the prisoners rehearse in *Bolívar* never moves beyond rehearsal, it never fully realizes the temporal multiplicity David George describes, remaining instead trapped in the static moment of terror.

Sabina Berman's *Águila o sol* approaches the performance of history in a more satirical fashion, presenting Cortés's conquest of Mexico in terms of translation and performance. Although the stated perspective of the play is that of the conquered, Berman's satire is directed at Moctezuma as well as Cortés. The play is composed of fifteen sections, beginning with the "Presagios" that announce Cortés's arrival and continuing through the death of Moctezuma. As in other history plays, Berman opens by citing her sources of historical information, as well as theatrical influences, among which she stresses contemporary street theater. The acknowledgment of sources is also an acknowledgment of point of view; Berman writes that her play "se fundamenta en las crónicas indígenas de los suce-

---

[22] David George argues that "a Performance consists of, at least, three, co-existing strata of time–simultaneously: i) the present (a parallel present: now-but-not-now and, as Schechner would have it, also not-not-now either); ii) a past (for the re-enacted event has implicitly occurred, at the very least in rehearsal and is now recuperated, re-presented); iii) and, therefore, a cycle (for the event has, can be and will be repeated, will recur, differently, but nevertheless . . .)" ("Performance" 3).

sos, recopiladas por el maestro León Portilla en la Visión de los Vencidos. Así, es el punto de vista de los conquistados el que se expresa" (225) [is based on the indigenous chronicles of events, compiled by León Portilla in *The Broken Spears*. So, it expresses the perspective of the conquered].

The translator's role, in particular the live, simultaneous translation offered by Malinche is essentially a performance. The series of names by which La Malinche is known is emblematic of her role: herself endlessly translated, renamed, reapportioned. In this she shares with Bolívar, and with Juana la Loca in Sabido's play, the potentially oppressive catalogue of names.[23] The translator simultaneously interprets and performs–improvises–the translated speech. The role of translator can be related as well to an understanding of theater as mediating practice. The speech to be translated might be viewed as the script, the translator's rendition the performance of that script. In this case, the text/performance relation is particularly charged, complicated by the power relationships between speakers as well as the cultural context of the historical and literary treatment of Malinche as prototypical traitor/translator.[24] (Traditional treatments of Malinche have rendered the translator's mediation as necessarily traitorous.) At the same time, in keeping with the subversive potential of performance, Malinche has a degree of power in that Cortés has no way of being certain how he is translated.

The highlighting of Malinche's role as Cortés's translator points to the historian as translator, a relation discussed by Bixler in her analysis of *Martirio*.[25] The playwright is a translator as well. Like Malinche reworking Cortés's speech for his Indian listeners, the historical play reshapes its source material–in this case indigenous chronicles of the conquest–into a theatrical language. This reshaping extends to an open violation of historical details. An author's

---

[23] Malinche's multiple names are a recurring motif. Carlos Fuentes's play *Todos los gatos son pardos* opens with Malinche (listed as Marina in the cast of characters) reciting: "Malintzin, Malintzin, Malintzin . . . Marina, Marina, Marina . . . Malinche, Malinche, Malinche" (13; sc. 1). Later she cries: "No, no, no más nombres" [No, no, no more names] (176; sc. 9).

[24] Sandra Cypess's *La Malinche in Mexican Literature* discusses in more detail the development and transformation of the figure of La Malinche.

[25] Bixler concludes that Leñero's play presents an "unresolvable clash between opposing translations of facts" through which "Leñero foregrounds the changing faces of 'history'; facts are made (events), recorded (translated into a text), read, interpreted, and ultimately rewritten or re-translated" ("Historical" 94).

note admits that "por razones teatrales aquí se incluye a Cortés en la llamada 'matanza del Templo Mayor.' En verdad él se encontraba ausente en esos días de la Ciudad de México" (260) [for theatrical reasons Cortés is included here in the so called 'massacre of the Main Temple.' In fact he was absent from Mexico City at that time]. It is necessary to take liberties with the historical record, liberties dictated not solely by interpretive intent but by theatrical advantage. In Berman's text, the "facts" at issue are retranslated in part through the image of an active translator on stage. The tenuousness of any translation is manifest in the person of an interpreter whose persona has undergone a variety of translations of its own as different aspects of the Malinche myth–traitor, victim, foremother–have been emphasized. The connection between translator in the history represented and the view of historian as translator can be seen as the historian's performance "translates" the historical material in question into either an official or an alternative version.

Other forms of mediation in the play include open narration and framed performances. In the first section of the play, El Narrador describes signs brought to Moctezuma, switching in the process from past-tense announcement–"otro prodigio fue el que llevaron los laguneros de la laguna mexicana" [another wonder was the one that the lagoon inhabitants took from the Mexican lagoon]–to the present-tense narrative, following the entrance of two Indians carrying a strange bird: "qué ave extraña llevan, ave de agüero malo / Admirable es su multicolor plumaje" (229) [what a strange bird they carry, bird of bad omens / Admirable in its multicolored plumage]. In this opening scene, narrative is foregrounded both through the presence of a narrator and because the narrator is the dominant speaker. There is a chorus but no initial dialogue between the *laguneros* and Moctezuma. Narrative foregrounding serves, in turn, to emphasize the recreation of past events, as no "live action" approximation is readily available without the intervention of a historian/narrator.

Berman's Cortés speaks gibberish; it is the Indians, in this play, who speak intelligible Spanish. This device foregrounds the Indians' perception of the conquest. At the same time, the linguistic inversion makes a grotesque figure of Cortés. The treatment of Malinche as the holder of order and logic contrasts sharply with the traditional portrait in which, according to Rosario Castellanos, "encarna la sexualidad en lo que tiene de más irracional, de más irreductible a las leyes morales, de más indiferente a los valores de la cultura" ("Otra vez" 26-27) ["incarnates sexuality in its most irrational aspect, the one least reducible to moral laws, most indifferent to cultural values" (223)]. Still, Cortés's speech is variable. At times it sounds like nonsense Spanish, at others there is a clear discrepancy between what Cortés says and what Malinche "translates," and at still other times he makes no sense whatsoever. His first speech to Moctezuma's emissaries, "¿Gato por liebre, sucios negros trajinantes? Mas cus-cus ¿io?: nieve de orozuz" [Pulling the wool over our eyes, dirty black swindlers? But cus-cus, me-o?: licorice snow], is rendered by Malinche as "¿no es una emboscada?" (234) [isn't it an ambush?]. In this instance, Cortés seems to make more sense before Malinche's translation rather than afterward, for the discrepancy between what he says and her version of the statement undermines the initial partial intelligibility of his words. Later, Cortés proposes a morning tourney: "Morgn morgn cascarita: hispanuss versus mexicanuss" (237) [Tomorrow tomorrow little shell: Hispanic versus Mexican]. Neither of these "gibberish" speeches is entirely incomprehensible. Following the massacre in the Templo Mayor, when Cortés speaks to his own troops, no translation from Malinche is necessary. It is significant that this speech occurs after he has shot the last standing Indian, so that the narrator's voice is symbolically silenced, reduced in his final speech to the stench of dead warriors: "Apesta hasta el cielo la sangre de los guerreros" (262) [The blood of the warriors reeks to the sky].

The play's language moves among a variety of idioms. Cortés's semi-intelligible speech contrasts, in its bald ambition, with Malinche's prettified translations. The formal elegance of the *requerimiento* and the attempts at missionizing reside in the translation, not in Cortés's swift, domineering mumblings. Cortés announces: "Espíritu Santus pater di Cristus. Cristus pater di Carlus Quintus. Carlus Quintus pater di Cortés. Y Cortés, io, pater di todus estus nacus, ¡ostia!" (251) [Holy Spirit father of Christ. Christ father of Carlos V. Carlos V father of Cortés. And Cortés, I, am father of all of these nations, damn!]. Malinche explains this–prefacing her translation, as usual, with "Dice el Cortés" [Cortés says]–as "Su señor Carlos V por pura compasión de ustedes, almas perdidas, lo ha enviado a salvarlos. ¿Quién quiere ser salvado? ¿Quién quiere no perecer? ¿Quién desea bautizarse?" (251) [His king Carlos V, through pure compassion for you lost souls, has sent him to save you. Who wants to be saved? Who wants not to perish? Who wants to be baptized?]. Malinche's own speech is also subject to variability and dissonance. At the close of "Bautismos," she joins Cortés and El Cura in crossing herself "¡A la bio, a la bao, a la bim bom bam!" (253). The hip, hip, hooray tone, appropriate enough at a football game, here produces a clash of expressive registers.

The disjunction of language is presented again when a soldier mispronounces Indian names. His error is represented orthographically in the script and later replaced by Moctezuma's correctly rendered names. Of course, all of the spellings represent attempts to render native names or languages into Spanish. As with the quasi-Spanish that Malinche translates, the contrast presents the invaders as linguistically less adept, reversing the tendency to view the Indians as those unable to speak. Where the soldier says, "Meksicanus, tenoshkas, tlalteloltecas," Moctezuma says, "Mexicanos, tenochcas, tlatelolcas" (262). However, while Moctezuma may be linguistically more adept, he is not more admirable than the invaders. Sending his emissaries to meet Cortés for the first time, Moctezuma attempts to use the difference of language to his own advantage, charging his representatives: "al hablarles, mezclen en el lenguaje común maleficios" (233) [when talking to them, mix curses in common language]. Later he urges his followers not to fight. Cypess concludes that "the incoherence of Cortés on the one hand and the incomprehension of the political reality by Moctezuma on the other show that both patriarchal leaders are empty signs–they do not signify the authority and command with which history has invested them" ("From Colonial" 502). As Ronald Burgess points out, "Mexican coins have an eagle on one side and a sun on the other, the equivalent of 'heads and tails' in English" ("Sabina" 157). Thus, the play's title suggests that there is not much to choose between Cortés and Moctezuma, and underscores the element of chance in all of the events represented. The rejection of both patriarchal leaders resonates with the destabilization of all versions of Morelos's story in *Martirio*.

Meléndez takes the idea of the coin toss a step further, arguing that Berman's "title presents the choice between the two sides of the coin not as query but as a categorical answer to the prevalence of doubt" ("Co(s)mic" 26). For this reason, "It is not a case of seeing if the balance of history will lean fortuitously toward the triumph of the Spaniards or toward the reevaluation of the role of indigenous groups. It is rather a case of stressing how the work itself offers a singular and paradoxical answer that suggests that both historical and theatrical reality *are* at once 'eagle or sun.' These realities reveal, in other words, their unity and their plurality simultaneously" ("Co(s)mic" 26). In Meléndez's view, *Águila o sol* does not "seek to be a mere attack on official historiography, nor to understand its historical present. Rather, it proposes a vision in which the coin is still in the air, in which the either/or choice between eagle and sun is not resolved" ("Co(s)mic" 21). The elements of simultaneity and indecision that Meléndez describes are linked to performance: to the performer's multiple roles, to the diverse perspectives introduced by multiple spectators, and most of all to the intrinsic contingency of performance, never unmediated, never fully resolved.

Águila o sol contains several framed performances. In "Teatro callejero" [Street Theater], two actors (specified in a footnote as either two men or a man and a woman) enact a frequently obscene burlesque that serves at the same time to inform the spectators (of both the interior and exterior plays) of the progress of the conquest. The play within the play serves an informative purpose for the interior spectators, similar to that of the exterior play, although the former (the street theater) centers on current events rather than historical reinterpretation.[26] The translator's role is similar to that of the theater as mediator, a function fulfilled by both the play within the play and by *Águila o sol*. That these mediations are far from neutral is evident throughout the play in, for example, Malinche's modification of Cortés's verbal aggression and the use of entertainment for the purpose of indoctrination. In the scene titled "Bautismos," Ixtlixuchitl informs the audience: "Esta es la historia de mi bautismo y el de mis hermanos" (249) [This is the story of my and my brothers' baptisms]. What follows is a proselytizing puppet show: "Tres indios se arrodillan junto a él. Se descubre el tablado mientras se canta atrás: 'En nombre del cielo, yo os pido . . .' En el tablado: Malinche hincada, flanqueada por un cura y Cortés. Entre sus tres pares de manos viajan los muñequitos con que ilustran la prédica" (249) [Three Indians kneel down with him. The stage is uncovered while they sing behind them: 'In the name of heaven, I

---

[26] Of course, as José Ignacio Cabrujas's *Acto cultural* takes pains to point out, "current events" eventually become "history."

ask you . . .' On stage: Malinche kneeling, flanked by a priest and Cortés. The small puppets, with which they illustrate the sermon, move between their three pairs of hands]. The street theater and the puppet show establish a clear parallel with the informative capacity of the overall play for a contemporary audience while underscoring the historical continuity in the uses of theater to inform as well as to distort. According to Meléndez, the conquest, in Berman's play, "is theatre and its reverse; it is a schema whose apparent coherence recreates an absurd and unintelligible drama and whose principal communicative structure–theatre–is an illogical and incoherent language. Theatre, then, turns out to be as deceptive and manipulative as historiography has been" ("Co(s)mic" 31-32). The use of theater to convey the official version–and the instability of this strategy–has already been seen in *Bolívar*. In *Águila o sol*, particularly in the case of "Teatro callejero," the performance occurs not within the coercive confines that limit the prisoners' "Bolívar" but in the relative freedom of the street, a freedom marked through ironic sexual innuendo. The tone of "Teatro callejero" is highly critical not only of Cortés but of other tribes that have allied themselves with the invaders. The puppet show, in turn, presents an immediate visual doubling of the protagonists, as Malinche, Cortés, and the priest manipulate hand puppets of themselves. Cortés's unintelligible speech becomes further distant as it is translated not only by the character Malinche but through the puppet's voice. The visible doubling in this scene underscores the distance between actor and character, as the puppets function as mobile masks through which Cortés, Malinche, and priest speak. The implication is that the three are always performing (as) themselves, with or without the tangible puppet as prop.

Malinche's speech here provides its own instabilities, and at one point she is uncertain how to proceed: "Los misterios no se explican. Además ustedes son indios y . . . ps . . . ps . . . Unos guerreros llamados romanos crucificaron a Dios" (251) [Mysteries are not to be explained. Also, you are Indians and . . . ps . . . ps . . . Some soldiers called Romans crucified God]. Cypess reads Berman's text as a thoroughgoing revalorization of the figure of La Malinche, underscoring the ease with which the character moves between Hispanic and indigenous societies and emphasizing the fact that she "exercises the traditional masculine prerogative of language dominance"

("From Colonial" 503). [27] Yet while her intelligence is amply demonstrated in Berman's portrayal, La Malinche's stance vis-à-vis the other Indians is ambiguous in that she does not question the doctrine she translates. No longer passive, traitorous, or submissive, La Malinche remains a complex figure. The destabilization of linguistic signs that Cypess discusses extends to La Malinche's speech as well: to the extent that her language dominance allows her to move between worlds, it facilitates the undermining of all claims to authority or truth.

Águila o sol deals less with the historian's translation than with the translation of performative acts in the historical event. The possibility of objective truth behind received versions–official or revisionist–is eliminated as the events themselves are presented as translations, contingencies, improvisations. For "La masacre de Cholula" [The Cholula Massacre], Cortés rides a horse made up of two other actors. At the end of the scene, "el caballo se desarma en jinete y dos hombres armados de varas. Cada cual se va contra un cholulteca. Estos quedan inertes en el suelo. Caballo y jinete se reintegran. Salen lenta, elegantemente" (247) [the horse dismantles itself, becoming a rider and two men armed with sticks. Each one attacks a Cholultec. These remain inert on the ground. Horse and rider are reintegrated. They leave slowly, elegantly]. The transformation of the horse is in keeping with another of Berman's source texts, the pre-Columbian and colonial codices in which the figure of a single soldier might stand for an army. The elegant retreat of the reintegrated horse reflects as well the machinery of conquest. In his performance of (as) the indigenous illustration, Cortés redraws his own figure, multiplying as necessary, reforming to make an unruffled exit with the elegance appropriate to a stylization.

Puppetry and framed history plays also serve the purpose of internal narration in Miguel Sabido's *Falsa crónica de Juana la Loca*. The play is divided into a prologue and seven scenes. The disjunction between history and fiction is made clear in the title, "falsa

---

[27] Cypess concludes that "Berman dramatizes the acculturation of La Malinche, her ability to move freely in both worlds, not as a negative connotation of *malinchismo*, of selling out to the foreigner, but in resonance with the view of some Chicana writers, as an indication of her empathy, intelligence, and revolutionary spirit" ("From Colonial" 503).

crónica," as well as in Sabido's preface. White distinguishes between chronicle and history and comments that "the chronicle usually is marked by a failure to achieve narrative closure. It does not so much conclude as simply terminate" (*Content* 5). Despite its fragmentation, Sabido's chronicle does achieve closure, although it is a closure at odds with the historical record and so, again, false. Sabido writes that he labels the play "falsa" because "esta obra no intenta ser la biografía de Juana de Castilla, La Loca. Se trata de presentar el mundo desorbitado y fuera de todo límite–como las pasiones que en esta reina hicieron nido y que yo quiero adivinar en el personaje" (8) [this work does not attempt to be a biography of Juana of Castile, the Mad. It tries to present a world carried to extremes and outside of all limits–like the passions that made a nest in this queen and that I want to explore in the character]. Moreover: "Es una falsa crónica porque no va de acuerdo con las interpretaciones tradicionales, si bien todos los datos y elementos que se utilizan son perfectamente ciertos" (9) [It is a false chronicle because it does not agree with traditional interpretations, although all of the facts and elements that are used are perfectly true]. Unlike the plays already discussed, Sabido's text makes no pretensions to historical accuracy, and the offering of an alternative to traditional interpretations is labeled false. However, as was the case with Leñero's detailing of textual source material, this claim of falsehood is disingenuous, masking the introduction of what is framed as a "deeper" truth. The falsity lies not in the details but in the emphasis. "Falsa crónica" becomes "falsa" with a wink, an interpretation not necessarily more false than earlier or more traditional versions. And if this false interpretation can be constructed from "datos perfectamente ciertos" [perfectly true facts], the traditional interpretations of the same data may be false as well. "Falsa crónica" is then itself contradictory: Sabido claims to have falsified not the content of the chronicle but rather the reading of those facts.

Falsa crónica uses highly theatrical means–elaborate stage games, lights, figurines–to condemn a kind of cultural theatricality. Only Juana and Mariana remain in a single role; all of the other characters are identified with an additional role, so that, for example, Isabel de Castilla is "al mismo tiempo la hechicera" (13) [at the same time the witch].[28] In the first scene, the politically motivated

---

[28] Minor characters are doubled as well: "Los monjes al quitarse el hábito resul-

marriages of Fernando el Católico's children and grandchildren are represented through a puppet show in which "los cortesanos manejan muñecos de un metro de altura que van sobre una pequeña plataforma con ruedas" (30; sc. 1) [the courtiers operate puppets of one meter in height that move over a small platform with wheels]. Fernando begins to choose among the dolls using a sing-song chant that echoes those of children's games. Launching arrows at the various suitors, Fernando becomes a grotesque Cupid. His system of alliances is recreated through a combination of game and performance: a game of chance in which Fernando challenges Death, who neatly picks off princes one by one, and the performance of the courtiers with their giant dolls and mobile stage. The superficiality of the game contrasts the level occupied by Fernando and the courtiers with that of Juana, who refers repeatedly to her position as chess pawn and insists, "para mí no hubo juego, Felipe" (38; sc. 1) [for me, there was no game, Felipe]. A second game is that of the swings, in which the disembodied voices tormenting Juana with rumors of Felipe's infidelities are revealed as belonging to actors "sentados hablando en columpios que cuelgan del techo. Se impulsan unos a otros como en un juego de niños monstruosos mientras vuelan sobre ella" (43; sc. 2) [seated on swings hung from the ceiling and talking. They prod each other as if in a monstrous children's game while they fly over her]. The games present a combination of fixed roles and chance, emblematic of an enforced but uncontrollable performance. While nonparticipation is not an option, the live-action immediacy of performance introduces a degree of instability. The disembodied voices, suggestive of Juana's alleged madness, are also a symptom of the societal ventriloquism through which individuals become puppets. Thus, in the fourth scene, Felipe appears to speak, but the voices the audience hears are in reality those of Isabel, Fernando, and Cisneros, extolling the virtues of a Europe united under a single crown. In keeping with Taylor's conception of social theatricalization, the ideology underlying Fernando's theatrical manipulations is questioned and transformed. At the

---

tan ser damas de la corte, moras, soldados, cortesanos" (13) [Upon taking off their habits, the monks become ladies of the court, moors, soldiers, courtiers]. Becky Boling discusses the use of two actors, in Sabido's theatrical production, to play the role of Cisneros/La Muerte, identified as a single actor in the printed text ("Spectacle" 88). The play as printed almost dictates such a change, as Cisneros and La Muerte appear on stage together in the final scene.

same time, as performance–with all its intrinsic variability and uncertainty–is highlighted, the inherent instability of the theatrical state is revealed.

The refiguration of Juana la Loca begins in the prologue as she pulls the funeral cart. The accompanying monks address the audience to list Juana's titles and the deeds of her parents, Fernando and Isabel, and her son, Carlos V, until Juana interrupts the accumulation of adjectives–"La Santa. La Bendita. La Elegida" [The Saint, the Blessed One, the Elected One]–with a desperate: "¡¡Basta ya!!" (20) [Enough!]. After being nearly crushed under this barrage of ritual praise, she offers her own catalogue, this one addressed to Felipe's coffin: "Tú, el único; Tú, el primero; Tú, el de siempre; Tú, el amadísimo; Tú, la única razón de cualquier existencia; Tú el deseado" [You, the only one; You, the first; You, the eternal one; You, the loved one; You, the only reason for existence; You, the desired one]–the list goes on (20). The official vigilance that framed the world of the prisoners in *Bolívar* is here clearly voyeurism. The dream-like tone of Juana's erotic, lyric speech to Felipe is destroyed as the two "empiezan a escuchar carcajadas obscenas de los cortesanos. [. . .] Los dos actores desnudos tratan de taparse, de defenderse de las miradas insultantes" (38; sc. 1) [begin to hear the obscene laughs of the courtiers. {. . .} The two nude actors try to cover themselves, to defend themselves from the insulting looks]. As Felipe leaves the stage, Juana alone faces the laughing, pointing courtiers. The scene of Juana's passion made the object of ridicule by the court mirrors that of Mariana's songs and rude remarks, meant to prod the audience to laughter at Juana's expense.

Historical information is presented through performance, not only of the play as a whole, but within the play. Mariana, a dwarf "vestida de 'menina' de Velázquez" [dressed like Velázquez's "menina"], frequently acts as narrator; her first song, accompanied by a dance, offers the traditional story of Juana's madness and her refusal to bury Felipe's corpse (21; prologue). Magnarelli maintains that "the official rendition of the historical events manifests itself in the narrative frame, the unofficial, in the internal plays, those depicted as plays within the narrative frame plays, in the plays recognized as such" ("Dramatic" 51). Yet despite the "clash of genres" that Magnarelli sees in the narrative frames, it is significant that even the official version is presented by the court buffoon, a stock performer. Although Mariana acts as narrator, her narration is delivered as performance, both in the obvious sense of singing and dancing and in the sense of being unstable, as revealed in the moments when her language slips, when she questions her own pronunciation. This instability serves to undermine the official version Mariana represents even in its presentation. The play of linguistic inadequacy that in *Águila o sol* marked the invaders, in *Falsa crónica* contaminates the official history of Juana's madness. The interrelation of unofficial and alternative history is more complicated than a simple and thorough privileging of one over the other.

Magnarelli points out that Mariana tends to perform "somewhat spatially separated and distanced from the scene being represented, as she symbolically embraces an intermediary position between us and the action, often commenting on the latter" ("Dramatic" 52). This intermediary position corresponds to the role of character/narrator who addresses the audience directly, participating in the action yet also stepping back to comment. Such a narrator often undermines the authority of other characters, offering an alternative version of events or openly contradicting others' affirmations. This dual role underscores the narrator's function as a bridge between the audience (which is to say, toward an observer external to the play's action) and the other characters in a way the use of a narrator unconnected with the play's action would not. In all four plays under discussion, performance is presented not as an attempt at achieving unmediated experience but as an (inescapable) form of mediation, present from the outset. This is doubly so given the necessarily mediated reality of the historical discourses that form the bases or pretexts for these plays. Although Sabido's play does not attempt to achieve an unmediated experience, the performer/narrator appears emblematic of the impossibility of that escape.

Mariana torments Juana with the distorted, official version of her madness. Her performance contributes to the impression of Juana as hemmed in on all sides by an exaggerated theatricality epitomized by Fernando's theatrical state. At the same time, Mariana's limited abilities, combined with the inevitable instability of performance, subvert the official version she represents. Yet the relation between Mariana's performance and the official history goes beyond her obvious technical inadequacies. Mariana's narrative is certainly depicted as unreliable, based on gossip, possibly contrary to fact, and characterized by "incompetence with language"

(Magnarelli, "Dramatic" 53). However, I see, in the "unnecessary repetition" Magnarelli criticizes, an opening of performance rather than strictly ineptitude ("Dramatic" 54). Despite her linguistic inadequacies, Mariana is at least partially aware of her errors. Ending a verse "don Fernando con sus hijos jugo" [Don Fernando palayed with his children], she realizes that something is wrong with what she just said and tries again: "No: ¿jugo? ¿jugo? No: juagaba . . . juagaba . . . juagaba . . ." (30; sc. 1) [No: palayed? palayed? No: was plaiying . . . was plaiying . . . was plaiying]. To the extent that her errors are an index of the official version's distortion of Juana, Mariana's discomfort with her own lapses hints that she is at least partially aware of the distortion in which she participates. It is also, as were the actor/prisoners' rebellions in *Bolívar*, an indication of the slipperiness of performance as a means of constituting or transmitting an absolute version of historical events. Even the official spokesperson, foregrounded as narrator and visually connected to the official painter of the historical court recreated on stage, cruelly provoking Juana with her insinuations and jabs, is unable to sustain her role. At one level, Mariana's shortcomings simply intensify the play's criticism of the official version by giving that version an incompetent representative. Still, the spokesperson's incompetence is not merely idiosyncratic. No attempted version, especially given the falsity of the one constructed here, could be flawlessly executed.

In keeping with the identification of the play from the outset as a false chronicle, the performance calls both versions into question. As Magnarelli observes, the play ends "with an inversion of the roles of the opening scene as [Juana] triumphantly whips those representatives of society who had exploited her. Patently, however, the irony is bidirectional, for we knew Juana's historical destiny all along, and her final ascendant role in this work is a direct product of literature" ("Dramatic" 49). Once again, alternative histories are invoked on stage not only through revisionary narratives but as tangible objects. In *Falsa crónica*, the alternative text is presented as textile: Juana "frente al telar comienza a entretejer hilos de colores que cuelgan de lo alto. Tienen que ser estambres o cordeles de lana para que puedan ser vistos por el público. En torno a Juana hay seis muñecos. Que representan a sus hijos" (41; sc. 2) [in front of the loom begins to weave colored threads that hang from above. They should be worsted or woollen yarn so as to be seen by the audience. There are six dolls around Juana, representing her children]. Weaving is itself a performative activity, a construction of representation through the horizontal sweep of weft. Juana's cradling of the bloody rags from Felipe's coffin recalls, with its textile imagery, the weaving scene, as do her costume changes from sumptuous robes to simple shifts. The dolls representing Juana's children in turn contrast with the dolls earlier employed in Fernando's game of marriage alliances. The fraying of the text, the bloodying of the rags that represent Felipe's end and Juana's destruction, carry a graphic portrayal of the hopelessness of the false chronicle's attempt to definitively amend past events.

In his preface, Sabido discusses the relevance of the figure of Juana for a contemporary Mexican audience. This question of relevance is common among history plays, in which past events are frequently taken, implicitly if not explicitly, as a way of interpreting the present. Sabido observes that "Juana fue la verdadera reina durante los años en los que Cortés conquistó la Gran Tenochtitlan, se dio el prodigioso teatro evangelizador franciscano, se sucedieron los hechos guadalupanos, arribó el primer virrey, se organizó la primera audiencia y se sentaron las bases culturales de lo que sería la vida de la Nueva España durante los tres siglos siguientes" (7-8) [Juana was the true queen during the years in which Cortés conquered the Great Tenochtitlan, the prodigious evangelical Franciscan theater was established, the Guadalupan events occurred, the first viceroy arrived, the first royal "audience" was organized and the cultural base was developed for what would be the life of New Spain during the next three centuries]. A parallel arises with *Águila o sol*, which recreates an evangelizing theater (the puppet show) in which Cortés takes Carlos V for legitimate king.[29] Sabido continues: "lo que ahora es México se descubrió, se conquistó, se organizó como país bajo el reinado de una reina reputada como loca. Estremecedora visión que explicaría, quizás, infinidad de hechos inexplicables. Carlos nunca pensó, siquiera, en venir a conocer las colonias americanas: ella lo pidió varias veces. ¿Hubiera sido diferente el brutal proceso de conquista si Juana hubiera tenido real autoridad?" (8) [what is now Mexico was discovered, conquered, organized as a country under the rule of a queen reputed to be crazy. This disturbing vision might explain, perhaps, an infinite number

---

[29] See Adam Versényi's *Theatre in Latin America* for an extended discussion of evangelical theater during the colonial period.

of unexplainable facts. Carlos never even thought of visiting the American colonies: she asked to do so several times. Would the brutal process of conquest have been different if Juana had had real authority?]. In Sabido's wistful meditation, Juana, would-be traveler, becomes a sort of patron saint of Mexico, a potential addition to the triumvirate of Mexican femininity described by Castellanos.

In keeping with the emphasis on Juana's being the legitimate queen during the conquest of Mexico, the prologue, in which Juana takes the place of horses hauling Felipe's funeral car, offers a suggestive parallel to the treatment of the Indians; while Juana "jadea y arrastra con dificultad el carro, el que la azota hace restallar el látigo sobre su espalda" (16) [gasps and starts the cart with difficulty, he who flogs her cracks the whip over her back]. Although she later expresses a desire to visit the far corners of her realm, Juana is also presented as at some level anti-imperialist: "me importa España, mi reino. No conquistar otros que no me pertenecen" [Spain matters to me, my kingdom. Not the conquest of others that don't belong to me] (62; sc. 4). Sabido proposes Juana as alternate or additional Mexican foremother, and as such her potential investment in overseas conquest is minimized. Boling argues that "rather than being the cause of 'marginality' like *la Malinche*, Juana is its sign. The play asks the audience to identify with the feminine insofar as they experience the 'marginality' of being Mexican" ("Spectacle" 90). While it is enforced by her gender, Juana's marginality is not strictly feminine but potentially universal. The figure presented as an alternative to Malinche in this analysis shares with the latter an overwhelming sexuality, although the suggestion that Juana's seeming obsession was in fact a necessary stratagem reclaims her capacity for logic as well as love. Juana's sanity is repeatedly presented, for example, in the contrast between her admission, "sé que estás muerto" (23; prologue) [I know that you're dead], and Mariana's refrain, "pero la reina insistía, insistía, insistía" (25; prologue) [but the queen insisted, insisted, insisted]. As Boling argues, "Juana's madness is just the name for an ideology that is proscribed" ("Spectacle" 92). *Águila o sol* and *Falsa crónica* present the (anti)histories of women whose only recourse in the face of danger was a performative role: translator or pretended madwoman. The traps inherent in such strategies are evident in La Malinche's transformation as myth and Juana's relegation to the camp of the insane. These roles are in turn foregrounded, and reconsidered, through the self-conscious theatricality of the two plays. Similar pitfalls constrain women performing in a hostile context, as in Gambaro's *El campo*, and the women who feign paralysis in Mariela Romero's *El juego*. Feigned madness parallels feigned paralysis in that, in an attempt to escape strictures or oppression, it demands the representation of an equally limiting role in a sort of frying-pan-to-fire paradigm of personal defense. Performance is often thus: an inadequate defense, but frequently the only option.

The historical plays discussed here, all of which use highly self-conscious performance formats as a means of historical narration and of commenting on that history, do not so much establish watertight alternative narratives as destabilize official and revisionist versions alike. The litany of names by which many of the characters are known, both within and beyond the confines of the texts under consideration, exemplify the multiplicity of roles, and the multiplicity within their roles, the impossibility of absolute definition, the slipperiness of their performance. *Martirio de Morelos* calls into question the authority of historical documentation. In *Bolívar*, the attempted performance of historical material is foregrounded and with it the physical violence perpetrated by the forced imposition of a preset mythic script. *Águila o sol* emphasizes translation, between languages but also between narrative and theatrical idioms, as the historical (narrative) information of the Teatro Callejero scene is presented in terms of contemporary theatrical practice. This emphasis on translation continues the undermining of authority and original documents observed in the first two plays, as the supposed "original" of any official or accepted version–and by the same token, any alternative version–becomes more and more unstable. In *Falsa crónica*, there is a greater emphasis on play in the destabilization of accepted history, but the games remain horrifying grotesques.

The historically based play has two texts prior to any proposed performance: received history and playscript. In a sense, the historical playscript is a textual performance of the prior text of the historical record. Lindenberger argues that "the sources of many plays consist less of the historical materials on which they are purportedly based than on the theatrical conventions which give them their essential form" (4). By this argument, the sources of Leñero's *Martirio de Morelos* lie more accurately in the conventions of documentary theater than in the legal documents relating to Morelos's trial and execution. Similarly, Berman's use of contemporary popular theatrical practices becomes a more immediate source than the accounts collected by León Portilla. In this case, the argument for accuracy–attacking Leñero for bad faith, for instance–is misplaced, for what is at stake is not so much the recreation of historical material as the readaptation of theatrical traditions. Lindenberger's observation is perhaps particularly apt in a discussion of the self-conscious performance practices highlighted in all four plays. He proposes that "the only contemporary convention which seems generally viable for historical matters is Brechtian epic theater, which, with its constant reminders to the audience not to lend too wholehearted a credence to the events depicted on stage, creates a kind of frame through which we can view the past from an unashamedly present-day vantage point" (17-18).[30] Yet these plays insist on their self-consciousness, not always in strictly Brechtian ways. The visually complex, pageant-like games of *Falsa crónica* have as much in common with baroque elaboration as with epic theater. The violence of the histories reworked in these texts contrasts with the frequent playfulness of their theatrical adaptation. The implication of the use of performance in these plays is that historical source material and theatrical convention cannot be neatly separated, as the histories –both in their written form and in their occurrence at a given time–are already colored by a performative structure. Performance's multiple instabilities–temporal, spatial, personal–reflect the character of all historical discourse, whether in the form of drama, novel, or historical treatise. In this way, the self-conscious foregrounding of performance illuminates both the events and individuals recreated on stage and the nature of historical understanding.

---

[30] Nevertheless, Lindenberger also suggests that the Brechtian mode may have become "a convention which has outworn its potential to the point that self-consciousness will work to inhibit the very self-consciousness of its devices" (18).

Chapter 2

FEIGNED PARALYSIS: PERFORMANCE AND GAMES

IMAGINATIVE games duplicate theatrical performance in their linkage of freedom and control: improvisation within a rigid framework, insistent repetition, determinate yet arbitrary roles. Even games invented by the players as they go along take on a life of their own, establishing the boundaries of the game context, solidifying a seemingly casual choice into an incontrovertible rule.[1] The metaphor of ritual game playing has provided many playwrights with a vehicle for theatrical exploration and sociopolitical commentary. Games have been presented as an escape from an unbearable reality, as a self-contained and often violent reality in themselves, and as a representation of the empty or commercialized relations between individuals in an impersonal society. Games are also a staple of playwrights, such as Samuel Beckett, associated with the theater of the absurd. Latin American plays that employ the game motif include *La noche de los asesinos* by José Triana (Cuba, 1965) [*Night of the Assassins*], *El cepillo de dientes* by Jorge Díaz (Chile, 1966) [The toothbrush], *¿A qué jugamos?* by Carlos Gorostiza (Argentina, 1968) [What shall we play?], *El juego* by Mariela Romero (Venezuela, 1976) [*The Game*], and *Extraño juguete* by Susana Torres Molina (Argentina, 1977) [Strange toy]. Many of these plays present metatheatrical performances, as the games in question consist of the representation of alternative scenarios or ritualized, repetitive scripts.

Enclosure and paralysis often frame the lives of characters physically confined or mentally immobilized by hopelessness or oppres-

---

[1] I will turn shortly to a discussion of the theoretical literature on games.

sion. At the same time, immobility and constraint define many of the games such characters play. In this chapter I will concentrate on a specific instance of game-marked representation, the exploration of feigned paralysis in Romero's *El juego*. Feigned paralysis is also significant in Mexican playwright Maruxa Vilalta's *Pequeña historia de horror (y de amor desenfrenado)* (1985) [*A Little Tale of Horror (And Unbridled Love)*] and, in a rather different way, in Colombian Esteban Navajas's *La agonía del difunto* (1977) [The agony of the deceased]. The latter two plays will serve as counterpoint for a discussion of the image of the false paralytic in Romero's text. Romero's play focuses attention on an underlying element of theater, its spatial/temporal definition as something apart, like reality but not reality itself. The struggle to overcome this separation, to eliminate the perceptual boundaries between the two has been a focus of much contemporary theater, performance art, and performance theory. My aim is to consider both the form of the game as paradigm and the content of the game as performance: the implications of the specific scenarios depicted through ritualized play between theatrical characters.[2] Focusing on the image of paralysis within the context of game playing invites consideration of the ambiguity of performance as a subversive practice: a practice which reproduces the relations and patterns it attempts to undermine, a process particularly visible in these circular, ritual reenactments. To feign paralysis is, at some level, to be paralyzed, but maintaining the discrete separation implied by "at some level" is by no means straightforward or guaranteed.

The play is divided into two scenes in which the characters, Ana I and Ana II, act out a series of situations, often of great violence. Transitions between games are frequently fluid and unmarked. For Ana I and Ana II, the games are an escape, a pastime within a miserable life, yet their games also partake of that situation, producing a metaphorical reflection of their violent existence. The games further produce genuine abuse between the two. This reflects a dilemma inherent to game plays. The discrete reality of the game must be recognized by all players in order to remain in force; at the same

---

[2] Drawing a connection between role playing and certain games, Eugene Moretta stresses "the idea of game playing as a double-edged sword" so that "the playing is a means of privileged access to what is most deeply real, yet at the same time a participation in the real that overwhelms and devours rather than frees" ("Spanish" 21).

time, the imaginary space is not so unreal that blows suffered in jest are painless. In *El juego*, the characters repeatedly move in and out of the game mode, and the status of the game as game is questioned. The game becomes the only reality that exists for these two characters; it is not, in fact, a game.

The image of the child's game produces a deceptively innocent front. Children's play often incorporates varying degrees of violence at the same time that it reflects the adult reality with which the children are surrounded. The theatrical play of ambiguously child-like adults, already distanced from childhood reality, invites us to read their games as allegorical or symbolic.[3] Jacqueline Bixler suggests that "the games being played on the Latin American stage today are not the chaotic, seemingly nonsensical games of absurdist drama, but rather organized, purposeful games that reflect metaphorically an extratextual, socio-political reality. While pretending through play to escape from their banal, miserable existence, the characters unconsciously produce a distorted, mirror image of that very same reality" ("Games" 22). Those elements of performance that most characterize the game–repetition, variation, ritual, and rules–are highlighted in games that present alternate, only slightly varied scenarios of repression and fantasy or escape. Games mirror yet question oppressive social realities, as the players' scripts reproduce the oppressions to which the individuals are subject. As performances, games incorporate role playing, self-consciously fictive acts, script destabilization, repetition, and narrative undermining. Enclosure and paralysis are reflections of performance as well, logical extensions of the limited space of the stage and the limitations of the script.

Generally understood as the impossibility or impairment of motion, paralysis may be physical or psychological. As portrayed dramatically, the two are often intertwined. Paralysis may be the result of an incapacity to overcome oppressive circumstances, as in Osval-

---

[3] Such readings may not be at all difficult or subtle. With reference to Polish-Argentine Roma Mahieu's *Juegos a la hora de la siesta* (1976) [Games at nap time], Bixler observes that "the similarity between stage events and the Argentine military state was apparently too obvious to the censors, who banned the work in late 1977. The pronounced contrast between victim and victimizer, the defenseless and the empowered, reflects clearly the Argentina of 1976, the year in which Peronismo and personal freedom came to an end, usurped by a military dictatorship" ("Games" 29).

do Dragún's *El amasijo* (Argentina, 1972) [The jumble], *La noche de los asesinos*, and to a lesser degree *El cepillo de dientes*. While the immobility imposed by outside forces is not identical to individual paralysis (if nothing else, because the source of immobility is identifiable and, potentially, mutable) the psychological effects may be similar. In *El juego*, the performance of physical paralysis is most evident. However, the use of physical immobility in Romero's play has implications for the psychological immobility explored in other game plays. Paralysis may be understood as both a physical inability to move and an existential inertia, either of which may be exacerbated by outside pressures such as institutional enclosure, stereotyped roles, or individual violence. In *El juego*, paralysis provides not only the context for the games but the material with which the characters play. *El juego*'s rituals extend beyond the representation of the violence between two individuals to the dramatization of paralysis itself. Romero's drama explicitly treats a ritual paralysis that, although it appears in the games of many of the works mentioned, does not become a central element. In its presentation of women in the role of pseudoparalytic, Romero's play delineates the potential pitfalls of the appropriation of the pose of weakness: the effects of a pretended debility are potentially real.[4]

Because of the traditional associations of femininity and passivity, and the immobility imposed by traditional women's roles, the choice of paralysis as a pose of resistance is from the outset problematic. *El juego* represents neither an uncomplicated attempt to recuperate immobility as a positive means of resistance nor an unquestioning acceptance of paralysis as the victim's inevitable lot.[5] Instead, as with many of the performances discussed in this study, performance becomes a curiously entrapping yet liberating necessi-

---

[4] The image of female paralysis is not limited to theater. With the figure of the immobilized woman, Romero develops a concrete representation of a phenomenon alluded to in other genres. Short stories such as Clarice Lispector's "The Imitation of the Rose" and Luisa Valenzuela's "Cambio de armas" explore the ritualization of women's lives and the paralysis to which it can lead. Phyllis Zatlin discusses themes of enclosure and immobility in postwar Spanish novels by women. In *El juego*, however, paralysis is performed rather than, or as well as, being imposed.

[5] One possibility for recuperating passivity can be found in the resistance of political protesters who choose to go limp as the police arrest them. However, the pose of paralysis in *El juego* does not reproduce such a use of immobility. Both Ana I and Ana II discard immobility or passivity when challenged; paralysis is not a means to meet violence, but an attempt to postpone it.

ty. Through the distorted mirror image Bixler describes, false paralysis reflects Ana I and Ana II's nonplay reality. Their first possibility of escape lies in the distortion of performative reproduction, a border space that eludes both outside control and the dominance imposed within the game by each Ana in turn. The second break occurs at the close of the play, as the repetitive cycle of game following game is interrupted by the approaching footsteps of El Viejo. This second escape is a negative one, an "escape" back to the violence beyond the violent game.

Immobility or paralysis, physical or psychological, is not limited to plays that deal with games. In his study of violence in Latin American theater, Severino Albuquerque compares immobility in three plays by Griselda Gambaro, *El campo* (1967) [*The Camp*], *El desatino* (1965) [The mistake], and *Las paredes* (1963) [*The Walls*]. According to Albuquerque, "in *El campo*, Martín's movements are circumscribed not by a concrete object but by the workings of a sophisticated institution which, having taken control of a numbed society, is free to extend its tentacles beyond the camp's fences and into the homes of perfectly innocent citizens. As the play ends, Martín's immobility, like the Youth's and Alfonso's in the final moments of *Las paredes* and *El desatino*, signifies the definitive capitulation to the forces of organized repression" (132-33).[6] Entrapment may be seen as a form of paralysis, as the character unable to escape is also unable to move. Immobility is frequently associated with women, as in Enrique Buenaventura's *La orgía* (Colombia, 1968) [The orgy] and in other plays by Romero, such as *Rosa de la noche* (1980) [Rosa of the night], *El vendedor* (1981) [The salesman], and *Esperando al italiano* (1987) [Waiting for the Italian].[7] The preva-

---

[6] Although it does not directly treat the game theme, Gambaro's *El desatino* has strong ties to Romero's play in terms of paralysis. As in *El juego*, paralysis is represented literally and visibly. *El desatino* traces the story of Alfonso, who, digging through the garbage, gets his foot stuck in an iron "artefacto" that he is unable to dislodge and which leaves him virtually unable to move. Alfonso's paralysis is false because it is external, accidental, and absurd. Yet, once paralyzed, Alfonso is unable to escape and he dies during an attempt to remove the artifact. The attempt to free Alfonso is motivated more by El Muchacho than by Alfonso, who, ceding to his mother's pressure, tries to dissuade the youth from his efforts so as not to be a bother.

[7] All three of Romero's later plays portray women who, while not physically paralyzed, occupy sharply limited spaces that offer little possibility of change or escape.

lence of feminine immobility within Latin American texts is hardly surprising. Jean Franco discusses the "privatization" of women in traditional Hispanic society, arguing that "the mother's immobility is related to racism and to the protection of inheritable property" ("Beyond" 507). Immobility is at once a sign of value–only the virtuous woman immobilized within the family home can protect the bloodline–and a symptom of oppression, a penalty imposed in anticipation of transgression.

While the Juana of *Falsa crónica de Juana la Loca* is trapped within the hallucinatory games of the monstrously childlike courtiers who surround her, the Anas of *El juego* both participate in the game.[8] The characters struggle against one another but also against the imposition of the game. At issue is whether to play and also who will control the playing, who has the authority to set the rules and establish the boundaries. In the imaginative, acted-out games the women undertake, the rules of the game become the script for an enactment both playful and violent. The negotiation of the game scripts is a negotiation between characters, a tug-of-war between conflicting versions and interpretations, but it is also the negotiation of the script as obstacle, an effort to confront or overcome a prior text. The script appears in a variety of guises, as authoritative text within the games–hence the constant tension between the players over whose rendition of the script is adequate–and in the form of the social roles games both reproduce and distort.[9]

Through their repetitive yet varied games, Ana I and Ana II produce a tissue of representations that separates the world within their room from the dangers outside. The delicacy of this barrier is revealed by the gaps in their play and in the glimpses of a nongame reality suggested in some of their exchanges. The constant presence of the wheelchair visually underscores the paralysis of the protago-

---

[8] Albuquerque classifies *El juego* with other representations of the "violent double" that "depict the intense and sometimes brutal relations of two individuals who, for all the differences between them, are complementary selves and therefore cannot exist apart from each other" (229). The interdependence of the protagonists is central to many of these representations of ritual violence.

[9] The difficulty of negotiating the script, both as obstacle and as bone of contention, is also addressed in José Antonio Rial's *Bolívar*, in which there is open discussion of what elements may or may not be included in the framed performance, and in which the manipulation and censorship of El Poeta's script is a site of violence. The script as obstacle appears as well in José Ignacio Cabrujas's *Acto cultural*.

nists rather than leaving their immobility an existential abstraction. The protagonists of Díaz's *El cepillo de dientes* or Torres Molina's *Extraño juguete* also use games to give meaning to a banal and tedious life. In Torres Molina's play, the games have as their basis the scripts that two sisters, Perla (Mónica) and Angélica (Silvia), purchase from Maggi (Señor Miralles), who takes part as well in the performance. The game is undone when Maggi leaves the scene at the climactic moment and all of the previous action dissolves in the dismantling of the set and a detailed settling of accounts. The possibility of a new game is introduced by Maggi's tentative offer, "tengo un nuevo material" (75) [I have a new subject].[10] Rather than being a series of improvisations around a single situation, the cycle of repetition here depends upon the purchase of new scripts. The games of *El juego*, in contrast, are less an attempt to give meaning to an empty life than a defense against external reality.

The parallels with Triana's *La noche de los asesinos* are clearer. Both plays are based on a series of ritual games played out by characters enclosed within substantially similar rooms, cluttered with cast-off furniture and general debris.[11] The characters are ambivalent toward their representations and alternate in the dominant role. At the beginning of the first act of *Asesinos*, Cuca states: "no estoy para esas boberías" (139; 1) ["I can't stand all this nonsense" (32)], but she herself opens the second act with the announcement: "ahora me toca a mí" (169; 2) ["Now it's my turn" (56)]. In a similar fashion, when Ana II oversteps the bounds, Ana I says, "no juego más. Esta vez has ido demasiado lejos" (88; sc. 1) ["I'm through playing. This time you've gone too far" (114)]. Later, however, Ana I proposes "uno de esos juegos que tanto te gustan" (93; sc. 1) ["another game. One of those that you like" (119)]. She elaborates: "yo trataré de imitarte . . . de comportarme como tú . . . y tú

---

[10] As Bixler notes, the "strange toy" of the title is Maggi himself, a man "reduced to a plaything of the bourgeoisie and forced to prostitute his dramatic skills in order to survive" ("Games" 29).

[11] Diana Taylor has questioned the privileging of the game structure in discussions of Triana's play. She argues that "Triana situates his work in the ground common to games, ritual and drama" (*Theatre* 70) so that "by blurring generic distinctions and forcing us to question the terms themselves, the formal antistructure of the work brilliantly echoes the play's thematic concern with boundaries of demarcation" (*Theatre* 73). Taylor's point is valid. However, Triana's play retains relevant similarities to *El juego* without requiring a strictly game-based reading.

tendrás que actuar como yo" (93; sc. 1) ["I'll try to imitate you . . . to act like you . . . and you can be me" (120)]. Although the dramatic worlds of both plays are constituted in reference to an absent authority, the relations between the protagonists and that authority–which in neither case physically appears on stage–are substantially different. Within the internal performances, Lalo, Cuca, and Beba play the roles of their parents, police investigators, and judgmental neighbors. Authority is the motive force behind the rehearsals for an endlessly deferred murder, as well as the power the individual protagonists arrogate to themselves in the course of the games. In *El juego*, El Viejo is mentioned for the first time near the end of the play and never appears represented within the games of Ana I and Ana II. The authoritative positions the two assume do not necessarily correspond to specific individuals but reflect above all an alternation of dominance. The authority experienced and performed by the women is thus more diffuse. Although both plays follow a structure of circular repetition, Romero's play ends as an apparently unconscious Ana I and a terrified Ana II await the imminent entrance of El Viejo. Triana's play closes with another beginning as Beba has the last word, repeating Cuca's earlier affirmation: "ahora me toca a mí" (201; 2) ["Now it's my turn" (81)]. In *El juego*, the cycle has been broken, at least temporarily.

In *Homo Ludens*, Johan Huizinga describes play as "a stepping out of 'real' life into a temporary sphere of activity with a disposition all of its own," although he notes that "the contrast between play and seriousness is always fluid" (8). Play is characterized by "its secludedness, its limitedness. It is 'played out' within certain limits of time and place" (9). A free, pleasurable activity, play is nonetheless associated with order and repetition, so that "play demands order absolute and supreme. The least deviation from it 'spoils the game', robs it of its character and makes it worthless" (10). The emphasis on rules seems especially applicable to organized games rather than to play more generally (although free-form play may have its rules, too). As Elizabeth Bruss notes, "rules of play 'constitute' as well as regulate the game" (158). The rules of the game parallel the limiting effect of the "script" in games that center on dramatic enactment. The necessity of agreed-upon rules is crucial to the games played out in *El juego*, and disagreement as to the form of the games themselves and the adequacy of the other player's participation contribute to the tension between the protagonists.[12] The rules of the game become the text of the performance and as such are open to the negotiation and adaptation inherent in the script/performance exchange.

Huizinga's model has been complicated by subsequent theorists. Gregory Bateson suggests that play, in both humans and animals, is framed by a metacommunicative message, "this is play," that sets it off from the nonplay actions it resembles. Thus, "not only does the playful nip not denote what would be denoted by the bite for which it stands, but, in addition, the bite itself is fictional" (70). The emphasis is on the imaginative qualities of play. Nevertheless, the effects may be quite real, as when "a man experiences the full intensity of subjective terror when a spear is flung at him out of the 3D screen" (71). In this case, the framing message–"this is play"–is displaced by the seeming reality of the moment. Natalie Schmitt observes that "in play events the metacommunication is not a single static signal. The whole of the behavior may be accompanied by some framing action or may be transformed in some way, as by repetition, exaggeration, timing, chanting or rhyming. The message 'this is play' acts as both a context and a text" ("Theatre" 221). The codes that signal play are not fixed but constantly in motion. The necessity of a metacommunication identifying play also carries with it the possibility of miscommunication, so that not only the rules but the state of playing may be disputed. Alternately, a player may recognize but disregard the play signal. A game entails multiple layers: the message designating play, the rules that constitute the game, and the varied stances the players may assume toward the play context.

Schmitt takes issue with the notion that play is clearly cut off from ordinary reality, noting that "children at play move from one mode to the other with relative frequency and ease" ("Theatre" 222).[13] Furthermore, not all play mimetically reproduces a nonplay reality. Schmitt therefore suggests that a shift in focus away from

---

[12] The tension between players as to the nature of the game and the game's subsequent rupture (expressed, for example, through a refusal to play or the accusation that others are "playing dirty") characterize other game plays as well, in particular *La noche de los asesinos*, *¿A qué jugamos?* and *Extraño juguete*.

[13] Moreover, "children may participate in both modes at once: they may drink orange juice and at the same time pretend to be drinking poison, or run an errand but be careful at the same time not to step on sidewalk cracks" ("Theatre" 222).

the imitative element of play allows one to emphasize in imaginative play "the distortion and exaggeration of reality rather than its simulation" ("Theatre" 223). Bixler argues that for Ana I and Ana II, "instead of providing an escape, their games invariably parallel or at least allude to their true situation. The brutal exchanges and the struggle for dominance that characterize all of the games are simply an imitation of life with El Viejo" ("Games" 25). Although the games in *El juego* reproduce the oppressive reality the two women experience outside the game, it is a reproduction characterized by the distortion and exaggeration Schmitt describes. The simulation inheres at an underlying emotional level of abuse and dependence rather than in the surface details enacted. Here, too, the borders are fluid: while certain games present a high degree of realism, others offer imaginative departures. Bruss argues that "a game, by definition, is the encounter between equally matched and equally creative participants" (154). The need for equally matched participants contrasts with the recurrent attempts of one player to dominate another, not only in *El juego* but in other game-centered plays as well. The struggle within *El juego* derives from the tension between assertions of individual power, which run counter to the gaming situation, and the alleged rules of the game. Bruss's discussion focuses on literary games in which the players are author and reader. However, her distinction between competitive and collaborative games is instructive in considering *El juego*, in which the series of competitive (antagonistic) games becomes, perhaps, a game-within-a-game, the outer game being the collaborative attempt of Ana I and Ana II to stave off El Viejo's abuse.

To assert that rules are a significant component of play is not a value free move. Catherine Larson argues that "games echo patriarchal relationships: they promote hierarchies in their opposition of winners and losers, stress the value of following rules, and emphasize the use of power (through physical strength, intellectual machinations, or emotional manipulation) to reestablish order" (78). Larson therefore views the adoption of the game metaphor by women playwrights as both risky and frequently ironic.[14] The troubling in-

---

[14] By contrast, in a collection combining theoretical reflection and the documentation of specific theatrical (often site-specific) events, Rosa Luisa Márquez revalorizes games and play not as thematic problem or formal representation but as technique, a point her subtitle makes clear: "el juego como disciplina teatral" [the game as theatrical discipline].

security Larson sees in games also applies to the image of paralysis. By adopting paralysis as pose, the characters inescapably insert themselves into the network of dominance and repression their games both mirror and resist. Paralysis appears intertwined with the development of alternative means of resistance, what Josefina Ludmer calls "tretas del débil" [feints of the weak]. Referring to Sor Juana Inés de la Cruz, Ludmer concludes that "el silencio constituye su espacio de resistencia ante el poder de los otros" (50) [silence constitutes her space of resistance in the face of the power of others]. Ludmer describes this silence as "no decir que sabe" (49) [not saying that she knows], a double gesture in which "se combinan la aceptación de su lugar subalterno (cerrar el pico las mujeres), y su treta: no decir pero saber, o decir que no sabe y saber, o decir lo contrario de lo que sabe" (51) [the acceptance of her subaltern space (women keep silent), and her feint are combined: to know but not to say, or to say that she does not know although she does, or to say the opposite of what she knows]. This chosen silence "combina, como todas las tácticas de resistencia, sumisión y aceptación del lugar asignado por el otro, con antagonismo y enfrentamiento, retiro de colaboración" (51-52) [combines, like all of the tactics of resistance, submission and acceptance of the place assigned by the other with antagonism and confrontation, withdrawal of collaboration]. For Ana I, feigned paralysis achieves a similar aim, although her paralysis seems more defensive shield than offensive tactic. When she imposes immobility on her opponent, Ana I becomes the aggressor. At other times, however, she uses her own immobility to fight back. Although it is tempting to posit a recuperation, from a feminist perspective, of weakness or passivity as a means of resistance, the relationships explored in *El juego* do not entirely vindicate such an attempt; ultimately, the characters are unable to extricate themselves from their predicament. The attempt to use a false paralysis to open a space of resistance is similar to the use of silence Debra Castillo proposes when she writes: "Silence, once freed from the oppressive masculinist-defined context of aestheticized distance and truth and confinement and lack, can be reinscribed as a subversive feminine realm" (40). However, like paralysis, silence has its limitations. Castillo concludes that "silence alone cannot provide an adequate basis for either a theory of literature or concrete political action. Eventually, the woman must break silence and write," just as eventually, the falsely immobilized woman must move (42). Her movement, however, may be a successful flight from prison or simply an evasion of the next incoming blow.

That the two characters are named Ana I and Ana II produces a lack of distinction that diminishes the possibility of individual development.[15] Yet despite the nearly identical names and the exchange of roles within the games, there is a certain differentiation between the two women, and Ana I is more strongly associated with paralysis than is Ana II.[16] The set's single room, cluttered with old newspapers, shattered glass and broken furniture, creates a claustrophobic atmosphere common to the work of Triana, Gambaro, and others. The sense of enclosure intensifies toward the end of the play, when the threat of El Viejo is introduced. Albuquerque concludes that "in the light of their oppressor's violence, the two women's destructiveness assumes a different significance, and their 'juego' can thus be seen for what it really is: a prolonged attempt at disguising their fragility and helplessness" (267). Yet there is more to the image of feigned paralysis than a manifestation of power and oppression. The false paralytic suggests the possibility of fragility or paralysis as act, as performance. The image also points to the use of passivity as refuge. To the extent that the games "disguise" fragility, they do so through resemblance, masking weakness with a superimposed pseudo- or apparent weakness.

There are four key episodes in an examination of the figure of paralysis in *El juego*: the revelation of Ana I's paralysis as false, the

---

[15] The effect of the doubled names is stronger for the reader than for the spectator. Between the two characters, a given name is used only once: the final line of the play is Ana II's cry, "¡Anita, mi pequeña!" (112; sc. 2) ["Anna, my dear little Anna!" (136)].

[16] Myron Lichtblau notes that in the play's premier, Romero played Ana II, thereby creating "una suerte de metateatro, en el cual se comenta sobre el proceso de escribir o, en este caso, sobre el proceso de representar un papel" (449) [a sort of metatheater, one that comments upon the process of writing or, in this case, the process of performing a role]. Karel Mena suggests that "El hecho de que ambos personajes lleven el mismo nombre, también permite la lectura de un solo personaje que se desdobla en facetas contrarias, como cuando niños jugamos frente al espejo, alternando el uno con el otro" (879) [The fact that both characters have the same name also permits a reading of a single character doubled into contrary facets, as when children play in front of the mirror, alternating one with the other]. In a film version of the play, both roles might be played by a single actor. In such an interpretation, the tension of the play would reflect an internal conflict, within which the ambiguous nature of the paralysis feigned by both women would become complicated at yet another level.

differing versions of the dream of the Príncipe Azul, the redefinition of the wheelchair as throne, and the begging lesson that occurs during Ana I's visit to Ana II in jail. These four moments situate paralysis within a complex matrix, alluding to a variety of social patterns and calling into question the connotations of an immobilized female figure. Paralysis–and false paralysis–appears linked to the danger of violent attack: as provocation or invitation, as that which makes the attack possible, and at the same time as that which ought to prevent attack, were it able to evoke the appropriate compassion. The various levels of paralysis present in *El juego* have their roots in the social limitations that surround the two women. The women's ritual representations are formulated in terms of a series of conventions, appropriating as dramatic material stereotypes such as the cripple unable to find work, the beggar who fakes her disability, and women vulnerable to rape because of weakness. The false paralytic is a different sort of leper, a social outcast medically defined but ultimately elusive. To the extent that Ana I is paralyzed (before her paralysis is revealed as part of the game), the physical cause of her immobility is never addressed. Feigned paralysis becomes a visual representation of women's weakened social status, so that paralysis might be seen as the logical extension of traditional roles that require an outward show of frailty.

The play's first stage direction establishes the presence of the wheelchair and a hospital bed, props that from the outset suggest illness and immobility. Although one might argue that a wheelchair becomes an extension of its occupant, offering mobility as a result, the use of the chair in Romero's text centers on a need to reach or occupy it, rather than on moving around once seated. The wheelchair remains more icon of paralysis than potential for movement.[17] The hospital-like furnishings visually allude to an institutional context and prefigure the later allusions to El Viejo, whose authority establishes the boundaries of the protagonists' lives. The

---

[17] Another interesting image of a woman in a wheelchair, although in this instance the paralysis is not feigned, appears in Jairo Aníbal Niño's *El sol subterráneo* (Colombia, 1977) [The underground sun]. This chair *is* a source of movement. In Niño's play, the chair itself, rather than the paralysis, is makeshift, "resultado del extraño maridaje de la pobreza entre un taburete de palo y dos ruedas de bicicleta" (159) [the result of poverty's strange combination of a wooden stool and two bicycle wheels]. Niño's play is a historical allegory of the massacre of Colombian banana workers.

clinical props also initially suggest entrapment of another sort, as if the two might be patients in an asylum, although the medical apparatus contrasts with the wooden crates, scraps of cloth, and broken glass that make up the rest of the decor.

At the first reference to Ana I's paralysis, there is no reason for the reader/spectator to doubt the reality of her handicap. Ana I insists that she is unable to stand, and Ana II forces her to drag herself across the floor to the wheelchair.[18] After Ana II seats her in the wheelchair, Ana I offers to relate "un sueño muy especial" (84; sc. 1) [a very special dream].[19] Her narrative provokes a violent reaction from Ana II, whose subsequent reformulation of the story highlights the image of paralysis. Ana I's version is one of romantic perfection. Still apparently paralyzed, she recounts her dream of a visit to a large city and a bicycle outing. When she is alone in the park, a prince appears and seduces her with his beautiful voice and soft hands. The prince's almost hypnotic gaze is underlined again and again: "estaba allí . . . a unos pocos pasos de mí . . . y me miraba. Me miraba con sus ojitos tan dulces" (85; sc. 1) ["He was right there . . . a few steps away . . . staring at me. His look was so soft" (112)]. His attraction lies, in part, in his eyes, in his willingness simply to look without acting. Yet it is Ana I's gaze that bewitches the prince: "no dejaba de mirarme ni un solo segundo [. . .] era como si yo le hubiera embrujado" (85; sc. 1) ["He didn't stop looking at me. Not for a second. {. . .} It was as if I had put a spell on him" (112)]. Even in this agreeable fantasy, there are notes of paralysis. The prince approaches when Ana I is lying on the ground, entirely still and consequently vulnerable. Describing the seduction, Ana I says, "yo me dejé llevar . . . no hice ni un gesto . . . ni un movimiento . . . me dejé llevar" (86; sc. 1) [I let myself go . . . I didn't make a move . . . not a single movement . . . I let myself go]. This paralysis

---

[18] The script, almost without stage directions, leaves a great deal of leeway for a director, and there are several options for the treatment of Ana I's initial paralysis. If she has remained on the floor until this moment–a choice that accords well with the rest of the action–the relation represented is simply that of strength against weakness. The revelation that Ana I *can* walk, that even her paralysis is part of the game, then produces a strong sense of surprise. If Ana I stands and later refuses to walk, the feigned quality of *all* of the play's action is evident from the first. The audience's sympathy for the abused invalid is negated by the falseness of her debility, and the symbolic associations of the paralyzed figure are reduced.

[19] Translations not appearing in quotes indicate that I have used my own rather than the published version of a given citation.

is no longer that of the wheelchair, but a pleasurable quiescence. In her telling, to surrender without movement is to cede to a gentle and trustworthy force. At the same time, the insistence of the prince's scrutiny and the emphasis on immobility reproduce, in fantasy, the paralysis that dominates her (apparent) reality. Her stillness is a necessary condition for the prince's approach, a necessity that may be read as empowering–he "catches" her only when she chooses to lie down–or as treacherous: the unmoving woman is vulnerable to approach by any and all.

Before Ana I is able to describe the consummation of the encounter, Ana II interrupts furiously and accuses her of changing the rules. She insists on imposing "la verdadera versión" ["the true story"] as Ana I begs: "no lo estropees" (87; sc. 1) ["don't spoil it" (114)]. Although Ana II repeatedly interrupts Ana I's narration to demand details, the exchange between the two also suggests repetition, as if all has been told before. Ana II is not responding in surprise to an unknown dream but to a set narration that, in her view, has been violated. The *telling* assumes paramount importance, and the force of rules in constituting the game is highlighted. Far from seeking new information, Ana II listens in order to make certain that the rules are observed. She protests at being left out and rejects as impossible Ana I's assertion that she was nowhere in sight during the encounter with the prince. Ana II's telling no longer resembles a dream but seems to recount actual events. In the retelling of Ana I's dream, narrative is foregrounded as a means of mutual abuse. The "script" of the story is openly an object of dispute, as the two claim ownership of both content and interpretation.

In Ana II's version, the prince becomes a syphilitic drunk, and his soothing gaze is replaced by "esa mirada sucia de sádico hambriento" (87; sc. 1) [the dirty look of a hungry sadist]. No longer false, a pleasurable manner of submission, paralysis is now the cause of violence. Ana I is unable to flee because of her paralysis, a paralysis that carries a clear measure of blame in the view of Ana II. Paralysis then invites violation: it is what allows the rapist to approach his victim and what prevents her from resisting. But the description of a woman awaiting her assailant, silenced by fear, anticipates Ana II's silent cry at the end of the play. The image of paralysis represents the vulnerability of both women, dominant only within the confines of their games and unable to escape the external control of El Viejo.

Also at issue in Ana II's retelling of the dream is the female spectator's reaction to the portrayal of violence against herself, as Ana II forces Ana I to observe, as spectator (listener), her own degradation. Myron Lichtblau writes, "el juego se vuelve tan sádico que la víctima no puede tolerarlo, ocurriendo así una forma de fantasía rechazada o fantasía negada porque el dolor, aunque no real, está profundamente sentido" (451) [the game becomes so sadistic that the victim is unable to tolerate it, leading to a form of rejected or negated fantasy because the pain, although unreal, is profoundly felt]. I would add that the pain, as performance, becomes real, and it is the force of performance that makes the pain unbearable. It is in reaction to the graphic description of her own rape that Ana I reveals that she does not in fact require the wheelchair. Accusing Ana II of going too far, she refuses to complete the game and instead retreats to her drawing table. Yet despite her initial refusal, Ana I is almost imperceptibly drawn into another game. Seated in the wheelchair, Ana II asks, first gently, then more forcefully, that Ana I undress. She urges: "mientras te desnudas me cuentas sobre tu príncipe de mirada azul" (90; sc. 1) ["while you are undressing, you can talk to me about your blue-eyed prince" (117)]. Once again caught up in the fantasy, Ana I begins to remove her clothing as she tells the story. Ana II, prompting the narrative, begins her own seduction until Ana I's resistance brings on a torrent of abuse: "esto no es ningún palacio, sino un burdel y yo soy la que manda en esta vaina" (92; sc. 1) ["This is no palace. This is a whorehouse, and I run it" (118)]. Ana I pays for the privilege of voice, of being heard, by stripping. Ana II appropriates a cliché and reelaborates it within her performance, explaining, "todas las putas son lesbianas y yo no soy precisamente la excepción" (92; sc. 1) ["All whores are gay and I'm no exception" (118)]. This remark is tied to Ana I's role as paralytic. The weak woman requires protection, even from an abusive patron; Ana II opened the queen/madam scenario under the pretense of offering shelter and a place to rest. But the falseness of the paralysis is important because Ana I only appears to need the madam's aid. The scene underscores again the interdependence of the two women, as well as the danger implied by Ana I's solo fantasy. While at one level Ana I's helplessness is only a pose, at another level Ana II continually strives to reinforce her dependence.

After a change of roles, Ana I directs Ana II to fetch the wheelchair, which has now become a throne: "desearía posar mi real trasero en los mullidos cojines de seda de mi trono imperial" (94; sc. 1) ["I want to feel those soft cushions caress my royal ass" (120)]. In this episode, the audience knows that Ana II is able to walk, although Ana I prevents her from doing so, and that Ana I's sole use for the wheelchair is as a prop for the dramatization of her fantasy. Appropriating Ana II's earlier role as sovereign, Ana I also reenacts the scene in which Ana II forced her to drag herself to the wheelchair. The redefinition of the wheelchair as throne superimposes a layer of associations on those the chair already carries. No longer an icon of immobility, the chair is the seat of power. The repetition of the queen motif echoes the fantastic, fairy tale imagery of the Príncipe Azul and extends the escapist possibilities of the game beyond the reenactment of mundane events to a world of luxury far from the sordid room the women inhabit. Still, the first queen (Ana II) transforms herself into a prostitute; the second queen is soon condemned as tyrant.

The allusions to a political context beyond the women's circumscribed world gradually become more insistent. Karel Mena argues that "Lo social es abordado desde la conducta moral de los personajes, sin referencias concretas a la re[a]lidad venezolana" (877) [The social is approached through the moral conduct of the characters, without concrete references to Venezuelan reality]. Although references to a specific historical moment are scarce, the women clearly invoke a world of dictatorship and generalized violence. The play premiered in 1976, at a time when repressive military regimes had overtaken governments in Brazil, Chile, Uruguay, and Argentina. In a warning that resonates with the feints Ludmer describes, Ana II has already cautioned that politics "es una de mis mejores armas. O mejor digamos, mi arma secreta" (89; sc. 1) [is one of my best weapons. Or better put, my secret weapon]. The wheelchair in turn literally becomes a weapon when Ana II throws it at Ana I. The "illegal" use of this symbol of paralysis and submission leads to Ana II's incarceration. She paints Ana I in the role of dictator, inverting paternalistic tradition to assure her captor, "estamos hartos de soportar tu maternalismo despiadado y cruel" (95; sc. 1) ["we've had it with your cruel and heartless maternalism" (121)]. The archetypal mother-as-nurturer is entirely absent. Employing the wheelchair, sign of paralysis within the game, as a physical weapon parallels the subversion of dominant forces in a broader context. The defining sign of weakness becomes the means of resistance. Although this shift is visually clearer here than in other instances, it recalls the way in which the overall game, imitating vulnerability and entrapment, postpones the terror of El Viejo's approach.

Ana I enters in the second scene seated in the wheelchair. The dialogue suggests that she is once again "inválida," although the fact that the episode occurs on the same set as the first scene implies from the outset another game, another performance. When Ana I visits her in jail, Ana II attempts to teach her to support herself by begging. She discounts the possibility that Ana I might find work and announces, "¡Pedir limosna! ¡Es su inevitable destino!" (100; sc. 2) [begging! It's your destiny!]. The inevitability of a career as a beggar is the logical result of the assumption that a weak woman requires external protection. The begging lesson further alludes to the image of the woman who must humiliate herself in exchange for support, an impasse that may occur at any social level (and which reflects the relation between the women and El Viejo).

In the role of a woman of the upper classes, Ana II resists Ana I's pleas and accuses her of not being genuinely paralyzed: "Se aprovechan de que uno es gente decente y tiene sentimientos para quererle sacar a uno los reales. Pero yo no me dejo conmover . . . además, yo conozco paralíticos que se mantienen haciendo manualidades" (102-03; sc. 2) ["You see a respectable person and then you play on her feelings. Well, it won't work with me. Besides I know a lot of people like you who work with their hands" (127)]. In desperation, Ana I kneels at the woman's feet, revealing once again that her paralysis is part of the fiction. Pretended paralysis moves beyond the strictly theatrical or performative context, for the woman's skepticism is yet another stereotypical reaction to apparently crippled beggars. The negotiation surrounding a (possibly) feigned paralysis depicted in the begging lesson has a concrete extratheatrical counterpart. In the economy of charity that the game reproduces, feigned paralysis (blindness, orphanhood, illness) is exchanged for sustenance, as the image of the incapacitated beggar, if successful, awakens the sympathy of the wealthy benefactor. The fact that paralysis is false–or is believed to be false–in the extratheatrical context calls attention to the degree to which other cases of fictive paralysis may be demanded by social constraints. The disability may or may not be real, but in order to resist the beggar's plea, the potential donor constructs it as unreal. The nongiver can then congratulate herself on having evaded the wiles of the beggar whose handicap is only a performance.

Ana I answers the suggestion of "manualidades" with the assertion, "yo sé pintar muy bien. Hago retratos," ["I can paint! I'm really good at doing people"] an offer scornfully denied by Ana II (in character as the upper class woman): "¡Sí, claro! ¡El retrato de la paralítica!" (103; sc. 2) ["I'm sure. Especially cripples" (127)]. In this encounter, Ana I's creative ability is reduced to a purely imitative capacity for manipulation. Nevertheless, Ana II admits that the ability to draw is the one thing she envies her–"realmente eres una artista" (106; sc. 2) ["You really are an artist" (130)]–although Ana II's admiration is at the same time another occasion for abuse. Yet the ability to draw is also a defense. When Ana II fails to recognize her portrait, Ana I informs her: "Yo no pinto lo que es . . . sino lo que veo" (107; sc. 2) ["I don't paint things the way they are . . . but how I see them" (131)]. Ana I's artistic self-awareness refracts her representation of herself within the games, producing yet another ground on which her perception is disputed. The self-conscious representation of paralysis, and the dramatic reenactment of the various scenarios that make up the game, is doubled in the treatment of Ana I as painter. While on one level she does indeed present the portrait of the paralytic, using her own body as canvas, on another level her art is described as nonrepresentational, or at least, "unrealistic." Her portrayal of the paralytic is not intended to reflect her actual physical capacity but an overall view of her position.

Issues of weakness, real and apparent, are evident early in the play. Ana II discounts Ana I's assertion that she is the weaker of the two with the explanation: "eres astuta, lo que viene a ser casi lo mismo. La astucia es a veces más peligrosa que la fuerza. Usas esa vocecita melindrosa y pones esa carita de niñita ingenua para conmoverme. Quisieras contagiarme tu debilidad" (81; sc. 1) ["you're smart, and that's almost the same thing. A smart person can be more dangerous than a strong one. You're trying to make me feel sorry for you . . . whining and pretending to be a sweet little girl. You'd love your weakness to rub off on me" (108)]. The threat posed by Ana I's weakness is not only the sympathy she garners or the lulling of her adversary to overconfidence; there is a danger of contagion, as if her immobility might by catching. Moreover, despite her generally subordinate position within the games, Ana I seems to enjoy relative safety from El Viejo. When Ana II points out that they will need to explain the day's idleness, Ana I reassures her: "yo te protegeré si puedo [. . .] a mí no me hace nada" (107; sc.

2) ["I'll protect you, if I can {. . .} he never does anything to me" (131)]. Unable to think of a suitable lie, Ana II resigns herself:

> ANA II: Es igual. Entonces le diremos la verdad.
> ANA I: ¡No te atreverás!
> ANA II: ¿Por qué hablas así? ¡Yo te protegeré . . . , no te atreverás . . . tú también estás metida en esto!
> ANA I: ¡Entonces digamos la verdad!
> ANA II: Sería capaz de matarme, tú lo sabes.
> ANA I: Sí, lo sé. Aunque no creo que te mate . . . en el fondo te necesita.
> ANA II: A ti también. Aunque nunca te lo diga, te necesita mucho. A las dos.
> ANA I: Eso le he oído decir. Una sola no es negocio. (108; sc. 2)

> [ANNA II: Then let's tell him the truth.
> ANNA I: You wouldn't dare!
> ANNA II: Why are you talking like that? "I'll protect *you*. . . *you* wouldn't dare." We're both mixed up in this.
> ANNA I: Then I agree. Let's tell him the truth.
> ANNA II: He'll kill me, you know that.
> ANNA I: Yes, he could. But I don't think he will . . . when all is said and done, he needs you.
> ANNA II: And you, too. He may never say it, but he does. A lot. He needs us both.
> ANNA I: Yeah, he even said so. He said he couldn't get by with one, but with two he could. (131-32)]

Again, the mutual dependence of the two is stressed. If one alone is not worth the bother, the departure of either clearly spells trouble for the Ana who remains. The interplay of contagion and representation further marks the women's (shared) weakness as a focus of negotiation. The possibility that Ana I's frailty is catching removes it, at least partially, from the ground of imaginary posturing. Yet her weakness retains a kernel of agency in Ana II's certainty that Ana I actively wishes to contaminate her. The threat of a contagious fiction reenacts yet again the work of a performative game that makes real, in the playing, that which it represents.

As the women attempt to fashion a story with which to defuse El Viejo, any division between their imaginative games and the reality they reflect is blurred. Ana I's description of what "really happened" recalls certain details of the begging scene, suggesting a correspondence between the dramatizations within the games and events outside:

> ANA I: ¿Por qué no le contamos lo de la violación?
> ANA II: No seas estúpida... no se lo creería.
> ANA I: Entonces lo del parque.
> ANA II: ¡Por favor, es en serio!
> ANA I: O mejor digamos lo que realmente pasó. Yo le iba a quitar la cartera a la vieja... pero tú te asustaste y la vieja se dio cuenta de la vaina y llamó a la policía.
> ANA II: ¡Sabes que sería capaz de matarme a golpes! (108; sc. 2)

> [ANNA I: Why don't we tell him about the rape?
> ANNA II: Don't be ridiculous... he'd never believe it.
> ANNA I: Then how about the park?
> ANNA II: Come on, this is serious!
> ANNA I: I mean let's tell him what really happened. That I was ready to grab the purse... but you got scared. Then she figured out what was going on and she called the police.
> ANNA II: If he knew that, he'd kill me with his bare hands. (132)]

Ana I's description of their encounter with the "vieja" hints that paralysis is a pose employed as part of their purse-snatching operation. When combined with the plots the two have earlier acted out, the summary of what "really happened" produces a layering effect. Certain elements are condensed, others expanded, as if the games represented fragments of reality fleshed out into more complete narratives.

The cooperative effort to protect themselves from El Viejo breaks down in mutual recrimination. Ana II proposes that they flee together, then insists that she will go alone. Even with El Viejo's steps approaching, the two are unable to leave behind the game, so that when Ana II demands to know where Ana I has hidden the purse, Ana I taunts her with the rhythm of a children's hunt, "Tibio ... tibio [...] Caliente, caliente..." (111; sc. 2) ["Warmer... you're getting warmer {...} Hot... now you're hot"] (134). Ana I collapses trying to prevent the flight of Ana II. Although Ana II holds a jackknife, it is not entirely clear whether she has used it. The paralysis Ana I performed in the first game has seemingly become real, breaking the confines of the "only a game" or "just pretend" space established earlier. Yet Ana I's collapse may be simply another stratagem to prevent Ana II from abandoning her.

Because they can, and do, move in and out of the play mode, the two move in and out of the wheelchair as well. Such movement allows them to reaffirm the temporary nature of their paralysis and, by extension, to dismiss their real entrapment, shifting their entire reality to the level of an implicitly escapable game. In this, the games mirror the theatrical situation, in which the actors necessarily move in and out of character, so that the pretended paralysis is false on more than one level.[20] A mobile actor plays the role of Ana I, a role that entails the representation of a paralysis neither actor nor character consistently suffer. At the same time, in her role as paralytic, Ana I tolerates considerable abuse. Because Ana I is *playing* the role of paralytic, there is a degree of acquiescence in her submission to Ana II's demands, an element of willingness revealed by its absence when she finally refuses to play. The charged nature of the games seems to produce an intensity of focus that allows the players to block out reality, so that the game structure is able to absorb a great deal of violence between the two before one of them calls "time." Alternately, the players are willing to endure the violence of the games in order to sustain their relation. Performance here is caught in a cycle of the reproduction of an abusive reality rather than providing a ludic escape.

The double-edged sword Moretta describes with regard to the game as vehicle for the characters becomes still more so for the woman dramatist. Larson argues that, for many women playwrights, "game-playing–whether literal or metaphoric–functions as a self-conscious technique for challenging such patriarchal notions as control and dominance" (78). She suggests that "playwrights use the game, itself allied with power and control, to portray the cultural and literary encoding that links women with manipulation, repression, and hierarchy. Nonetheless, games are curiously paradoxical choices for women to utilize in structuring their plays, at least in part because of the varied connotations that they generate" (85). Games reproduce the hierarchy Larson identifies as patriarchal, yet offer ample room for manipulation (the game structure is itself a

---

[20] The acknowledgment of the actor's presence as actor is also evident in the character/narrator of Dragún's *Historias para ser contadas* (Argentina, 1957) [Stories to be told] or in the alternation of control between Lalo and Cuca in *Asesinos*.

manipulation of reality), traditionally associated with femininity. The pose of female paralysis works in a similar fashion. Because of the connotations of feminine immobility, such a pose cannot function as an uncomplicated appropriation of repressive images to transformative ends. This is particularly so in *El juego*, in which the pose of passivity masks the characters' real situation only to the extent that it allows them to recreate with each other, instead of El Viejo, the unequal power relationships that delimit their lives. The pose reproduces the hierarchy but in the process allows each in turn to exercise her aggression against the other. Still, the mask is not ultimately liberating: the repetitive cycle of games is broken at the end of the play, but the women's link to El Viejo remains intact.[21] Larson concludes that "the playwrights evoke a kind of double-voiced discourse, inscribing their texts into male tradition while simultaneously using its very conventions to destabilize the literary and cultural myths that are encoded in the concept of game-playing" (86). Yet this argument seems equally applicable to *La noche de los asesinos*, if not in terms of gender relations, certainly in the use of existing conventions to destabilize cultural myths. The ironic undermining of the association of game-playing with childhood evident in Triana's depiction of adult children in a world of make-believe is a clear instance of the subversive assimilation Larson describes. Like performance, game-playing is inherently polysemous, conventional in its reproduction of rule structures, subversive in its refiguration of reality.

Although the operations Larson ascribes to games do tend to support patriarchal patterns, and the two Anas do join against the oppression of the unseen Viejo, the insistence of their violence toward each other points to a more complex questioning of power relationships than that produced in a strict reading of game as patriarchal construct. Nor is feigned paralysis in *El juego* inevitably expressed within a male/female relation. While we learn toward the end of the play that the games have been a defense against El Viejo, the absence of any mention of this authority in the first scene, and a large part of the second, gives the impression that the "violent dou-

---

[21] The use of games as a means to take out on one another the violence or abuse suffered outside the game or performance context is crucial to *Asesinos*. The game proposed by Federico in *¿A qué jugamos?* also provides the opportunity for the exercise of displaced aggression disguised as play.

bles" form a closed system. Within the games, a range of figures steps in to overpower the subordinate character: queen, madam, upper class matron, dictator, drunk. As often as not, the dominant figures are themselves socially marginalized. The majority of this play's violence occurs between women, even when they take on fictional roles within the games, although rival interpretations of an imagined male figure–prince charming/syphilitic rapist–shape their interactions. Still, rape, not the gender of the attacker, is the constant. The paralytic is presented as the dependent woman par excellence; the fact that the paralysis is fictive undercuts this dependence without entirely eliminating it. Paralysis in *El juego* is also valued as a means of exchange. The dominated member of the pair in effect concedes to her oppressor her capacity for independent movement. In exchange she receives a guarantee of protection, a nonaggression pact that will be immediately violated. The redirection of conventions Larson sees in game-playing is evident in the use to which Ana I puts her feigned paralysis, a conventionally female sign (immobility, passivity) redirected as a posture of resistance. Nevertheless, as in the case of the games Larson discusses, the strategic appropriation of false paralysis carries limitations.

   Schmitt suggests that "like post-modern performance, pretend play emphasizes process and improvisation, not resolution and a written text. In both, the performers may move in and out of the play mode and may serially transform objects, roles and actions. Both seem to be more rewardingly analyzed as perceptions of reality rather than as imitations of reality" ("Theatre" 230). The view of play as a perception of reality accords well with Ana I's own characterization of her painting as a depiction of what she sees, not necessarily what is. Ana I and Ana II perceive a reality governed by manipulation and abuse, a reality their games both reproduce and distort, amplifying certain elements, suppressing others. Although their games are not unrelated to their nongame lives, they are as much an exploration of the phenomena of paralysis and confinement as a detailed recreation of objective reality. The perception of paralysis as double-edged, both evasive and entrapping, is clear. Playing their paralysis as game reflects their sociopolitical context as well: even the confrontation between Ana II (as imprisoned subversive) and Ana I (as cruel dictator) takes on the quality of a verbal chess match as Ana II points out to Ana I the futility of either freeing her, unpunished, or providing a martyr for the revolution.

The treatment of paralysis in Romero's play demands a consideration of the female body as at once a site of violation and resistance. Ana I and Ana II use their bodies to represent in games the vulnerability of those same bodies in another context. Despite the distortions the games present, their performances quite literally reproduce the domination to which they are subject. The tensions between the game structure and the material represented within that framework are emblematic of the ambiguities of performance as liberating practice: while Ana I and Ana II temporarily displace their dreary existence through play, their games represent a reality as grim and violent as the one they attempt to escape. The hints of a reality behind the games, and the ambiguity of each of the contested versions, echo the questioning of historical knowledge discussed in the previous chapter, as the myriad events that make up history (small h) remain disputed or unknowable. The imaginative game is an ideal ground on which to question the text/performance relation. The struggle over the rules, over the correct rendition of the story of the prince, manifests a struggle over an implicit written text. These games are as much *about* their texts as of them. Likewise, despite the power of rules to constitute the game, many games in fact center more on achieving that constitution than on following the rules once established.

Through the substitution of stylized representations, the games that constitute *El juego* displace external (nongame) violence. Paralysis itself is emblematic of the situations portrayed in many game-centered plays. These performances, however, are not necessarily cathartic or liberating. In *La noche de los asesinos*, for example, the protagonists remain trapped in a cycle of repetition with variation: Beba will lead the next round. The back and forth of violence here associated with performance—individuals are coerced into performing, perform (act out) abuse, accept abuse in order to perform—recalls the comments on actors in concentration camps with which Rial prefaces *Bolívar*. As a space of negotiation similar to that of performance, games provide a partial liminal space, not quite as cut off from "ordinary reality" as Huizinga might suggest, but nevertheless restricted. In a wider social context, "paralysis" is the real condition of women, like Ana I and Ana II, dominated by forces that prevent them from moving.[22] The chance of resolution, or at

---

[22] Susana Castillo concludes that in *El juego* "el recinto cerrado es un sórdido

least closure, comes at the end with the imminent violence of El Viejo. Seen from the border between game and reality, the game (which dramatizes paralysis and is at the same time caused by exterior paralysis) is a tactic of resistance. Nevertheless, it is a resistance inevitably shaded by the paradoxical use of immobility as a means of agency. The presence of these unmoving women is as insistent as it is disquieting. The image of female immobility reconstructs female identity through an appropriation of dominant conceptualizations. The self-conscious adoption of the pose presents a performance of paralysis designed at the same time to break stasis in favor of escape. Still, although Ana I's immobility is false, she is unable to escape the broader paralysis that keeps her in the room, awaiting El Viejo. *El juego* ends with both women paralyzed, Ana I collapsed, Ana II silenced by fear. The feints of the weak, in this instance, displace but cannot eliminate oppression.

Maruxa Vilalta's *Pequeña historia de horror (y de amor desenfrenado)* and Esteban Navajas's *La agonía del difunto* also explore the notion of feigned paralysis in dangerous games, although the figure is less central than in *El juego*. In *Pequeña historia*, feigned paralysis is part of an extended play of horror conventions and sexual excess. *La agonía del difunto* makes the inherent risks of performing paralysis explicit, as the character who performs his own death is killed by his spectators, who at one level simply accept the superficial terms of the performance he has undertaken.

Pequeña historia de horror (y de amor desenfrenado) is essentially a farce, spoofing the conventions of television and melodrama with a bizarre sequence of murder plots within plots, dizzying sexuality and gender reversals, and a butler constantly cackling in the manner of El Monje Loco [The Crazy Monk]. The plot involves the arrival of Jonathan at an old London home with the purpose of making love to Mildred, whom he has observed through a window. The

---

microcosmos desde el cual se enjuician todas las instituciones sociales. Los personajes, manipulados y limitados por fuerzas socio-económicas, sobreviven en los rituales violentos de los juegos y las recreaciones. De ahí que su pequeña lucha–por muy fútil y desigual que parezca–es la única posibilidad de ruptura del círculo opresor" (32) [the enclosed space is a sordid microcosm from which all social institutions are judged. The characters, manipulated and limited by socio-economic forces, survive in the violent rituals of games and re-creation. However futile and uneven they may appear, their small fights become the only possibility of rupturing the oppressive circle].

house reveals a knot of would-be assassins, presumed or hopeful heirs, and interchangeable lovers. Set in England, although the characters "hablan todos en mexicano," [all speak Mexican] *Pequeña historia* is also a parody of the stage conventions of Englishness, with the inevitable butler and afternoon tea (22; 1).[23]

In Vilalta's play, the pretended paralytic is a man, known as Tía Emily, who alternates between the roles of giggling "ancianita," seductive woman, stock homosexual, and infuriated macho. Set against the extended treatment of false paralysis in *El juego*, the employment of the image in *Pequeña historia* is far less central. Feigned paralysis in Vilalta's text is part of the continual shifting of apparent motivation and intention. Tía Emily's pretended paralysis is an attempt at ingratiation, at concealing power and enmity. It is also openly acknowledged. When Jonathan expresses surprise at one of Tía Emily's transformations, Mildred informs him, "no es ancianita. Finge serlo por parecer indefensa" (21; 1) ["She's not a little old lady. She pretends to be one so people will think she's defenseless" (33)]. Later, under her breath, Mildred reminds Jonathan: "trata de parecer inofensiva, pero no está paralítica" (33; 1) ["She tries to seem harmless, but she's not paralyzed" (39)]. Tía Emily's giggling, wheelchair-bound "ancianita" is a role necessary to the script but one that is ultimately unsustainable. Rather than invite violence, Tía Emily's pose of weakness masks her threats and makes her own violence possible.

The characters' intermittent self-consciousness is closely tied to a sense of genre identification. More caricature than rounded character, Jonathan affirms: "me gustan [los melodramas] desde que soy personaje principal precisamente de un melodrama" (14; 1) ["I've liked them ever since I've had the lead role in one" (29)]. When Jonathan inappropriately addresses her as Margaret, Mildred's correction is greeted with a nonchalant "la historia se repite" (11; 1) ["History repeats itself" (28)]. Mildred's lack of understanding is in turn dismissed with Jonathan's admission: "me encantan las frases hechas" (11; 1) ["I love clichés" (28)], a more subtle suggestion of repetition that is continued as both plot and character are constructed from the "frases hechas" of generic convention. The stock

---

[23] Kirsten Nigro's translation of the play retains the necessary clash of accents for an English-speaking audience by rendering the passage as "these Londoners all speak like Yanks" (33).

character is made emotionally expressive not only in spite of but through his conventional mannerisms, so that Williams's chilling laugh is used "no siempre para indicar necesariamente algo siniestro sino también para significar estados de ánimo diversos: expresar burla, desafío, amenaza, complicidad, satisfacción, autoelogio" (16; 1) ["not just to indicate something sinister, but also a variety of moods: mocking, challenging, threatening, conspiratorial, self-congratulatory, and of satisfaction" (30)]. Implicit in this description is a questioning of the efficacy of language, as a single vocal expression is assigned a range of unexpected meanings. Williams's laugh functions as an all-purpose sign, in contrast to the giggle Tía Emily employs to mark her "ancianita" persona.

The parody of melodrama in Vilalta's play echoes the romantic fairy tale parodied in *El juego* through Ana II's retelling of the Príncipe Azul story as the antithesis of the romantic dream Ana I had enjoyed. However, the interactions among the cast as a whole do not present a repetition of past events. The game-like nature of their exchanges emerges in slippages from an implied text or in the obstinacy with which individuals hew to planned scripts in the face of obvious noncomprehension. Following an interruption, Jonathan asks: "¿En qué íbamos?" ["Where were we?"] only to reject Mildred's suggestion with a confident "No, eso ya pasó. Íbamos más adelante" (35; 1) ["No, I'd already done that. We were further along" (40)]. As he embraces Mildred, Williams informs the audience of his murderous intentions. Yet when he moves to stab her, his actions are misinterpreted: "Sin dejar de abrazar a Mildred, trata de sacar el puñal, pero no lo logra. Ella toma sus esfuerzos por movimientos eróticos" (49; 2) ["Still embracing MILDRED, he tries to get the dagger from his pocket, but can't. MILDRED takes his contortions for some kind of erotic play" (46)]. The play closes with an extended monologue in which Jonathan rehearses his possible madness and his wife Margaret's murder, after which he kills Mildred, Tía Emily, and Williams.

As a defensive pose, Tía Emily's paralysis is easily discarded, just as she shifts persona mid-speech according to need. When Williams advances on her, dagger in hand, Tía Emily leaps from the wheelchair brandishing a revolver. Nevertheless, Jonathan expresses surprise when he encounters Tía Emily standing up: "de modo que no está paralítica, digo, paralítico" (43; 2) ["So you're not a paralytic after all" (43)].[24] Tía Emily responds by reassuming her role: pretended paralysis is one more element in a repertoire of masks assumed as the occasion demands. Paralysis and an infantilizing take on old age are combined in Tía Emily's lisping, tantrum-prone "ancianita." As in *El juego*, paralysis is identified as a feminine pose. Tía Emily, employing several personas, would seem to blur gender roles. Yet the personas Tía Emily adopts remain discrete caricatures, rather than overlapping or running together. In both plays, paralysis is feigned in an attempt at self-protection. Here, however, the focus is on the inversion of melodramatic conventions rather than on an extended consideration of the implications of assumed immobility. The theatricality of Tía Emily's paralysis is even more strongly underscored than is that of *El juego*, for the performances within *Pequeña historia* point to no outside context, in the manner of *El juego*'s references to dictatorship, but instead occur within a frame of theatrical self-reference and melodramatic exaggeration.

Feigned paralysis is just one of the dangerous performances evident in *Pequeña historia*. Violence between characters is frequently tied to performance, as when Williams' attempts to stab Mildred are interpreted by the intended victim as an attempted seduction. The tale is so exaggerated and far-fetched that, as Sharon Magnarelli notes, "se nos prohibe una suspensión voluntaria de la incredulidad") ("Contenido" 77) [we are denied the willing suspension of disbelief]. With its emphasis on melodramatic convention, all of the events of *Pequeña historia* may be seen as a game in which Jonathan recreates, again and again, the murder of his wife. In his final monologue Jonathan, in the role of psychiatric patient, addresses various audience members directly as Doctor. His final words–"I'm hungry"–following upon a triple murder, are so banal and irrelevant as to call into question the already doubtful reality of the entire plot.

The play is filled with subtle and not so subtle references to theater. Jonathan protests that the cat that rapes Mildred every night is not even real: "Pero si es de utilería, de peluche" (21; 1) ["But he's a prop, a stuffed animal" (33)]. Tía Emily, on the point of killing Williams, addresses the audience: "¡Maldición! Intermedio" (42; 1)

---

[24] The gender confusion evident in the Spanish paralítica/paralítico is difficult to capture in English.

["Damn! The intermission" (42)]. The two freeze, and the second act opens as though not a moment had passed; Williams resumes his anguished cry "como disco que vuelve a empezar a girar bajo la aguja" (43; 2) [like a record that begins to turn again under the needle]. The entire set-up is played as a game, although it is one with ultimately murderous consequences. Characters frequently refer to their own actions as games. Jonathan, eager to get rid of Williams so as to be alone with Mildred at last, proposes multiple plots that might justify, to the muddle-headed butler, his departure. When Williams only becomes further confused, taking Jonathan's suggestions literally, Jonathan explains that it is all a game, "El juego de las suposiciones" (55; 2) ["The suppositions game" (49)]. Jonathan ultimately transposes his suggestion to the realm of television, that is, into terms Williams can understand. In the tone of a television annoucer, Jonathan offers: "Conecte su mente, Williams; ponga la televisión. [. . .] Le estoy dando una categoría de personaje . . . qué digo de personaje; una categoría de protagonista de una historia de horror" (60-61; 2) ["Plug your mind in, Williams. Turn on the television. {. . .} I am offering you the chance to be a character . . . what do I mean, character! The chance to be *the* protagonist in a tale of horror" (52)]. Williams' training as spectator–his devotion to television is repeatedly invoked–makes possible his performance in Jonathan's script. The mix of recorded and live performance is also striking, as this stage play attempts to approximate the stability and accessibility of phonograph records and television programs.

Closely tied to the endless plot reversals are questions of gender and sexual practice. No identity is stable, everyone seems to be sleeping with everyone else, and Williams complains frequently of his inability to satisfy the myriad sexual demands of the house's residents. Frustrated by the indeterminate gender of Tía Emily, Jonathan repeatedly asks for clarification, at one point demanding, mockingly, "Decídase de una vez: ¿es hombre, mujer, lesbiana o joto?" (32; 1) ["Make up your mind once and for all: are you a man, a woman or some combination or permutation thereof?" (38)]. Williams, ostensibly the quintessential English butler (he boasts of his lengthy pedigree), is also ambiguously gendered:

> WILLIAMS: ¡Mildred! (*Furioso, puñal en alto, está ante Jonathan. Trata de disimular. Inicia tímida carcajadita, que le resulta femenina.*) Uuuaa . . . (*De puntillas, como bailarina, da unos pasitos de ballet.*)

JONATHAN: ¡Ah, es usted bailarina! De modo que también el mayordomo resultó loca.
WILLIAMS: (*Macho*) ¡Yo soy muy hombre!
JONATHAN: ¿Y los pasitos de ballet?
WILLIAMS: (*Melodramático*) ¡Lady Macbeth! La escena del puñal.
JONATHAN: Oh, lee usted a Shakespeare.
WILLIAMS: ¡No! Veo la televisión. (51-52; 2)

[WILLIAMS: Mildred! (*Furious, he's left holding the dagger in mid-air, face to face with* JONATHAN. *He pretends that nothing is going on. He laughs a timid, feminine laugh.*) Uuuaaaaaaaaaa... (*He walks around on his tip-toes, like a ballerina.*)
JONATHAN: Oh, so you're a ballerina. So the butler's also a bit of a pansy.
WILLIAMS (*macho*): I'm every inch a man!
JONATHAN: And that little ballet routine?
WILLIAMS (*melodramatic*): Lady Macbeth! The dagger scene.
JONATHAN: Oh, you read Shakespeare.
WILLIAMS: No! I watch television. (47)]

Gender and performance are connected and again, conventions are undermined. Williams's recourse to Lady Macbeth to explain his prancing about with the dagger combines a well-worn allusion (the dagger scene itself is almost a dramatic cliché) with a reference to a deliberately unfeminine woman.[25] Significantly, it is an allusion available to Williams through television–he has not read the play. Intertextuality connects not only distinct texts, but diverse media. The internal spectators of Vilalta's play are at once over-prepared and unsophisticated, on the one hand trapped by melodramatic conventions they are unable to revise and on the other able to comprehend only that which reaches them via the television screen.

Yet *Pequeña historia de horror (y de amor desenfrenado)* can be read on several levels, for while the violence often takes on a slapstick quality, and the play of sexualities is always exaggerated and

---

[25] Lady Macbeth's invocation, "Come, you spirits / That tend on mortal thoughts, unsex me here" has been variously read; here it is sufficient to underscore the highly theatrical and ambiguously gendered ground of Williams's explanation (1.5.38-39). The play of gender and genre will be explored more fully in the next chapter.

unreal, three corpses are left on stage at the close of the second act. What seems a pell-mell crush of playfully shifting sexual identities and practices is the underlying justification for a well-worn plot–everyone is out to kill everyone else, and sex is largely an excuse to get close to the victim–and beyond that the ground of a distinctly violent game. Thus, while it appears at first that everything can be reduced to sex, in the end all of the characters' connections are reduced to violence. Magnarelli writes, "lo que pudo haber sido un trillado melodrama se convierte en una descripción poética de la agresión y violencia en la lucha por el poder y en las relaciones sexuales" ("Contenido" 78) [what could have been a trite melodrama becomes a poetic description of aggression and violence in the struggle for power and in sexual relations]. The illicit thrill of off-limits sex in fact camouflages the less commonly hidden, and so less immediately tantalizing signifier, aggression.

La agonía del difunto offers another counterpoint to the false paralysis of *El juego*. The action occurs in a single afternoon of pouring rain on a cattle ranch in northern Colombia, a region of vast haciendas and the site of numerous land invasions in the late sixties and early seventies. Faced with a peasant invasion of his property, landowner Agustino Landazábal fakes his own death in order to gain time while awaiting military assistance. His wife, Doña Carmen, aided by two campesinos, Ñora Otilia and Benigno Sampués, carries out the mourning rituals while Agustino does his best to keep still. In the process, Doña Carmen is also forced into immobility as Ñora Otilia and Benigno take a dominant role that she is unable to counter. The two prod her to kneel and force upon her their version of the widow's role she herself has assumed. As she complains after they have left the room, "parece que supieran que no puedo estarme ni cinco minutos arrodillada y lo hicieran a propósito" (700) [it seems as if they knew that I can't kneel for even five minutes and they did it on purpose]. Truly active spectators, Ñora Otilia and Benigno demand of Doña Carmen an adequate–by their standards–rendition of the role she has chosen. The campesinos work in stages, first commenting on the miraculous preservation of Agustino's body–three days with no sign of decay–later complaining of the stench despite Doña Carmen's insistence that she smells nothing. Over her objections, they wrap his body tightly for burial. Agustino's false paralysis becomes real when the campesinos pretend to take at face value the assertion of his death; he is sealed in a coffin and buried alive.

Games are also significant in *La agonía del difunto*, although Agustino's paralysis lies outside the game context and so within the play's reality. Rather than enacting a false paralysis, this play's games provide both comic and physical relief from Agustino's enforced immobility. The games further supply a justification for his death, as they reenact events to which the campesinos at his bedside have alluded more indirectly. Agustino and Doña Carmen ward off fear of their own deaths with games that recreate the deaths for which they have been responsible.[26] The couple's games represent flashbacks to a time before the action of the play. Unlike the fragmented hints of outside events the audience gleans from the dialogue of *El juego*, in Navajas's play the games provide straightforward background to the plot. In their own way, the games are as violent as those of Ana I and Ana II, although the violence is directed outward, rather than toward each other. Agustino and Doña Carmen's games once again take place within a context of enclosure, recreating events that have occurred outside the confines of the house the characters are unable to leave. According to Patricia González, "los juegos que les entretienen son macabros, donde la risa y el placer son producto de la carnicería que hacen los toros de los peones borrachos o descuidados. Agustino juega con la muerte sin saber que baila la danza de la suya propia" (29) [the games that entertain them are macabre ones in which laughter and pleasure are products of the butchery that the bulls make of drunken or careless workers. Agustino plays with death without realizing that his dance is that of his own death]. In the games, Agustino and Doña Carmen are the drunks, and Agustino's later hiccuping, after Benigno and Ñora Otilia's return, fails to puncture the illusion of his death only because Benigno and Otilia are determined to respect appearances while toying as much as possible with the landowners' fear of discovery. As moments of freedom from the limitations imposed by

---

[26] As González observes, "aunque recurren a una situación memorable y feliz del pasado, regresan a la necrosis: evocan las muertes ocasionadas durante la corraleja que festejó las nupcias" (29) [although they turn to a memorable and happy situation of the past, they return to necrosis: they evoke the deaths that occurred during the bullfights that celebrated their wedding]. The *corraleja* is an unusual local festival in which amateur bullfighters confront angry bulls, frequently resulting in the humans' maiming or death (often to the delight of the crowd).

the roles of widow and corpse, the games allow the two to play themselves, and the indifferent cruelty revealed in their amusements serves to further justify the tenants' retribution.

Both Benigno Sampués and Ñora Otilia have lost family members to the Landazábals' greed and arrogance. As he coaches Doña Carmen in her widow's role, Benigno recalls the death of his wife Natalia and the bittersweet persistence of his memories. Later, playing with Agustino, Doña Carmen reenacts the death of Demetrio, Ñora Otilia's father, who expired during the wedding: "*comienza a bizquear y se arrodilla entre convulsiones extrañas, sacando notas cada vez más destempladas del bombardino*" (711) [she begins to cross her eyes and kneels in strange convulsions, blowing increasingly discordant notes on the baritone]. Agustino, initially frightened by her appearance, is delighted when he solves the puzzle and begs an encore: "Estuvo genial. La muerte del viejo Demetrio. ¡Repítelo!" (711) [It was brilliant. The death of old Demetrio. Do it again!]. Demetrio's death was one of those that "made" the wedding for, as Agustino shouts, "¡Si no hay muertos no hay fiesta buena!" (710) [It's not a party unless somebody dies]. It was, moreover, a grotesque and unnecessary death, as can be seen in Agustino's savoring of the details: after three days of drinking and playing, "le estallaron los pulmones. Nunca había visto nada igual. La sangre y pedazos de bofe salían a borbotones por la trompa del bombardino. [. . .] Llené cien veces su bombardino con ron blanco y todos bebimos a su memoria" (711-12) [his lungs exploded. I'd never seen anything like it. Blood and pieces of lung gushed out of the horn of his baritone. {. . .} I filled the baritone with white rum a hundred times, and we all drank to his memory]. Adding insult to injury, Agustino gave Demetrio's widow a heifer in exchange for the baritone that Doña Carmen now plays. In the final scene, Ñora Otilia triumphantly reclaims her father's instrument, placing it atop the sealed coffin as she and Benigno bear Agustino's body away.

Ironically, Agustino and Doña Carmen are undone by their own performance of weakness. Agustino gloats, "sólo hay algo que me alegra: que yo sé qué está pasando y ellos no. Tengo el as en mi mano derecha y conozco el final de la historia" (701) [only one thing makes me happy: that I know what's happening and they don't. I have the ace in my right hand and I know the end of the story]. Yet as his anxiety increases, he asks his wife: "¿Crees que todo este teatro me salvará de la muerte?" (706) [Do you think that all this theater will save me from death?]. Like Ana I and Ana II, feigning paralysis to escape, or displace, their real entrapment, Agustino plays possum in a desperate attempt to avoid death. Yet all of the aces Agustino imagines up his own sleeve are already in Benigno's pocket: after hammering the nails into Agustino's coffin, (ignoring the blows of the "dead" man against the lid) Benigno pulls out a fuse and casually repairs the radio on which Agustino and Doña Carmen had tried to summon help. Albuquerque describes the play's "gradual revelation of the victimizer's entrapment in the repressive machinery of his own device" (132). The dramatic irony of Agustino's remarks about theater contrasts with the uncertain fate of the characters at the close of *El juego*. In a sense, the paralysis adopted by Agustino, and its effects, are the inverse of the paralysis played out by Ana I and Ana II. Where Agustino is trapped in his own "repressive machinery," Ana I and Ana II are trapped in the machinery of their oppression. Agustino adopts a pose of weakness in an attempt to evade the payback for his own abusive activities and is trapped by the attempt. Ana I and Ana II adopt, with no greater success, poses of immobility that seek to evade their actual immobility. *La agonía del difunto*, then, displays two levels of game: the games played by Agustino and Doña Carmen when they are alone, and the game played by Benigno and Ñora Otilia, a game of pretended ignorance, of knowing but not saying, as in Ludmer's formulation. *La agonía del difunto* further points to the vulnerability of false paralysis: the ease with which the representation of immobility can become entirely real. The "feints of the weak," however, triumph here in a way that Ana I and Ana II's stratagems do not.

El juego, *Pequeña historia de horror (y de amor desenfrenado)*, and *La agonía del difunto* all reflect the dangers of performing illness or, in the case of the last play, death. The campesinos carry to its logical extreme the willing suspension of disbelief: if Agustino looks dead, he must be dead, and the performance literally infects the actor. The blue leper has taken over–the space of performance absorbs the non-dramatic or non-theatrical reality and obliterates or erases it. I return to the image of the blue leper–a figure of staged contamination, of unwitting infection–as a reflection of the risks of the paralysis feigned in these three plays. One danger of performing an outcast role is the risk of being forced to maintain that role, to take it up and make it one's own. The contagion of weakness is also the contagion of performance, the self-realizing performative lurking in any fully realized role, however fictive. None of these performances of immobility are fixed. Instead, like that half-remembered, not-quite-real girl in the bright blue dress, they represent what cannot be finally pinned down. The solidification of played stasis points to performance's intrinsic instability: I play at immobility so that you will overlook me and move on to the next victim, so that I can slip out of range. But if the act is too convincing, I may be left unable to move. Alternately, it may not be how convincing the act is that is important, but when it takes place, whether the pretended immobility coincides with violent attack. The problematic temporality of performance plays into this uncertainty. The audience is invited to witness a dangerous spectacle of vulnerability and must decide whether to remain passive or to intervene. And the layering of multiple moments, multiple texts, expands the vulnerability of the seemingly immobilized performer across the auditorium and beyond the stage.

CHAPTER 3

PLAYING GENDER

IN Rosario Castellanos's perhaps over-long farce, *El eterno femenino* (Mexico, 1974) [*The Eternal Feminine*], the protagonist Lupita ("focal point" might be a better term for her) experiences the rapid-fire play of future possibilities–bride, mother, scorned wife who kills her husband's secretary–much like a spectator in a theater: the play she watches is her own (potential) life. A sequence of socially sanctioned outcomes, exaggerated for comic effect, combined with the "true confessions" of female historical figures ordinarily distorted by official history, call into question all of Lupita's expectations. *El eterno femenino* does not so much question the idea of gender as highlight the various "performances" a woman is obliged to produce in keeping with her social role or position. The respectable woman becomes a construct of manipulation, motherly advice, and artful appearance, a productive process in which she is often implicated as a more or less willing participant. Castellanos's play is also a dramatization of her own essays, and establishes an intertextual dialogue with her previous writings as well as with the social conventions she takes as texts.

Although Castellanos questions the roles assigned to women rather than the gender category "woman," the performance of gender roles, and of gender as role, parallels the concerns of writers such as Judith Butler, who argues in *Gender Trouble* that "there is no gender identity behind the expressions of gender; that identity is performatively constituted by the very 'expressions' that are said to be its results" (25). Gender categories come in for greater questioning in Sabina Berman's *El suplicio del placer* (Mexico, 1978) [The torture of pleasure], particularly the first part, "Uno," and in Susana Torres Molina's *. . .Y a otra cosa mariposa* (Argentina, 1981)

[And that's enough of that]. In "Uno," an androgynous couple recreates the events of the previous evening, in the process blurring gender and individual roles. . . . *Y a otra cosa mariposa* follows four male friends from childhood to old age. Both plays present complex scenarios of transvestism, formally and thematically. The transvestism of "Uno" combines an androgynous costume with a mobile mustache coded male but variously interpreted. In Torres Molina's play, cross-dressing establishes the representational frame of the play when the four female actors assume the costumes of their male characters. Transvestism also occurs within the frame, as part of the interaction of the four protagonists.

All three plays depict, in differing ways, relations between gender and performance, including the performances demanded in accord with a presumably given gender and the construction of gender through–and as–performance. Cross-dressing is not necessarily limited to literal instances of male-to-female or female-to-male impersonation. Thus, Marjorie Garber, while acknowledging that the readers of certain how-to magazines for the male-to-female transvestite have "bought into the concept of woman as artifact, assembled from a collection of parts: wig, painted nails, mascara and 'blush,'" contends that "the social critique performed by these transvestite magazines for readers who are not themselves cross-dressers is to point out the degree to which *all* women cross-dress as women when they produce themselves as artifacts" (49). As a variety of transvestism, the roles Lupita assumes in *El eterno femenino* illustrate Castellanos's contention that feminine roles are artificial and constructed rather than naturally given. The stereotyped and frozen images Castellanos mines for comic effect correspond to the reification of femininity in the male-to-female transvestite whose costume depicts an exaggerated and distorted "femininity" with little real-world analogue.

A consideration of gender and performance suggests two areas of analysis: the roles imposed by gender (roles which must be performed) and the possibility that gender itself is a performance, a possibility that effectively erases the "itself" of the last phrase. A model of gender as performance is complicated by the traditional view of women as inherently superficial or unreal. The recognition of the element of performance in gender is both a critique of the given system–a critique accomplished in *El eterno femenino* through the ridicule of the "performances" imposed–and, in other models, a rejection of the "agent" of those performances, that is, of the woman who deceptively performs. The critique of feminine roles or identity as performance may follow two distinct trajectories: a dismissal of woman "herself" as duplicitous, always deceptively "made up" (both imaginary and cosmetically adorned) and a rejection of the demand or necessity for that performance. Connecting gender specifically to performance also recalls the long history of opposition to professional female actors.

Transvestism becomes an important tool for the representation of gender and its destabilization on stage because, unlike frequently invisible (because customary) normative male and female roles, it is immediately recognizable as a performance. Garber argues that the significance of cross-dressing lies, in part, in the manner in which, as a "third term," transvestism "offers a challenge to easy notions of binarity, putting in question the categories of 'female' and 'male,' whether they are considered essential or constructed, biological or cultural" (10). To view Tía Emily's cross-dressing in Maruxa Vilalta's *Pequeña historia de horror (y de amor desenfrenado)* as a "third term" illustrates the way in which her tricky gender identification destabilizes the game of mistaken identities and concealed ploys of the work's hybrid horror-melodrama. Garber stresses, however, that "the 'third term' is *not a term*. Much less is it a *sex*, certainly not an instantiated 'blurred' sex as signified by a term like 'androgyne' or 'hermaphrodite,' although these words have culturally specific significance at certain historical moments. The 'third' is a mode of articulation, a way of describing a space of possibility" (11). Garber's third that is not a term recalls the axis David George sets up between actor and role, in which the process of relating, rather than any resulting relationship, is paramount. Yet Tía Emily's occasional transvestism is an act in the strongest sense: it is something she does, not a distinctive state or object. This episodic transvestism underscores the fact that gender is always a performance, at once assumed and imposed.

For Garber, transvestism is fundamental to representation. She concludes that "the more I have studied transvestism and its relation to representation the more I have begun to see it, oddly enough, as in many ways normative: as a condition that very frequently accompanies theatrical representation when theatrical self-awareness is greatest. Transvestite theater from Kabuki to the Renaissance English stage to the contemporary drag show is not–or not only–a recuperative structure for the social control of sexual behavior, but also a critique of the possibility of 'representation' itself" (353).[1] As I have argued earlier, however, to question the possibility of representation is not to eliminate it. Like performance more broadly understood, cross-dressed representation is yet another means of critique implicated in the very structures it sets out to destabilize.

Like Garber, Severo Sarduy views transvestism as irreducible, a sign in itself rather than inevitably a "metaphor for." In a discussion of José Donoso's *El lugar sin límites*, Sarduy argues that "El travestismo, tal y como lo practica la novela de Donoso sería la metáfora mejor de lo que es la escritura: lo que Manuela nos hace ver no es una mujer *bajo la apariencia* de la cual se escondería un hombre, una máscara cosmética que al caer dejara al descubierto una barba, un rostro ajado y duro, sino *el hecho mismo del travestismo*" (74) ["Transvestism, as Donoso's novel practices it, is probably the best metaphor for what writing really is: what Manuela makes us see is not a woman *under whose outward appearance* a man must be hiding, a cosmetic mask which, when it falls, will reveal a beard, a rough, hard face, but rather *the very fact of transvestism itself*" (33)]. Elaborating the writing-transvestism comparison, he concludes: "Estos planos de inter-sexualidad son análogos a los planos de inter-textualidad que constituyen el objeto literario. Planos que dialogan en un mismo exterior, que se responden y completan, que se exaltan y definen uno al otro: esa inter-acción de texturas lingüísticas, de discursos, esa danza, esa parodia es la escritura" (74) ["Those planes of intersexuality are analogous to the planes of intertextuality which make up the literary object. They are planes which communicate on the same exterior, which answer each other and complete each other and define each other. That interaction of linguistic textures, of discourses, that dance, that parody, is writing" (33)]. To some degree, Sarduy's characterization of writing seems compatible with the revalorization of surface that Debra Castillo proposes: "the cultivation of a polished superficiality suggests a willed, willful transvaluation of values which surpasses mere rever-

---

[1] Jill Dolan, however, criticizes Garber for "shortsightedness about theatrical performance," observing that "she engages with very few, and mostly mainstream, examples of performance to make her point about the transvestite as the 'third term' in binaries of gender" (434).

sal" (52). Still, in the plays under discussion here, transvestism continues to function as metaphor, if only to the extent that it represents the degree to which all gender acts incorporate cross-dressing, whether conventionally recognized or not. Cross-dressing in the plays I will examine points up the constructedness of gender, the instability of apparently inevitable categories. The transvestite "as such," however, is less central; the instances of cross-dressing, I would argue, are in fact allusions to something else, to something that is disguised in drag, rather than a free-standing or independent third term or articulation.

Jean Franco has observed in the work of Latin American women writers "the emergence of certain *topoi*–in particular, the *topoi* of the stigmatized female body and that of the liberated artist or performer" ("Self-Destructing" 108). Franco frames her discussion with the differential weight the adjective "public" carries when attached to women rather than men: "To describe someone as a 'public woman' in Latin America is simply not the same as describing someone as a public man–and therein hangs a tale. The public woman is a prostitute, the public man a prominent citizen" ("Self-Destructing" 105).[2] She writes: "Both *topoi* respond to a system of representations found in works by male authors; in the first [case] to the representation of sado-masochistic relations and in the second case to the 'immobile' and fixed spaces of femininity (house, brothel, convent) which the actress alone transgresses. Yet performance is also a problematic metaphor for liberation. [. . .] Women can never forget their looks as males can. Thus, for women writers to depict creativity in terms of a performance inevitabl[y] exposes the painful contradiction that, to be creative, she must become a public woman, a public woman whose shame and failure are exposed to ridicule" ("Self-Destructing" 108). The immobility that Franco describes is also that depicted in Mariela Romero's *El juego*, transposed or transgressed by the female actor's refusal of paralysis, a refusal realized in the apparent freedom of performance. Yet there is a dual danger in the depiction of creativity as performance: the danger of the figure (of the too-quick appropriation of an un-

---

[2] The emphasis on the distinction between public man and public woman is pervasive. Garber notes in passing that "like the dissymmetry of reference in Spanish between a 'public man' (a statesman) and a 'public woman' (a whore), 'making a man' and 'making a woman' mean two very different things, culturally speaking" (93).

questioned model of theatricality, of a seemingly transparent figure that proves opaque) and the danger the figure represents, the danger to the performer. Performance is an uneasy ground for the representation of liberation not only because it demands public exposure, but because it is often far from free. The "public woman" exposed to ridicule is but one highly visible example of the potentially coercive dynamics of performance.

None of the plays discussed here present women as performers in the public, professional sense–that is, the actor, the singer, the musician. Castellanos's protagonist is a "typical" bride-to-be. Torres Molina's characters likewise present easily identifiable social stereotypes while Berman's play focuses on the private lives of a somewhat sketchily defined couple. Franco's analysis is nevertheless useful in considering the view of even the nonactor as inescapably performing. In the exploration of the degree of performance inherent in gender, the plays present other facets of the dangers Franco cautions against or, more generally, of the instability of performance as a liberating metaphor. Finally, although the characters in these plays are not professional actors, they must obviously be represented –performed–by actors. The plays then necessarily occupy that space both forbidden to and excessively identified with women: the stage on which one makes a spectacle of oneself. If gender itself is a performance, the problematic figuring of creative action as performance represents a double bind, and the danger Franco describes is unavoidable.

Laurence Senelick writes, categorically: "Gender *is* performance. [. . .] Whatever biological imperatives may order sexual differentiation, whatever linguistic patterns may undergird it, it is outward behavior that calibrates the long scale of masculinity and femininity in social relations" (ix). Theatrically self-aware representations of gender, then, would appear to face an impasse, being on the one hand inescapable, on the other caught in the complexities of performance itself as either means toward or metaphor for liberation. Butler defines gender as "the repeated stylization of the body, a set of repeated acts within a highly rigid regulatory frame that congeal over time to produce the appearance of substance, of a natural sort of being" (*Gender* 33). The assertion of a regulatory frame immediately places gender–and the performance of gender–outside a space of free-play variation. The performance of gender is not freely chosen, but coercively imposed, "a performance with clearly punitive consequences" (*Gender* 139). Butler's argument extends to males Franco's view of performance as a questionable metaphor for liberation: if all gender is entirely performance, no one, male or female, can forget their looks. Butler suggests that gender be considered "an 'act' [. . .] which is both intentional and performative, where 'performative' itself carries the double-meaning of 'dramatic' and 'non-referential'" ("Performative" 272-73). She contends that "gender cannot be understood as a *role* which either expresses or disguises an interior 'self,' whether that 'self' is conceived as sexed or not. As performance which is performative, gender is an 'act,' broadly construed, which constructs the social fiction of its own psychological interiority" ("Performative" 279). Thus, gender has no existence prior to its performance. Not only is the performance enforced by the regulatory frame of social sanction, but there is nothing behind the performance. The representation of gender is at once its constitution and its mirror; there is nothing else.

Such a view of gender as performative act is complicated when the performance, always present in "real" life, occurs on stage. Senelick observes that "the actor is concerned with conveying not a personal code of gender but a set of signals that are at once more abstract and more graphic than those transmitted in standard social intercourse" (ix). If the gender represented is already nonreferential, an act whose appearance is its only substance, the representation of gender on stage is doubly distanced from any essential "reality." Echoing the dual nature of the critique of gender performances, Senelick notes that "gender roles performed by 'performers' never merely replicate those in everyday life; they are more sharply defined and more emphatically presented, the inherent iconicity offering both an ideal and a critique" (xi). This duality may be observed in each of the plays under discussion, as, for example, when the traditional roles of the idealized Mexican mother are viewed ironically through Lupita's performance in *El eterno femenino*.

Franco's emphasis on the public/private space dichotomy is also significant in examining the ways in which women perform roles designated feminine or, in a performative sense, the roles that designate them, allow them to be designated, feminine. By claiming the right to perform, women claim public space, space reserved for men. This is a liberating act in that it allows women to escape the confines of their private spaces, act on a public stage, and communicate in ways formerly unavailable. However, it is also a dangerous practice. As she shucks off her private identity, a woman becomes public, open to ridicule and worse. In her discussion of political demonstrations by groups such as the Madres de la Plaza de Mayo, Franco notes that "in countries in which women's public behavior has been carefully circumscribed, they made spectacles of themselves" ("Self-Destructing" 108). This idea of making a spectacle of oneself, a clearly pejorative epithet in its customary usage, is interesting in light of the suggestion that the self is to some significant degree already a performance, a spectacle. The woman, as woman, cannot help making a spectacle of herself: to make herself is to make a spectacle. Of course, male gender identity is no less a performance. However, the implications of claiming public space or of making oneself visible have been constructed differently for men.

The duality of ideal and critique also applies to transvestite performance. In claiming male space, women may also claim male roles and, in the case of cross-dressed performances, male costumes. Stage transvestism has a long history, including the boy actors in female roles of Shakespearean theater and the female "breeches role" of Restoration comedy. Female actors in male dress were popular in Spanish theater as well. In an essay comparing English and Spanish Renaissance drama, Ursula Heise notes that "detractors of the stage in both countries agree that the transvestite actor/actress is an object of irresistible erotic enticement" (367).[3] Heise concludes that "transvestism in English as well as Spanish theatre thus can be understood to owe its continued existence and popularity to its curious social ambivalence: whereas it enhances on one hand a basically patriarchal structuring of the relationship between audience and performance, it becomes on the other hand precisely the moment which projects an alternative structure as a viable option" (372). In her study of Lope de Vega's honor plays, Yvonne Yarbro-Bejarano

---

[3] Citing a variety of antitheatrical polemicists, Heise suggests that their "almost hysterical preoccupation with the effeminizing influence of the theatre reveals a deep apprehension that female sexuality, which finds a space of its own in the free social intercourse of the actors and actresses, the performance of love plays and the adoption of male disguise, might ultimately not only de-humanize the male spectators by turning them into beasts or dogs but also emasculate them. The assumption seems to be that when the male is confronted with unconcealed, un-covered femininity, he reacts not by asserting his difference but by imitating and adjusting to the female" (369). She continues: "transvestism in the theatre turns out to be a one-way street: it always leads to greater femininity, never away from it" (371).

argues that "the increasing efforts to confine respectable women to the home and the increasing visibility of nonrespectable women in public spaces may also have contributed to the appeal of the woman dressed as a man, who claims male space for female spectators" (105). The charged dichotomies of public and private space, public and private men and women, are reflected in the ambiguous figure of the female performer, regularly identified as a "public woman" in the derogatory sense, dressed as a (respectable) man.

Questions of visibility and invisibility are complicated in the figure of the cross-dressed woman, whose femininity, hidden beneath male clothing, is nevertheless excessively visible.[4] Pat Rogers comments that "it was attractive actresses who were given the chance to play breeches parts–that is, women who had been found attractive to men" (248). Heise argues that to contemporary commentators, "a woman in male attire appears even more attractive than in her usual clothing–so much so, in fact, that she comes to epitomize the dangers of theatre in general" (367). Male costume reveals female legs ordinarily obscured by long skirts, so that, as Rogers observes, "the display of leg enhances the sexual display of womanhood even as it pretends to mimic manhood" (248).[5] The visibility of this type of cross-dressing contrasts with the *in*visibility supposedly afforded, in Berman's "Uno," by the mustache which serves to deflect unwanted attentions. Visibility is also important in . . . *Y a otra cosa mariposa*, both in the initial, visible, costuming of the female actors and in the protagonists' exhibitionist games and overriding concern

---

[4] Marion Jones describes the various motivations behind the breeches part on the Restoration stage: "first, of course, came revivals of old plays with parts written for boys playing women, where the plot demanded assumption of male disguises at times during the action: with the advent of actresses, titillating dénouements with bared bosoms and flowing tresses became popular, and new plays were written to exploit this 'disguise penetrated' motif. Next, increasingly popular after Nell Gwyn played the madcap Florimel in Dryden's *Secret Love* (1667), came the 'roaring-girl' type of part, where the heroine adopted men's clothes as a free expression of her vivacious nature" (148).

[5] Oddly enough, Kenji Inamoto interprets the concrete *visibility* of the cross-dressed woman represented on stage as a determining factor in Cervantes's use of the motif in narrative but not in drama; Inamoto concludes that "la mujer vestida de hombre existía ya como recurso novelesco que no pretende el efecto erótico visual" (143) [the woman dressed as a man already existed as a novelistic recourse that does not claim an erotic visual effect]. This argument seems to discount entirely the erotic potential of narrative; it is difficult to see how a reader, imagining the cross-dressed woman in her oh-so-revealing breeches, would find the image less erotic (or necessarily less visual) than the theatrical spectator.

with appearances. The visibility of the female body is of course different for a contemporary audience, in that trousers no longer of themselves constitute male disguise. Within lesbian aesthetics, however, the "butch" role may be viewed as just such an erotic disguise: Garber cites a definition of "butch" as "knowing how to stand on a streetcorner and catch a femme's eye" (148). The cross-dressed stage role exacerbates the threat of making a spectacle of oneself, coyly highlighting the female body through male dress. The image of the actress in drag both reinforces an essentialist view of gender distinction (try as she might, the performer's "true" gender remains evident) and destabilizes those very divisions through its excessive visibility.

Franco suggests that for women writers, "the figuration of woman as performer [. . .] becomes a device that permits them to explore the traditional limitations on creativity even though [. . .] it also opens up ambiguities that invite parody" ("Self-Destructing" 115). Again, performance is not an unproblematic metaphor for freedom. In a discussion of Griselda Gambaro's *El campo*, Franco asserts that "Gambarro's [sic] plays are not written as feminist works; but they are important because they allow us to understand that the social construction of the feminine position within the overall sexual politics of sado-masochism is symptomatic of the State's manipulation of the erotic in order to secure obedient subjects. [. . .] Further, women incline to perform this script written by the State because their creativity is often a desire for performance. Indeed, the concert performance in *The Camp* is one of the most powerful and pitiless representations of women's desire seeking to liberate itself from sado-masochistic performance only to find all other forms of expression closed" ("Self-Destructing" 110).[6] Cre-

---

[6] As Franco's emphasis on the construction of the "feminine position" makes clear, she is concerned with female roles rather than with a construction of gender as performance. As to whether Gambaro's plays are "written as feminist works," it is worth noting her own observations on the subject. In an essay entitled "¿Es posible y deseable una dramaturgia específicamente femenina?" [Is a specifically feminine dramaturgy possible and desirable?] Gambaro rejects a view of women's writing as distinct but argues: "Sólo cuando las mujeres conquistaron un medio social, aunque fuera a medias, aunque todos sus derechos no le fueran reconocidos, pudieron franquear el bloqueo que les impedía escribir para el teatro, y casi paralelamente pudieron llegar a la dirección" (19) [Only when women conquered a social sphere, although it was only partially, and although not all of their rights were recognized, could they overcome the blockade that prevented them from writing for

ativity presented as a desire for performance corresponds to a need to perform openly or publicly the representation in which the individual is already engaged. I will argue later that Emma's concert may be better understood as "nonperformance," a clearly coerced yet equally impossible recital. What is important here is the manner in which performance may become both torture and reward, Emma's highest aspiration–a means of creative action–and her most humiliating moment. Similarly, the recognition of the performance inherent in all gendered identities, on or off stage, presents a liberating opening, a reclaiming of the process and material of performance, that as often as not leads to an awareness of an unvarying cycle of performance that begets only more performance.

For women in particular, given the historical associations of women on stage, the theater may be a fraught space. Women are already charged with superficiality and dissembling; to view gender, in this instance womanhood or femininity, as performance, seems to cater to such charges. Alternately, an emphasis on gender as performance redeems the dissembling or acting with which women are traditionally identified: it becomes the nature of gender itself (hence, both male and female), a necessity rather than a moral flaw. Stage performance both allows and forces a woman to occupy public space, a physical placement that has complex cultural implications. In her introduction to the appropriately titled *Making a Spectacle*, Lynda Hart argues that "the theatre is the sphere most removed from the confines of domesticity, thus the woman who ventures to be heard in this space takes a greater risk than the woman

---

the theater and, almost in tandem, they began to direct]. Gambaro describes women's texts "en las que cada palabra elegida ha sido producto de una doble transgresión: como creadoras, como mujeres. Aunque se llegue al mismo lugar, es en la travesía y en la manera de encarar la travesía donde se producen y existen las diferencias" ("Respuestas" 149) [in which every word chosen has been a product of a double transgression: as creators and as women. Although you arrive at the same place it is in the crossing and in the manner of facing the crossing that differences are produced and exist]. Of her own vocation she writes: "El hecho de ser mujer no ha condicionado mi temática, lo que sí ha modificado es el punto de partida de esa temática, lo que llamaría 'el lugar de ataque' de esa temática" ("Respuestas" 149) [The fact that I am a woman has not conditioned my themes. What has been modified is the point from which the themes arise, what I would call 'the place of attack' of the themes]. However, Gambaro's view of the feminist text is broad: "as far as I am concerned, a work is feminist insofar as it attempts to explain the mechanisms of cruelty, oppression, and violence through a story that is developed in a world in which men and women 'exist'" (Castedo-Ellerman 19).

poet or novelist, but it may also offer her greater potential for effecting social change" (2). The dangers of the performance metaphor, necessarily multiplied on stage, also represent an opening for change. The spectator is a key element in this transformative potential. Franco observes that in the demonstrations of the Madres de la Plaza de Mayo, through the use of white kerchiefs and family snapshots, "'private life'–as an image frozen in time–was represented publicly as a contrast to the present, highlighting the destruction of that very family life that the military publicly professed to protect." Moreover, "the women turned the city into a theater in which the entire population was obliged to become spectators, making public both their children's disappearance and the disappearance of the public sphere itself" ("Going" 67).[7] The performance of the Madres openly undercut the gender constraints surrounding the demonstrators, a move that has implications for aesthetic as well as political representations. As Franco argues, the Madres redefined public and private spaces, a division strongly implicated in the problematic of female performers in general and in particular in the representation of gender as performance.

Susan Noakes analyzes the long-standing trope of the superficial female reader who is chastised for "an inability to 'penetrate' words, that is, a habitual cessation of interpretive activity prior to arrival at a suitable endpoint (a hermeneutic defect) and a failure to comprehend the complexity of sign production (a semiotic defect)" (340). The view of the female reader as superficial, with its troubling implications, might profitably be extended to the female performer. The performer's interpretation of her script is of course a reading, a reading whose adequacy may be judged lacking. Franco's caution about the dangers of the female performer as a figure for liberation is then apt, for it is the perceived potential for a superficial reading or performance that opens the door to the (self-)parody Franco observes. Moreover, Noakes contends, according to the model of women as inadequate readers, "woman as seducer behaves like woman as reader; thus, woman reads in the same way she seduces" (344). Woman as performer has also been read as seducer;

---

[7] Diana Taylor observes that for the Madres, "visibility was both a refuge and a trap–a trap because the military knew who their opponents were, but a refuge insofar as the women were only safe when they were demonstrating. Attacks on them usually took place as they were going home from the plaza" ("Performing" 286).

when performance is added to the mix, the woman's seductive reading becomes seductive performance, a performative act of seduction. Rather than explore the specific dangers of figuring feminine creativity in the performer, *El eterno femenino*, *El suplicio del placer*, and . . . *Y a otra cosa mariposa* force an understanding of the traps in the requirement that all women (and men) perform. Because it is imposed, regulated (as Butler argues), and inescapable, simply to recognize the performance is not sufficient to effect a liberation. At the same time, if acting one's gender is an inevitable necessity, what is required is not to unmask and thus eliminate the performance but to transform it. Castillo's discussion of Castellanos's "cultivation of superficiality" offers one possibility for reconfiguring the terms: "implicitly recognizing and taking into account once again a tradition that marks women readers as superficial and morally deficient, she realigns the terms to right the misappropriation of the reading woman as immoral, while reversing the negative charge on the accusation of superficiality" (50). Similarly, women performers must take into account both the transgressive possibilities of a deliberately assumed public stage and the ground of often invisible or unacknowledged performance on which it rests.

By foregrounding the degree to which *all* women perform, in the home as well in the plaza, plays such as *El eterno femenino* blur the private/public separation, an erasure of boundaries that suggests that all women are in effect "public." In Castellanos's play, nearly all of the roles offered Lupita occur in private–or at least indoors, as at the beauty parlor–with the exception of the quintessentially public prostitute of the third act. The public or professional performer that *is* visible in the play is the main attraction at a circus freak show, advertised as "el fenómeno más extraordinario del mundo: la mujer que se volvió Serpiente por desobediente" (72; 2) ["the most extraordinary phenomenon in the world: the woman who was turned into a serpent because she disobeyed!" (297)]. She is subsequently revealed as Eve herself, eager to tell her story of boredom in paradise.

When the gender roles (or genders) performed are blurred, as in *El suplicio del placer*, space begins to dissolve. The action of Berman's play occurs in private, in a hotel suite, house, or apartment. However, in the first act, it is the action on the public stage of the hotel restaurant, discussed by the protagonists the next morning, that provides the ground on which the majority of their gender games are negotiated. An element of class privilege is also required, as their relative wealth and status affords the two a free space of experimentation. At the same time, although roles are freely shifted, they are not in all cases transgressive: Él's enjoyment of his polished, active seduction is pointedly contrasted with Ella's restraint.

In Torres Molina's . . . *Y a otra cosa mariposa*, female performers claim the public space of the plaza, not *for* women but by playing men. They also construct private enclaves through the displacement of women, such as the characters' wives, who never appear on stage. The cross-dressed actors function as butch figures as well, for whom a doubly disguised actor in female drag provides a foil. Gender play in Torres Molina's text occurs both in the satirical critique of the male roles the performers assume and in the subtle layering of genders in or by those performers. Because all such performances require an audience, the protagonists perform for each other as self-consciously as the actors presenting Torres Molina's script perform for the theatrical spectator.

El eterno femenino opens with the installation, in one of the salon's state-of-the-art hair dryers, of a device designed to prevent the unoccupied women from accidentally thinking. Lupita, who has come to have her hair set for her wedding, becomes (unwittingly) the gadget's first subject. Gender in this play is presented as a limited spectrum of available, sex-specific roles, reflected in the menu of "dreams" that the salesman promises his "aparato" will provide: "Hay un catálogo completo de variantes: sueña que es la mujer más bonita del mundo; que todos los hombres se enamoran de ella; que todas las mujeres la envidian; que a su marido le suben el sueldo; que no hay alza de precios en los artículos de primera necesidad; que consigue una criada eficiente y barata; que este mes queda embarazada; que este mes no queda embarazada" (29; 1) ["There's a complete catalog of possibilities: she dreams that she is the prettiest woman in the world; that all men are falling in love with her; that all women envy her; that her husband gets a raise in salary; that there's no price increase in the basic cost of living; that she finds an efficient and inexpensive maid; that she gets pregnant this month; that she doesn't get pregnant this month" (276)]. *El eterno femenino* does not so much question the idea of gender as highlight the various "performances" a woman is obliged to produce in keeping with her social position or in order to acquire a position. Because the production demands that she be in several places at once, the role of Lupita cannot be played by a single actor. This is in keeping with Castellanos's assertion at the outset that hers is "un texto no de caracteres sino de situaciones" (*Eterno* 21) ["a text, not of characters but of situations" (273)]. The need for multiple performers to play Lupita also points up, in highly visual fashion, the interchangeable nature not only of the roles assumed but of the women who fill them. There need be no visual continuity between one Lupita observing another; they need not "be" the same person to fulfill the same role.

As framing device, the salon provides a doubly theatrical setting. Kirsten Nigro has observed that in addition to being a theatrical space in which women "get into their roles," "*this* beauty parlor is one where women perform for other women. As the heroine Lupita goes in and out of her multiple identities her audience is first of all the other women at the beauty parlor" ("Breaking" 129). Linda Kintz defines the salon as "a kind of threshold space, a temporary location in which women perfect their masquerades; it is neither private nor is it public in the sense in which *public* refers to a place where men valorize themselves through activity" (256). The beauty parlor is the jumping off point for the plays within the play as well as the dressing room for the social ("real life") performance to take place at Lupita's marriage later that afternoon. When in the third act Lupita, her own hair an irredeemable mess, tries on a series of wigs, the donning of the wig is the assumption of the role. The plays within the play establish multiple layers, multiple audiences: the audience of the beauty salon viewing Lupita; Lupita as spectator to the performances of others, in the circus tent and wax museum scenes of the second act; and Lupita as audience to herself, spectator to the vignettes representing her future possibilities. When the persona of Lupita is split within those vignettes, Lupita becomes audience to herself at yet another level. In "Crepusculario" ["Twilight"] the stage direction reads: "Hay dos focos de atención en este sitio: la jaula del perico y la pantalla de la televisión, en la que se ve el rostro interrogante de Lupita. De una silla se levanta, en pantuflas, pelo gris, gorda y fodonga, la misma Lupita, sólo que mucho más vieja" (57; 1) ["There are two focal points in this room: the parrot cage and the television screen on which Lupita's questioning face is seen. Lupita herself gets up from a chair: she is in house slippers, gray-headed, fat, and slovenly, but now much older" (290)]. Kintz argues that Lupita "is both subject and object of the spectacle, doubling the space of the spectator as she acts the role of spectator" (269). Moreover, by the end of the play, Lupita becomes "the mirror that makes the audience possible" (273). The show, then, is constitutive for both performer and audience.

That Lupita performs first for other women–and, through the splitting of the Lupita role, for herself–implies a certain complicity among this initial audience with the social arrangements Castellanos ridicules. Feminine roles are not mandated solely by a disembodied patriarchal order but fostered and reproduced by women as well, as is evident when Lupita's mother transforms her into the suffering, self-sacrificing mother-to-be or when Lupita counsels her daughter (Lupita II) on the ways of respectable women. Mamá provokes Lupita's morning sickness by giving her warm salt water to drink; afterwards, "la despeina, le quita el maquillaje, la deja hecha un desastre y luego contempla, con la satisfacción del artista, su obra" (41; 1) ["musses her hair, removes her makeup; she leaves her looking a wreck, and then she contemplates her handiwork with the satisfaction of an artist" (282)]. Here the artist unpaints her canvas, so that the creation of the ideal woman is explicitly a process of erasure. Although the "mujer decente" ["decent woman"] plays her role in private, she is never without an audience. When her daughter asks: "¿Quién te ve? Estás siempre encerrada" ["Who sees you? You are always shut inside"], Lupita lists "el abarrotero, el tintorero, el lechero, el cartero" (58; 1) ["the groceryman, the man from the dry cleaners, the milkman and the mailman" (290-91)]. When Lupita II dismisses this public–"¡Qué auditorio tan distinguido!" ["What a distinguished audience"]–Lupita adds: "el abogado, el médico de la familia, la gente visible, en fin" (58; 1) ["the lawyer, the family doctor, the visible people, I guess" (291)]. Within the privacy of her own home, she makes an acceptable spectacle of herself; invisible behind her prim lace curtains, she is nevertheless seen by the "gente visible," all of whom are male. Her relegation to a private space is again more apparent than real: it is not that a woman does not perform, is not seen, but that the space of her performance must be controlled, the audience carefully selected. If a woman in fact cross-dresses as a woman, she must select the audience before whom she can "pass" undetected. Her carefully orchestrated appearance is designed to produce the invisibility of the respectable woman who never calls attention to herself.

Gambaro has suggested that the relationship between text and performance should become a "canibalismo amoroso" [loving cannibalism] through which the dramatist's idea is deciphered and appropriated by the director in a process that recognizes that the dramatic author "no proporciona un pretexto, proporciona una visión y una filosofía sobre el mundo" ("Voracidad" 63) [does not provide a pretext, but a vision and a philosophy about the world]. Castellanos's play, frequently referred to as "unperformable," at once enacts the performance of the critic (as, at least by reference, Castellanos becomes a character in her own play) and the critique of feminine identity as an obliged performance.[8] Castellanos posits women as forced performers, interpreters of an assigned script. Gambaro's essay, about the relation of the director and the dramatic text, suggests a parallel for the performer-script relation, so that the cannibalism she describes for the director may work for the individual performer as well. The humorous critique in Castellanos's play presents one way of realizing that cannibalism: devouring the text, understanding its "sign" as Gambaro indicates, but redirecting it. One might read Castellanos's play as itself performing that cannibalism,

---

[8] Nigro and Barbara Aponte both note the excess of episodes; as Nigro argues: "While the individual episodes for the most part are finely wrought, highly economical dramatic moments, there are just too many of them. [. . .] Because the play badly needs a judicious pruning, the accumulation of vignettes ends by being a variation on a single theme, which wears thin as the work progresses through its three lengthy acts" ("Rosario" 98). Aponte agrees: "hay demasiada materia y la estructura libre no mantiene la atención a través de todos los cuadros" (57) [there is too much material and the open structure does not hold our attention through all of the scenes]. However, after commenting on the technical difficulties presented by Castellanos's script, Nigro concedes: "This is not to say that *El eterno femenino* is unstageable. [. . .] Yet no matter how these difficulties in mounting the work are tackled, the fact is that in terms of its potential for stage enactment, *El eterno femenino* is not a wholly successful piece of playwriting" ("Rosario" 99). In a footnote she suggests that the play "is too small in its scope to merit the rather complex mounting the text suggests" ("Rosario" 102). Debra Castillo refers to the play as "nearly unproduceable" (144), while Mónica Szurmuk categorizes it as "de difícil puesta en escena" (37) [difficult to stage]. Maureen Ahern notes that when "[Rafael] López Mirnau and [Emma Teresa] Armendáriz prepared to stage the play, they realized that the complete script was too complicated to present as it was written, posing many difficulties for the director as well as the actress who must play multiple roles. Act II was omitted" (54-55). Nigro is likely right when she suggests that Castellanos's technical requirements are "definitely more filmic than theatrical" ("Rosario" 99).

taking as the original "script" the social mores she satirizes. Gambaro proposes her model of cannibalism as a means of ultimately being "faithful" to the text, defending the word in performance, the role of the dramatic script. Nevertheless, Castellanos's observation that "con una persistencia que no disminuye ante ningún fracaso, la mujer rompe los modelos que la sociedad la propone y le impone para alcanzar su imagen auténtica y consumarse–y consumirse–en ella" ("La mujer" 19) ["with a persistence that does not diminish in the face of disaster, woman breaks the models that society proposes and imposes upon her in order to achieve her authentic image and consummate herself–and be consumed–in it" (243)] elaborates a parallel possibility of a confrontation with the script that is at once consummation and consumption. As Nigro and others point out, Castellanos's demystifying project tends toward overkill. Yet Castellanos herself notes that "el proceso mitificador [. . .] es acumulativo" ("La mujer" 7) [the mythmaking process {. . .} is cumulative]. Perhaps the demystifying process requires a similar, if inverse, accumulative process. The episodes that make up *El eterno femenino* reproduce one another in multiple variations, and the latest technology–the hair drier that prevents thought–is only the most recent version of a timeworn strategy: in the second act, the Corregidor describes his policy of keeping his underlings, including his wife, from reading in order to prevent them from thinking (113; 2).

The resistance of Castellanos's text to an imagined performance suggests that the loving cannibalism Gambaro describes as the text-director relation becomes here a lump impossible to swallow. Or perhaps the cannibalism–eating one's own species and hence, at some level, consuming oneself–occurs earlier, in the play between observation and experience, Lupita watching (dreaming) her own transformation into the series of exaggerated stereotypes Castellanos offers. Castellanos herself describes traditional roles in terms of an unrealizable performance: "Quitémosle, por ejemplo, la aureola al padre severo e intransigente y el pedestal a la madre dulce y tímida que se ofrece cada mañana para la ceremonia de la degollación propiciatoria. Los dos son personajes de una comedia ya irrepresentable y además han olvidado sus diálogos y los sustituyen por parlamentos sin sentido" ("La participación" 39) [For example, let us take the halo from the severe, unyielding father and the pedestal from the sweet, shy mother who offers herself every morning for the ceremony of the propitiatory throat-cutting. Both are characters of an already unrepresentable comedy. They have forgotten their dialogues and substitute for them nonsensical speeches]. Castellanos's play satirizes in performance the social norms Castellanos elsewhere describes as unperformable.

Gayle Austin's essay, "Creating a Feminist Theatre Environment: The Feminist Theory Play," provides a model for reading *El eterno femenino* as a "theory play" in which Castellanos's own essays, in particular "La mujer y su imagen" ["Woman and Her Image"] and "La participación de la mujer mexicana en la educación formal" [The participation of the Mexican woman in formal education], establish the prior theoretical text. Austin describes her "feminist theory plays" as a response to "long discussions of feminist theory, theatrical practice, and how the two so rarely blend" (49). She writes of her first such experiment, "Resisting the Birth Mark":

> I assembled the performance text from the short story, "The Birthmark" (1843) by Nathaniel Hawthorne, various feminist theory texts (chiefly sections of Fetterley's book), and my own interpolation of actions, movements, sounds, and visual effects. The securely canonical short story concerns an eighteenth-century scientist who, obsessed with a red birthmark on his wife's cheek, devises a potion. While it fades the mark, it kills the wife. The student actors framed the thirty-minute piece as performers, taking on various roles over the course of ten brief scenes. Narrative sections of the story read by a male voice were played on tape and dialogue sections were enacted, but interrupted by segments of theory. (49)[9]

Castellanos's "theory play" does not read a male canonical text such as Hawthorne's short story. She is, however, "reading" canonical female (and male) roles. Historical texts and interpretations are also reread, particularly in the second act in which historical figures such as Sor Juana Inés de la Cruz and La Malinche attempt to set the record straight. As Sor Juana puts it, "ahora vamos a presentarnos como lo que fuimos. O, por lo menos, como lo que creemos

---

[9] Austin refers to Judith Fetterley's *The Resisting Reader*. Austin's essay is part of another performance context as well, that of the conference paper; of the feminist conference she writes: "the way women interact there is a form of feminist theory," and she concludes: "My next stop: the environmental feminist conference play" (54).

que fuimos" (87; 2) ["now we are going to present ourselves as what we were. Or, at least, as what we think we really were" (304)]. The last line makes clear that the newly animated wax figures have no greater monopoly on historical truth than other historians, and their reenactment of memory will be partial. Interestingly, Sor Juana chooses to represent herself cross-dressed, revealing "un aspecto equívoco de efebo" (101; 2) ["the equivocal appearance of an adolescent boy" (311)]. Reflecting the distorted, invariable images of them presented in official records, the historical figures are here objectified, literally, as statues. At the same time, as *wax* figures, they are potentially more malleable than sculptures of granite or marble.[10] Barbara Aponte also underscores the narrative elements of the second act, arguing that "paralela a la actuación dramática, hay una función narrativa que puede comentar, anticipar, o resumir la acción. Ésta se halla ejemplificada en las mujeres históricas del segundo acto quienes cobran vida para re-representar teatralmente momentos críticos de su pasado. Todas ellas comentan aspectos de esta actuación, o entre ellas mismas o para el beneficio de Lupita" (52) [parallel to the dramatic performance, there is a narrative function that is able to comment upon, anticipate or summarize the action. This is exemplified in the historical women of the second act who come to life to theatrically re-present critical moments of their past. All of them comment on aspects of this performance, either among themselves or for Lupita's benefit]. Performance here is read as re-performance and narrative as a means of performing.

Lupita herself is marked as part of the triumvirate of Mexican femininity Castellanos traces in "Otra vez Sor Juana" ["Once Again Sor Juana"]: "En la historia de México hay tres figuras en las que encarnan, hasta sus últimos extremos, diversas posibilidades de la femineidad" (26) ["There are three figures in Mexican history that embody the most extreme and diverse possibilities of femininity" (222)]. All three are present in *El eterno femenino*. Sandra Cypess notes that Lupita's name "is a reference to the Virgin of Guadalupe, icon of Mexican national identity and the opposite pole with respect to the bad woman represented by La Malinche" (*La Malinche* 124). As the theatrical embodiment of the icon of feminine perfec-

---

[10] I tend to associate wax museums with horror, which makes the image of these sculpted, frozen women in their niches still more troubling, though this may be an idiosyncratic connection or the effect of too many cartoons.

tion, however, Lupita plays student to La Malinche's bad influence, listening respectfully to her version of events. Like the more specifically historical revisions of the Malinche figure already discussed, in which the "truth" of various versions of historical events was contested, Castellanos's reexamination of La Malinche, along with other figures of Mexican history, concentrates as much on subsequent interpretations of the women as national icons as on what "really happened."

More than interpolating sections of theory, Castellanos's play seems an illustration of what her essays call for: the play is an enactment of the theory. Castellanos rejects

> lo más inerte, lo más inhumano, lo que se erige como depositario de valores eternos e invariables, lo sacralizado: las costumbres. La costumbre de una relación sado-masoquista entre el hombre y la mujer en cualquier contacto que establezcan. La costumbre de que el hombre tenga que ser muy macho y la mujer muy abnegada. La complicidad entre el verdugo y la víctima, tan vieja que es imposible distinguir quién es quién.
>
> Ante esto yo sugeriría una campaña: no arremeter contra las costumbres con la espada flamígera de la indignación ni con el trémolo lamentable del llanto sino poner en evidencia lo que tienen de ridículas, de obsoletas, de cursis y de imbéciles. Les aseguro que tenemos un material inagotable para la risa. ¡Y necesitamos tanto reír porque la risa es la forma más inmediata de la liberación de lo que nos oprime, del distanciamiento de lo que nos aprisiona! ("La participación" 38-39)

[that which is most inactive, most inhuman, which sets itself up as a depository of eternal and invariable values, the consecrated: customs. The custom of a sado-masochistic relationship between men and women in whatever contact they establish. The custom that a man has to be very macho and the woman self-sacrificing. The complicity between the executioner and the victim, so old that it is impossible to distinguish one from the other.

With this in mind, I would suggest another approach: not to attack customs with the flaming sword of indignation nor with the lamentable quivering of tears but rather to expose their ridiculousness, their obsolescence, their vulgarity and their imbecility. I assure you that we have inexhaustible material for laughter. And we so need to laugh, because laughter is the most immediate form of liberation from what oppresses us, of achieving distance from what imprisons us!]

As theory play, *El eterno femenino* might be read as the answer to this call to satire, an exemplary case of the humor Castellanos demands. This humor extends to self-parody, expressed in the reactions of a group of "cultured" women to Lupita's (here in the role of professor) description of Castellanos's play as an outrage "dirigido contra la abnegación de las madres; contra la virtud de las esposas; contra la castidad de las novias; es decir, contra nuestros atributos proverbiales, atributos en los que se fincan nuestras instituciones más sólidas: la familia, la religión, la patria" (*Eterno* 182; 3) ["directed against mothers' selflessness, against wives' virtue, against brides' chastity, that is, against our proverbial attributes, the attributes that form the base of our most solid institutions: family, church, and country" (350)]. After rejecting the play on technical grounds, given "la arbitrariedad de las secuencias, la inverosimilitud de las situaciones, la nula consistencia de los personajes" (183; 3) ["the arbitrariness of its progression, the unrealistic situations, the utter inconsistency of its characters" (351)], Lupita-Profesora concludes that the author of the offending piece nevertheless deserves "el regalo de nuestra lástima, teniendo en cuenta que es una pobre resentida, envidiosa, amargada" (184-85; 3) ["the gift of our pity, keeping in mind that she is a pitiful, resentful woman, envious and bitter" (352)]. As Maureen Ahern observes, Castellanos's self-criticism "is an effective way of defusing hostility by anticipating the attacks that she knew this play would arouse in Mexican social circles" (55). As a play, moreover, the text might provoke especially strong attacks. Ahern argues that "enactment confers a power that other literary modes do not achieve" (56). The performance of gender, inescapable but regularly masked outside the theater, becomes excessively visible on stage. The subsequent critical chorus of "unperformable" only replays Castellanos's performance as critic within her play.

The discussion of Castellanos's play is not her only entrance as author, nor are her essays the only prior texts. Castellanos's own poetry and popular genres such as the *corrido* are also invoked. For example, in the third act, one of the wigs Lupita tries on is "Jornada de la soltera," the title of one of Castellanos's poems which is subsequently recited. As the poem title becomes the wig, the wig creates the role, so that the poem is as much a performative as it is a text performed. To wear the wig (derived in this case from the poem) is to become the woman designated by that wig. The multivoiced portraits of another of Castellanos's poems, "Kinsey Report," also resonate with the menu of female roles presented to Lupita. In an analysis which approaches certain of the troubling nodes of the performance/self-destruction/liberation matrix, Mónica Szurmuk argues: "asombra que, aun en [*El eterno femenino*], [Castellanos] se cuestione el derecho a producir literatura. No es casual que las mujeres aspirantes a intelectuales del tercer acto no sólo desconozcan a [Castellanos], sino que también necesitan la información pertinente sobre su vida privada para determinar si la obra es tan cínica y desvergonzada como pretende la profesora" (38) [it is remarkable that even in {*El eterno femenino*}, {Castellanos} questions her right to produce literature. It is not by chance that the aspiring women intellectuals of the third act are not only unfamiliar with her work, but also need pertinent information about her private life to determine if the work is as cynical and shameless as the professor claims]. Szurmuk's argument echoes Franco's caution about the ambiguity of the image of female artist as performer. This metatheatrical moment (only here does Castellanos explicitly name herself) puts one in mind of Lionel Abel's suggestion that "Hamlet's philosophizing about action is a projection into the play of the playwright's difficulty in making his hero tragic" (45). Transposing entirely the terms (and not for a minute thinking that Castellanos is after tragedy), this moment of feminist metadrama seems to reflect not only the process of playwriting but Castellanos's own process of self-creation. By making the play–and, by producing the play, performing as author–she makes herself playwright. At the same time, says Szurmuk, "que el debate haya sido generado por *El eterno femenino* y su autora en algo así como una autoparodia de Rosario, indica que [Castellanos] tenía confianza en [*El eterno femenino*] como apertura de un foro de discusión" (44) [that the debate was generated by *El eterno femenino* and its author, in something of a self-parody by Rosario, suggests that she had confidence in the play as a means of opening a discussion]. Self-parody, then, is not an uncomplicated index of self-doubt.

Castellanos brings this self-parody to her other textual performances as well. In the essay "A pesar de proponérselo," she makes fun not only of her monolingualism, allegedly unique in Israel, but of her "misuse" of the one language she does speak. Appropriately enough, the joke comes as a parenthetical dramatic aside: "¡Zas! ¿Qué es ese ruido? Es el portazo que, una vez más, me da en las narices la Academia Mexicana de la Lengua por el no sé si impropio, pero sí inseguro uso de un vocablo" (270) [Bang! What's that noise? It's the bang, once again, of the Mexican Academy of Language slamming the door in my face for the maybe not improper, but certainly uncertain usage of a term]. This self-reflexive aside is in keeping with the self-referential turns so common in Castellanos's writings. Taking "A pesar de proponérselo" as her point of departure, Debra Castillo underscores "an autobiographical gesture–'I was putting on makeup'–that concentrates on a consciously constructed self, a staged performance that comments on, challenges, or exposes role playing and posits life as a staged aesthetic performance, a production valuable not for its hidden depths but for its style of presentation" (151). Castellanos's essays demonstrate both thematically and formally the premise of *El eterno femenino*: that a woman's life is both constituted and circumscribed by her performance of various preestablished and overdetermined roles. The autobiographical "aside" reveals the degree of performance as it mimics dramatic convention. Castillo's argument suggests finally that the performance may be valued for its own sake, read neither as devious dissemblance nor as enforced falsity.

Castellanos's play sets out a ground of gendered role playing against which to read the transformations of transvestism explored by Berman and Torres Molina. Castellanos's exhaustive series of vignettes hammers home the argument that the roles believed to transparently reveal a natural gender are in fact artificial constructs imposed by social sanction and even inertia. The reanimated figures of the second act place this demystification within a historical context. The dilemma of the separation of public and private space–and her public and private persona–confronts Lupita at every turn, as the public space of the beauty parlor serves to prepare her for the private performance of her wedding night, a performance which, in the event, is no more private than that of the salon and indeed is designed with an audience in mind: "En un sofá, cubierta con un velo y vestida con el más convencional y pomposo traje de novia –al fin y al cabo es para una sola vez en la vida– está Lupita. En la cola del traje hay una mancha de sangre que no resultaría muy visible si ella no arreglara cuidadosamente los pliegues de modo que la mancha resalte a la vista" (32; 1) ["Lupita is sitting on a sofa, with a bridal veil covering her face and dressed in the most conventional and pompous bridal gown imaginable

–after all, it is only once in a lifetime. On the train of the dress there is a bloodstain, which would not be clearly visible if she had not carefully arranged the folds so that the spot would be in full view" (278)]. As in the cross-dressed transformations that follow, placement and display are everything: the stain must be the appropriate color and size, the fabric arranged just so.

Sabina Berman's *El suplicio del placer* is subtitled "Tres obras de un acto sobre un tema" [Three one-act plays on a theme]. I will concentrate on the first of these plays, "Uno," as most relevant to a discussion of "playing gender," although all three deal with male/female roles. Each piece has two characters; despite the insistent blurring of genders, they are identified only by the pronouns "Él" [He] and "Ella" [She]. "Uno" takes place in the sitting room of a hotel suite, where a "varón afeminado" [effeminate man] and a "mujer masculinoide" [masculine woman] recall the previous night's seductions as a shared false mustache is passed back and forth between them. In the second piece ("Dos"), Él is identified as "un hombre maduro, obsedido por su propia importancia, vestido ostentosamente" [a mature man, obsessed by his own importance, dressed ostentatiously], while in her case, "5-90-60-90 son sus medidas –de la cabeza, el pecho, la cintura y las caderas, respectivamente" (282) [5-90-60-90 are her measurements–of her head, her chest, her waist and her hips, respectively]. "Dos" recalls a vignette from *El eterno femenino*, "Usurpadora" ["The Usurper"], in which a maid both comforts and ridicules the kept woman soon to be discarded. In "Tres," a husband and wife attempt to discover the reality behind an apparent dream involving a pistol that may or may not be loaded, may or may not exist.[11]

"Uno" figures gender as defense, as exchange, as interchangeable. Implicitly, ambiguity heightens desire at the same time that it necessitates the eye of the other for self-definition. The mustache

---

[11] A revision of the play, published in 1994, adds a fourth section. In addition, the sections are given titles rather than numbers. The new section, "Los dientes," relays a fantastic dental appointment in which the stage is dominated by an enormous mouth: "la enorme boca se abre a medias y a través del hueco vemos el cubículo, al dentista y a la enfermera observando la boca" (*Entre Villa* 207) [the enormous mouth opens halfway and through the opening we see the cubicle, the dentist and the nurse observing the mouth]. Changes to "Uno"/"El bigote" [The mustache] are minor.

alternately disguises, enhances, or transforms the "real" gender behind it, working as a visual cue, or as visual performative–to wear the mustache is to become/perform a gender. The movement between genders is the more fluid given the visual resemblance between the two characters: "llevan el pelo corto y pintado en un color rojo caoba. Son esbeltos, bellos y elegantes –y lo saben. Hablan y se mueven con una lenta soltura. Se parecen asombrosamente" (268) [They wear their hair short and dyed mahogany red. They are slender, beautiful and elegant–and they know it. They speak and move with a slow ease. They look frighteningly alike]. In addition to their physical similarity, the two are identically dressed in white pants and white silk shirts. Because the mustache is false, the gender performances are always marked, at least for Él and Ella, by an inherent fictionality. A stage prop, the mustache can be owned, and is in fact generally designated as the private property of Ella, although Él also refers to it as "ours." The mustache is employed for specific, even strategic purposes: to avoid the desire of others as well as to excite it. Gender, with the mustache as visual performative, is invoked according to need.

As the act opens, Él finds a terse Ella reading the newspaper and observes: "Te noto extraña. Como si algo te faltara" [You seem strange. As if something were missing]. After a few moments he realizes: "Ya sé lo que tienes de raro. No traes tu bigote" [I know what's strange. You're not wearing your mustache], to which she replies, "Por supuesto que no traigo mi bigote. Mi bigote lo traes tú" (269) [Of course I'm not wearing my mustache. You're wearing it]. When Ella rejects his offer to return it, Él states: "Creí que te gustaba traerlo puesto" [I thought you liked to wear it]. Her reply is brusque: "Sabes perfectamente bien que lo uso solamente para no ser importunada. Solamente para eso. Para que no se me acerquen hombres a cortejarme cuando no me da la gana" (269) [You know perfectly well that I only use it so as not to be bothered. Only because of that. So that men don't approach and court me when I'm not in the mood]. In this initial moment, Ella insists that pleasure plays no role in her use of the mustache and that she "performs" in public (by wearing the mustache) only to protect her private self. As a performer, then, her public persona is male. However, this easy identification is gradually complicated. In response to Él's demand for a promise that, once tempted, she will drop the mustache and let herself be seduced, Ella assures him that *she* will do the seducing: "te aseguro que el día en que desee que un hombre se me acerque y me seduzca, antes me le acerco yo y lo seduzco y tan rápido que ni se da cuenta que ya lo usé y lo tiré al olvido" (276) [I assure you that the day I want a man to come up to me and seduce me, I will approach and seduce him before he even has time to realize that I've already used and forgotten about him]. Even without the mustache, her behavior is more in keeping with that of the men from whom she hides than with the docile, innocent "morena" [brunette] of Él's dalliance.

The mustache is also an index of tension between the two. As the last night's events are replayed, it becomes clear that Él borrowed the mustache so as to make himself more attractive to a young woman, in effect, to heighten his masculinity. In the face of his nonrecollection, Ella offers a detailed description. Él suggests that Ella was the one interested in the woman, to which she replies, "Ser mujer no me impide disfrutar la belleza de otra mujer" (270) [Being a woman does not stop me from enjoying the beauty of another woman]. Él's insinuations that Ella's desires tend more toward women than men are repeatedly rejected. Ella continues the story of the previous night, "mimando su relato de manera que actúe como si fuera él y él fuera la morena" (273) [miming her story so that she acts as if she were he and as if he were the brunette]. The gender role playing becomes more complex as the two switch genders for the performance of this small drama of which they are the only audience. Although Ella *acts* as though she were Él, she speaks in her own voice, saying of the girl: "Dulce niña. Te miraba como desde un sueño" (273) [Sweet girl. She watched you as if from a dream]. The story of the previous night becomes a scene of intermingled voyeurism and exhibitionism as Él suggests: "Lo viste todo" [You saw everything], and Ella replies: "Me hubiera gustado verlo todo, pero lo peor sucedió a puerta cerrada" (274) [I would have like to have seen everything, but the worst of it happened behind closed doors]. In Ella's narration, what is admired–indeed, all that she directly observes–is the performance of the seduction, the astute selection of a Strauss waltz, the effectiveness of "their" mustache in action.

Ronald Burgess suggests reading Berman's early plays, including *El suplicio del placer*, in terms of "creative acts," by which he means "a kind of play 'written' by one character for himself or herself and other characters. In these plays, others are expected to participate by accepting the role and reciting the dialogue written by the first character. These alternate realities become sources of conflict that destabilize personal relationships as well as what normally passes for reality" (*New* 81). Burgess concludes that in the case of "Uno," "the elaborate 'play' that they have written for themselves has erased their identities instead of liberating them" (*New* 82). Granted, the freedom for which the two congratulate themselves is not without difficulties. (Nor is the "writing" of roles limited to the interaction between Él and Ella: the young woman at the next table is clearly slotted into a previously devised scenario of seduction.) The two argue about their differing interpretations of their freedom and the guilt Él suffers because he acts on a temptation Ella claims not to feel. She responds furiously: "¿Quieres limitar mi libertad pidiéndome que actúe como una mujer libre cuando soy tan absolutamente libre que no necesito actuar como si fuera libre?" (275-76) [Do you want to limit my freedom asking me to act like a free woman when I am so absolutely free that I don't need to act as if I were?]. Already free, Ella does not need to act as though she were; the demand that she act is as overbearing as the social norms of monogamy and fidelity that she is *not* constrained to observe. Yet Él's insistent desire to witness such action indicates his awareness of a performative level. While Ella may feel so unconstrained that she need not act out her liberation, Él recognizes action as the only proof–even the only existence–of that freedom.

However, the process is not simply one of erasure: the two have created a new, fused identity. As effeminate man and masculine woman, Él and Ella present a variation on the butch-femme couple. Sue-Ellen Case suggests that "the butch-femme couple inhabit the subject position together–'you can't have one without the other' [. . .]. These are not split subjects, suffering the torments of dominant ideology. They are coupled ones" (283). Nevertheless, the "torments of dominant ideology" remain all too present, in Él's doubts about Ella's lack of sexual adventures or his dominating, abusive tone with the brunette. The shifting identities not only are a means of relating (or not) to others, but both destabilize and motivate the relationship between Él and Ella; each functions as mirror to the other. And this mirroring is another source of tension, so that Él complains: "Solo puedo ver qué soy en tu mirada" (277) [I can only see what I am in your look]. The ambivalence at the root of their relation is evident as Él announces: "te odio siempre en esos momentos en que sé que tú me has empujado a enfrentarme con el asco de otro" (279) [I always hate you at those moments when I know that you have pushed me to face the disgust of another]. The mirroring that each provides to the other is interrupted by the hostile looks of outsiders, the humiliation of self-exposure on a public stage. Moreover, in public the couple's performances require certain props–they are not automatic or in any way unmediated. "Liberated" as the pair might be in private, in order to do without the authorizing male companion in public, Ella needs an effective substitute. In an ironic take on the traditional roles satirized by Castellanos, here a woman alone requires only a mustache, not the man that might come with it, to protect her.

The repetition of almost melodramatic phrases, in particular the description "como un relámpago de seda negra" [like a lightening flash of black silk] attached to the young woman's hair and ultimately to the mustache, places the pair's reconstruction of the previous night within a frame of heightened self-awareness (270). Their use of language reflects Burgess's notion of creative acts in that the recreation of the events, as well as the events themselves (such as Ella watching), are self-consciously dramatized. The refrain "un relámpago de seda negra" extends the ambiguous doubling of Ella and the brunette occasioned by Ella's dreamed return to childhood, a dream that coincides (temporally) with Él's verbal upbraiding of the woman he addresses as "Niña" and whom both describe as "dulce niña." The self-consciousness of their language contributes to a sense of repetition, as if the scene, or one very like it, has been played out many times before.

A certain level of economic privilege and the comforts it affords make possible these games of gender ambiguity.[12] Butler questions the possibility of isolating gender as a discrete category, arguing that "it becomes impossible to separate out 'gender' from the political and cultural intersections in which it is invariably produced and maintained" (*Gender* 3). The specific blurring of categories in

---

[12] This applies to other sections of *El suplicio del placer* as well. In the second play, the businessman never lets his mistress forget that his money makes everything possible: "Como las manecillas de tu Cartier estoy duro y dale, duro y dale sin parar todo el santo día. Y ¿para qué? Para mantener mujeres inútiles. Mujeres cuyo único trabajo es ser mujeres, carajo" (284) [Like the hands of your Cartier, I'm at it nonstop all the blessed day. And for what? In order to support useless women. Women whose only job is to be women, damn it].

"Uno" seems to stem as much from the possibilities afforded by privilege as from an inherent instability of the overall notion of gender. That is, the exchange and redefinition of roles is something Él and Ella choose to indulge, constructing their freedom in terms of superiority over those trapped by foolish conventions of monogamous fidelity. All the same, they find plenty of willing partners; both women and men find them irresistible. Still, a vague sensation of guilt occasionally intrudes. Él confesses: "A veces me siento culpable de ser tan bello y tan refinado y tan libre y de tener a todos los otros al alcance de la mano. En el fondo soy un socialista. . . Pero aún más al fondo estoy convencido de que la pobreza no debe combatirse" (275) [Sometimes I feel guilty for being so beautiful and so refined and so free and for having everyone else within reach of my hand. Deep down I'm a socialist . . . But even deeper down I am convinced that poverty should not be combated]. Él's poetic ramblings are received sarcastically by Ella and quickly forgotten. His confident domination of the restaurant stage–sizing up his prey, ordering the right vintage, selecting just the right waltz–reflects, if nothing else, long experience in elegant hotels. With Él's cry of "¡qué cursi!" [how corny!] at Ella's mention of Strauss, the scenario elaborated in pursuit of the brunette becomes by implication a cynical ploy (272). His "masculinity," fluctuating with his possession of the mustache, is a consciously contrived act reformulated according to its intended audience. Yet his discomfort with this instability is evident in the alcohol-induced memory lapses he suffers in the mornings.

Sexuality is also at issue, as categories of both social role and sexual object are blurred:

> ÉL (*maliciosamente*): ¿Has visto cómo te miran las mujeres? ¿Cómo te sonríen? . . . Eres irresistible con el bigote y lo sabes. Y lo disfrutas.
> ELLA: ¿Qué estás insinuando, cariño?
> ÉL: Pues a veces me das qué pensar. Sólo tienes ojos para las mujeres bellas. Me las señalas, me aconsejas cómo acercármelas . . .
> *Ella lo mira con fijeza. Él se arrepiente de haber dicho lo que dijo.*
> ÉL: Bromeaba. No me mires así. No soporto que me mires así. Es evidente que no te gustan las mujeres. Si no te gustaran los hombres no te gustaría yo, ¿verdad?, y es evidente que yo te

> gusto porque soy un hombre. Contéstame. Dime que te gusto porque soy un hombre.
> ELLA: Me gustas. Es evidente.
> ÉL: Dilo completo. Dí: me gustas porque eres un hombre. (276-77)
>
> [HE (*maliciously*): Have you seen how women look at you? How they smile at you?. . . You are irresistible with the mustache and you know it. And you enjoy it.
> SHE: What are you implying, dear?
> HE: Well, sometimes you make me think. You only have eyes for beautiful women. You point them out to me, you advise me how to approach them . . .
> *She looks at him firmly. He regrets having said what he said.*
> HE: I was joking. Don't look at me like that. I can't stand it when you look at me like that. It's obvious that you don't like women. If you didn't like men, you wouldn't like me, right? And it's obvious that you like me because I'm a man. Answer me. Tell me that you like me because I'm a man.
> SHE: I like you. It's obvious.
> HE: Say the whole thing. Say: I like you because you're a man.]

Ella is almost a "better" man than Él (women find her irresistible); her masculine performance is more effective than his supposedly masculine "self." At the same time, she is his only guarantee that he *is* a man, a fact both of them recognize. While Él accuses Ella of knowing that with the mustache she is irresistible, earlier he has himself acknowledged, "sé que cuando traigo puesto nuestro bigote soy irresistible" (273) [I know that when I wear our mustache, I'm irresistible]. More than anything that lies behind it, the mustache itself excites desire and the other's affirming gaze across the room. In a sense, the mustache is the "third term," the transvestite that is ultimately only a sign of itself. Embodied in the mustache, transvestism is both camouflage and lure. The mustache serves to make Ella invisible to the "galanes" [gallants] who approach her against her wishes, yet visible, and desirable, to women; it allows Él to seduce the brunette at the next table but leaves him invisible to men. Yet as the piece closes, after Ella has denied her interest in women, the mustache that earlier was to fend off unwanted male attention seems designed to allay her own temptation and finally to transform her into the "he" to Él's "she":

> ÉL: Eres bella. Fría y bella como una diosa de mármol. Con el bigote eres de carne, pero aún peligrosa: ¿lo quieres?
> ELLA: No. ¿Para qué? Esta noche no hay otra mujer que me tiente. Pero si tú quieres quitártelo . . . Tal vez haya un hombre que te guste y si quieres que se te acerque tienes que quitarte el bigote.
> ÉL: No. No hay otro hombre que me guste tanto como tú. Eres irresistible con el bigote puesto. Póntelo.
> *Él mismo se lo pone. Le acaricia el bigote.*
> ÉL: Como un relámpago de seda negra . . .
> *Se besan en los labios.* (280)
>
> [HE: You're beautiful. Cold and beautiful like a marble goddess. With the mustache you're made of flesh, but you're still dangerous: do you want it?
> SHE: No. Why? Tonight there's no other woman who tempts me. But if you want to take it off . . . Maybe there's a man that you like and if you want him to approach, you'll have to take off the mustache.
> HE: No. There's no other man I like as much as you. You're irresistible with the mustache. Put it on.
> *He puts the mustache on her. He caresses the mustache.*
> HE: Like a lightening flash of black silk . . .
> *They kiss on the lips.*]

Though both finally acknowledge same-sex attraction, it remains an attraction based on difference: the mustache will enhance her seduction of women just as it undermines his seduction of men.

Gender as category is blurred or questioned from the outset in Susana Torres Molina's *. . . Y a otra cosa mariposa*. The play's five scenes follow four characters, El Flaco [Skinny], El Inglés [The Brit], Pajarito [Little Bird], and Cerdín [Piglet] from age twelve or thirteen through their late sixties.[13] Each scene depicts a "typical" moment in the lives of this group of childhood friends. A note following the *dramatis personae* specifies: "Esta obra tiene como única condición para su representación, que los cuatro protagonistas

---

[13] As Jacqueline Bixler, from whom I have borrowed these translations of the characters' names, points out, Pajarito's name "also refers to homosexuality and the male organ" ("For Women" 222). The implication of homosexuality is already present in the title of the play; the word "mariposa" [butterfly] also connotes homosexuality (Seda 110).

deben ser representados por actrices" (11) [The only condition concerning the performance of this work is that all four protagonists be represented by actresses]. The play's performance–and performance within the play–is dependent on a particular inversion of expected gender roles. The audience is aware of this shift: "la obra comienza cuando una luz muy tenue ilumina a las 4 actrices que lentamente comienzan a desvestirse de mujeres y vestirse como chicos" (11) [the work begins when a tenuous light illuminates the four actresses who slowly begin to undress themselves as women and dress themselves as boys]. Completing the frame, the play concludes as "los cuatro protagonistas se van quitando el maquillaje y las ropas masculinas" (56) [the four protagonists take off their masculine makeup and clothes]. The women take off stage makeup in order to reveal themselves as women, just as the made-up woman (made up as a woman) removes makeup to reveal the "real" face beneath the mask.

The four female actors play highly stereotypical roles: boys looking at a pornographic magazine; teenagers berating "effeminate" tendencies; married men establishing a "bachelor pad" complete with prostitutes and inflatable doll. Somewhat similarly to Austin's "feminist theory play," with its use of Fetterley's "resisting reader," the women actors playing men foreground the constructed–performed–nature of their machista roles. This is not to say that Torres Molina's is precisely a theory play. However, one way of reading the female roles–women playing men–is to note the parallel with the woman reader trained to read as a man. Although casting women in the male roles underscores and satirizes the characters' machismo, there is a degree to which the female voices repeating machista cant mimic the complicity of women in the perpetuation of such attitudes, a difficulty alluded to as well in *El eterno femenino*. An issue in staging the play must be the degree to which the actors might disguise their voices, as more or less "masculine" voices would tend to underscore the irony of these "male" lines pronounced by women. The cross-dressed illusion may be partial as well. According to Jean Graham-Jones, the "male costume is never entirely masculine: the fabrics are shiny and soft, the makeup exaggerated" (102). The use of female actors undermines even the most strident assertions of masculinity by separating the individual embodying the character from the character's represented "self."

Torres Molina describes the effect of having women play the male roles in somewhat contradictory terms. Of the play's first performance, she says: "fue representada por cuatro actrices amigas. Se vistieron de hombres y los trabajos de las cuatro fueron tan maravillosos que el público olvidó que eran mujeres. Ellas mismas, después de ensayar y actuar en la obra dijeron que se sentían como si fueran hombres" (Eidelberg, "Susana" 392) [it was performed by four actress friends. They dressed as men and the work of the four was so marvelous that the audience forgot that they were women. They themselves, after rehearsing and acting in the play, said that they felt as if they were men]. Yet the motivation behind the cross-gender casting would seem to be undercut by the erasure of difference–both actors and audience "forgot" the players were women. It is precisely in the contrast between performed and "real" (biological) gender that Torres Molina sees critical potential: "si hubieran sido actores, sería una comedia graciosa, tal vez, pero se habría perdido lo incisivo de la crítica" (Eidelberg, "Susana" 392) [if they had been male actors, it would have been a funny comedy, maybe, but it would have lost the incisiveness of the critique]. Nevertheless, the contradiction is to some degree more apparent than real. Jacqueline Bixler concludes that "By casting women in the roles of men, Torres Molina conveys in parodic style not only how men perceive women, but also, and more importantly, how women perceive men" ("For Women" 231). Although the audience might temporarily forget the "true" gender of the female actors, the closing scene in which they remove their male costumes deliberately destroys the illusion. At that point, the constructed nature of all gender roles, male as well as female, must be doubly apparent to a spectator recently persuaded that female performers were in fact men.

Case argues that the femme "foregrounds her masquerade by playing to a butch, another woman in a role" (291). She contends that "from a theatrical point of view, the butch-femme roles take on the quality of something more like a character construction [. . .]. Thus, these roles qua roles lend agency and self-determination to the historically passive subject, providing her with at least two options for gender identification and with the aid of camp, an irony that allows her perception to be constructed from outside ideology, with a gender role that makes her appear as if she is inside of it" (292). Case further suggests that "the butch, who represents by her clothing the desire for other women, becomes the beast–the marked taboo against lesbianism dressed up in the clothes of that desire" (294). Butler asserts that "within lesbian contexts, the 'identification' with masculinity that appears as butch identity is not a simple assimilation of lesbianism back into the terms of heterosexuality. As one lesbian femme explained, she likes her boys to be girls, meaning that 'being a girl' contextualizes and resignifies 'masculinity' in a butch identity. As a result, that masculinity, if that it can be called, is always brought into relief against a culturally intelligible 'female body'" (*Gender* 123). In . . .*Y a otra cosa mariposa*, the butch has no femme to whom to play. This opens several possible interpretations. First, the audience may be placed in the position of the femme, attracted to the butch costume. At the same time, one female actor plays a man who is himself a transvestite, so that Pajarito, cross-dressed, may represent the femme to the other three. However, Pajarito is not (apparently) involved sexually with any of the other protagonists. The passion they play is not directed toward him but only toward a "femininity" that, in drag, he represents. His drag becomes an icon of displaced femininity, like the inflatable doll, displayed as contrast to the "masculinity" of the cross-dressed female actors. In a parallel with Castellanos's play, male–rather than female–posturing is stressed as performance.

Bixler writes that "women are simultaneously present in and absent from *Mariposa*. As invisible and defenseless verbal referent, they occupy most of the men's dialogue, which alternately portrays them as spendthrifts, temptresses, troublemakers, and idiots. Yet at the same time, women are continually present in the outer frame of *Mariposa* as actresses dressed in male garb" ("For Women" 226). In part given the rigidity of the roles critiqued, gender is not as slippery a category as it is in Berman's play. Nevertheless, the ambiguities of women playing men are underscored. In the first scene, "La prima" [The cousin], Pajarito tells the story of seeing his older cousin nude in her bath. During the narration, Cerdín takes on the role of Pajarito's cousin, "imitando una voz femenina" (17) [imitating a feminine voice]. In this instance Cerdín, not Pajarito, plays the doubly cross-dressed role. The only female figure actually appearing on stage (within the frame of the actors disguising themselves as boys) is an inflatable doll. Other women are invoked by reference–Cerdín complains about his mother, El Inglés about his wife–or suggested through the actions of the male characters: obscene gestures, leers.

In the fourth scene, the protagonists, now middle aged, assemble for an afternoon of pornographic films and illicit sex. While they wait for the "minas" to arrive, an inflatable doll that El Flaco has recently acquired becomes the focus of the ongoing rivalry between the four, as well the occasion for much joking at the expense of the women the doll is meant to represent or replace. El Inglés suggests that the doll may be the answer to Cerdín's prayers, trapped as he is at home with his aging mother and often unable to go out. Cerdín timidly fondles the doll, but pulls away as El Inglés begins to egg him on. Yet the doll, brought by a cousin from Sweden, can still be acquired or exchanged. El Inglés takes Cerdín aside to whisper, "si el Flaco te ve entusiasmado, seguro que te la regala" (47) [if El Flaco sees that you're excited, I'm sure he'll give it to you]. Cerdín then ingratiates himself with El Flaco, admiring the doll and finally speaking to her directly. Pajarito, who has remained on the sidelines, "se coloca detrás de la muñeca y le mueve los brazos y la cabeza, como si fuera un títere" (47) [places himself behind the doll and moves its arms and head as if it were a puppet]. As puppeteer, Pajarito also partners Cerdín, so that the doll functions, briefly, as an intermediary between the two men. Always conscious of his friends' reactions, Cerdín gives the doll a passionate embrace, continuing his "juego exhibicionista" [exhibitionist game] as El Flaco and El Inglés whistle and shout (48). Cerdín must prove himself in front of his friends, submitting, in the process, to a none-too-subtle humiliation as the "have not" among the sexual "haves" whose excess property includes not only regular partners but docile plastic mistresses. The exhibitionism of this scene contrasts with that of "Uno," in which Él is titillated by the possibility that Ella observed his entire seduction of the brunette, while her vicarious enjoyment of the young woman's beauty is such that Él accuses her of being the one intrigued. In "Uno," seeing and being seen are mutually enjoyable, unlike the more hostile one-upmanship of the four friends in Torres Molina's play.

Interrupting the game, Pajarito winks at Cerdín saying, "Hacé tu vida. Tranquilo. Como si no estuviéramos" (48) [Live your life. Calmly. As if we weren't here]. Cerdín is induced to lie down on the couch, and Pajarito places the doll on top of him. To cheers of "¡Dale gordo!" [Let's go fatty!] Cerdín "comienza a desabrocharse la bragueta frenéticamente. Tiene la cara muy colorada. El cántico de los tres es cada vez más exacerbado. Cuando Cerdín abraza a la muñeca y la rodea con sus piernas, Pajarito se acerca y con un solo y preciso movimiento, le saca el tapón. La muñeca lentamente comienza a desinflarse encima de Cerdín" (49) [frantically begins to undo his fly. His face is very red. The cheering of the three becomes continuously more urgent. When Cerdín hugs the doll and encircles it with his legs, Pajarito approaches and, with a single precise movement, removes the plug. The doll begins to deflate slowly on top of Cerdín]. Pajarito's role, participating in yet undermining Cerdín's "seduction," is ambiguous. His interruption of the first game (the "flirtation" with the doll) is in fact a substitution, for of course the three do not make themselves scarce, "como si no estuviéramos," [as if we weren't here] but rather encircle Cerdín, cheering. The doll is necessarily on top, perhaps because Cerdín's weight might pop it or in order to keep his red face visible for the audience, but also because the doll, even disinflated, obscures his fly, and prevents a visual revelation of what the audience already knows: the performer is a woman. Yet the inflatable/deflatable doll is more a figure of masculine than feminine genitality. When Pajarito acts as puppeteer, a woman, dressed as a man, activates a female figure that is, in fact, at once both more male than female and a male construction of ideal femininity. Cerdín's performance with the doll (and Pajarito's performance as the doll) make neither of them a "real" man. These uncomfortable and scarcely controlled games underscore the element of performance in all of the protagonists' dealings with the opposite sex, a performance directed more toward the observing male peers than toward the alleged object of desire. Even the plastic doll, lauded earlier as the ideal substitute for an impatient flesh and blood woman, is fallible, and the failure here is clearly linked to the interference of the audience that was supposed to validate the game. An inherent insecurity of performance lies in its dependence on outside validation from an audience that may or may not cooperate.

Homosexuality is a continuing theme as the four repeat, with variations, their posturing for one another. Pajarito's name itself bears the implication of homosexuality. In the first scene, El Inglés "camina imitando un marica" (14) [walks, imitating a gay man]. After Cerdín joins the game, "comienza un juego de seducción entre los dos 'maricas'. Los otros dos siguen el juego riéndose muy excitados. Cada vez que pasa Cerdín al lado de ellos, le pellizcan el traste" (14) [the game of seduction between the two 'queers' begins. The other two follow the game laughing with excitement. Every time Cerdín passes by them, they pinch his behind]. Here a female actor plays a boy pretending to be an effeminate boy. Later, in the scene "Despedida de soltero" [Bachelor party], Pajarito explains that he shares the apartment he has recently rented: "lo comparto con . . . un tipo. Un tipo que necesitaba guita y me lo ofreció. Vi el aviso en el diario y . . . pero el departamento es grande" (36) [I share it with . . . a guy. A guy who needed cash and he offered it to me. I saw the ad in the paper and . . . but the apartment's big]. Goaded by his friends with taunts such as "Me imagino que tomarás la píldora, ¿no?" (37) [I bet you take the pill!] and "¿Te vestís de mina?" (38) [Do you dress like a girl?], Pajarito insists on differentiating himself from women: "¡Soy marica pero no mina! ¡Entendieron, hijos de puta! ¡soy marica pero no mina!" (38) [I'm gay, but I'm not a girl! Understood, assholes? I'm gay, but I'm not a girl!]. The scene's violence is physical as well as verbal: El Flaco and Cerdín throw Pajarito face down on the table. Ultimately, however, the entire episode is taken as a joke. El Flaco recalls, "¿Se acuerdan la vez que [Pajarito] nos hizo creer que tenía parálisis infantil?" [Do you remember the time he made us think he had infantile paralysis?] and the four friends embrace (39). While the group is quick to "feminize" Pajarito, calling him "Palomita," "loca" (slang for an effeminate gay man), and "malita," they are just as eager to gloss the entire episode as yet another performance, that of the perpetual joker who can make his friends believe anything. In refusing his friends' labels, Pajarito rejects any suggestion that he takes a passive homosexual role. However, the conflation of passivity with effeminacy also recalls the absent but repeatedly invoked feminine figures against whom all four characters are defined. Castillo notes that "*Una loca* represents the most common appellation for any woman who crosses the threshold of the home and who steps outside the traditional bounds of a proper, womanly *pudor* (decorum, but also modesty, humility, and purity) and *recato* (prudence, caution, shyness, also coyness)" (16). The friends' shorthand for Pajarito's "feminine" persona relies entirely on pejorative terms for a transgressive femininity; however ingrained in ordinary slang those terms may be, the negative cast remains.

Pajarito's sexuality is more openly recognized later in the play. In "El bulín" [Bachelor pad], El Inglés suggests Pajarito date women "para . . . mostrarte, para que te vean" [to . . . show yourself, so that people see you], a performance that would publicly establish his masculinity (44). El Inglés insists he has no desire to meddle but points out that seeing them so much together, people might assume that all four "estamos en la misma" (44) [are into the same thing]. Naturally, El Inglés is only concerned for his family: "Uno tiene hijos. Hay valores. Costumbres" (44) [One has kids. There are values. Customs]. His acceptance of Pajarito is clearly partial. Nevertheless, when Pajarito leaves the room in search of the projector on which to show the pornographic films and returns in full drag, no one is surprised: "Se ha maquillado ojos y boca y está vestido de mujer, con tacos altos. Su aspecto es de 'travesti'. Nadie parece notarlo" (49) [He has put makeup on his eyes and mouth and is dressed as a woman with high heels. He looks like a transvestite. No one seems to notice]. The transvestite is, at least initially, invisible, overlooked. The treatment of transvestism here is at once more straightforward and more complex than in "Uno." In contrast to the ongoing instability that characterizes Él and Ella in their shifting aims and appearances, Pajarito conforms to a stereotyped construction of the gay man as transvestite. According to Bernhardt Schulz, "para la sociedad latinoamericana es menos inquietante y más aceptable enfrentarse con un homosexual en ropas de mujer" (218) [for Latin American society it is less disturbing and more acceptable to face a homosexual dressed as a woman]. Finally, transvestism may function as a double facade, one that destabilizes gender hierarchies at the same time that it eludes or diverts censorship. As Laurietz Seda has underscored, the implicit lesbianism introduced by the sexual interactions between (disguised) female actors must be masked due to the highly repressive period in which the play was written and staged.[14] Thus, lesbianism never becomes explicit in the way that Pajarito's identity as a gay man is revealed. At the same time, because of the cross-gender casting of the entire play, for the audience, Pajarito is not the only character in drag. The play of woman dressed as man dressed as transvestite complicates the absolute divisions between macho and effeminate that the

---

[14] Seda describes the censorship of the period of the *Proceso de Reorganización Nacional* (1976-83)–a repression that included, but was by no means limited to, gay practices and representations–and concludes that Torres Molina uses the theatrical convention of women dressed as men "para escapar de los males de la censura de la época, para enmascarar el tema del lesbianismo y para añadir de esta manera una dimensión transgresora a la obra" (109) [to escape the censorship of the period, to mask the theme of lesbianism, and to add in this way a transgressive element to the work].

four friends initially establish. The butch role is inverted, with woman-as-man-as-woman in the place of woman-as-man. (As no mention is made of special arrangements, such as a male prostitute, for Pajarito, we might assume at another level that he plays the femme to the butch roles represented by the other three.)

Torres Molina's actors not only assume male roles but male space, the cafés and park benches Franco describes as the male preserve, without becoming the public women of some of *El eterno femenino*'s episodes. Yet while traditionally women are often relegated to private spaces, here such spaces are owned by men. "Private" space in . . . *Y a otra cosa mariposa* is most clearly figured in the "bulín," a space where married men can safely bring "public" women. This privacy is acquired through the displacement of women: the bachelor pad enclosure evades the disapproving gaze of wives and mothers. Women are displaced in other ways as well. El Inglés brags about having set up his wife (herself a prop required by his respectable persona) in a boutique, ostensibly to cure her boredom but in fact to create a free space for his sexual adventures. Displaced to the shop, his wife is placed like so much merchandise, private property on suitably circumscribed public display. Men create their own private space–an ostensibly female space–by displacing women into the more public space of the well-heeled boutique. In the play's final scene, the four once again occupy a public area, as the aging friends, seated on a park bench, discuss physical ailments and dietary restrictions. Their occupation is partial, however, in that they are harassed by the sling-shot play of the surrounding children. One by one, the men leave the stage and return dressed once again as young boys. The circularity of this final scene, which echoes the first scene of the play, is itself repeated by the un-costuming of the female actors, who close the play by resolving the cross-dressed frame.

Castellanos's theory play, with its accumulative parody and no-stone-unturned approach to detail, provides a ground against which to read the more nuanced exploration of gender in "Uno" and . . . *Y a otra cosa mariposa*. Where Lupita is confronted pell-mell by role models and icons past and present, from the isolated housewife to the "public" streetwalker, romantic ideal to national traitor, the circumscribed space of the hotel suite occupied by Él and Ella represents an ambiguously private public stage on which to negotiate a reordering of unstable identities. The "breeches role" as recreated in . . .*Y a otra cosa mariposa* once again moves into public spaces. In Torres Molina's play, all four of the actors cross-dress when they "get into costume," but only Pajarito cross-dresses within the action framed by the female actors' initial disguise and final disrobing. While the transvestite is ultimately erased–Pajarito returns to his/her female attire–the uncertainty or instability revealed by his performance remains. In "Uno," both Él and Ella cross-dress. Their cross-dressing, however, is limited to and located in the mustache. Interestingly, the mustache, visible sign of masculinity, is patently false, a prosthetic hair piece that, physically, belongs to neither of them. When Ella uses the mustache to hide (in plain sight) from unwanted suitors, it functions as a more visible example of the "falsies" with which a male cross-dresser, such as Pajarito, stuffs his shirt. Within their private interaction, the mustache is used not to "pass" but as a token, an exchange of freedom or permission, an implicit invitation or dare.

Each of these three plays portrays gender roles, or gender itself, as dependent on individual performances validated by an audience. This exploration has two facets: subverting the view of gender identity as natural or given and revalorizing the element of performance traditionally recognized in gender, particularly feminine, identity. These elements, then, are connected: the prejudice against women acting in the theater; the prejudice against women for, supposedly inherently, acting or dissembling; the concern with accurate rendering of gender representations on stage, and hence the danger and titillation of women in men's clothes. A revalorization of performance in gender identity may recognize feminine performance as an inescapable imposition or accord it a positive value in itself, acknowledging the performance as in some sense "real." The recognition of the requirement of performance relieves the performer of the burden of duplicity, so that women's performances may be viewed not as an index of their deviousness but as a systematic imposition. At the same time, to recognize a tie between gender and performance opens up possibilities for new performances that rewrite or refine previous scripts. If one looks at women as necessarily performers, Gambaro's description of the director/text relation can be taken as a means toward a revalorization of performance as a liberating process that does not entirely reject the prior text but rather attempts to take the "pretext" and reshape it in performance.

Ultimately, the interplay of gender and performance is at once liberating and coercive. By consciously performing (a) gender, as the four female actors do in *...Y a otra cosa mariposa*, the actor underscores not only the contradictions or abuses within traditionally constructed masculine roles but foregrounds as well the degree of performance within those roles. Thus, the four friends are always conscious of their audience. The protagonists of Berman's play refine and rewrite their prior texts, but they also repeat, in the banal seduction of the starry-eyed girl, or in their seemingly inescapable differential monogamy, the scripts under revision. Franco argues that "the class privilege of the intelligentsia has always posed a problem for Latin Americans, but in women's writing it becomes particularly acute since women writers are privileged and marginalized at one and the same time" ("Going" 70). Furthermore, she suggests, "in order to challenge that privilege women writers have been forced to reexamine that hidden sphere of the public/private dichotomy–the private itself, which traditionally has been so closely linked to the subjective and the aesthetic" ("Going" 74). If gender (or gender roles) require a spectator, only very problematically can gender exist in private. As Franco points out, "The *private* is, in fact, a slippery term, used by economists to define private enterprise as opposed to the state and by social scientists to refer to the family or the household. But it also refers to the individual and the particular as opposed to the social. Even for male writers, however, the private was necessarily riddled with conflict; while seemingly the space for freedom and creativity, insofar as it was the space of the individual, the private revealed the limitation of death and mortality" ("Going" 74). The space of "freedom and creativity" here described as private is also connected to the attempt to claim the stage as a setting for liberation and points up yet again the paradox of the figure of performance as freedom. Making the woman "public," performance invades the private, so that the relation of public to private cannot be resolved into a simple separation of male and female. As inevitable performer, the woman is always public, because always on stage and observed. Suggestive as this is, however, gender "reduced" to performance does not do justice to the contextual matrices of these plays. Although gender roles are destabilized, this destabilization occurs always within the context of greater or lesser economic privilege and frequently political domination, as when the boys in the first scene of *...Y a otra cosa mari-*

posa echo the rhetoric of dictatorship gleaned from television and newspapers.[15]

In all three plays, questions of placement and display are recurrent motifs in the deconstruction of the roles and constraints of gender construction or gender play. Placement alludes to both the traditional spatial restraint of women, placed in the home, convent, or, in Torres Molina's updating, the upscale boutique, and the re-placement of women onto a public stage, either through political action or theatrical representation. Women may be literally replaced–dispossessed–on stage, as by the Elizabethan boy actor, or replaced in the sense of being newly placed or placed again. Display is at once what the respectable matron must never sink to–making a spectacle of herself–and a means of turning performance toward transformative ends. The visibility or display of the constructedness of gender, for example, undermines the acceptance of gender as natural or given. Display also partakes of the ambiguity of the tropes of visibility and hiding, as the visible mustache hides the woman behind it, as the audience forgets, provisionally, that a male character is played by a female actor, as the transvestite enters the room unobserved. Like performance more broadly, display may be double edged, exposing not only the constraints or assumptions the performer wishes to question but the performer herself to public scorn and physical attack. Similarly, placement, with its ring of passive submission to a dominant, "placing" agent on the order of a cosmic chess player, is liberating only to the extent that the specific placement raises questions or is actively undertaken by the individual so "placed." Placement and display encompass the two poles of the continuum of gender performance that these plays represent, combining the contradictions of the performance metaphor as one of liberation with the revalorization of performance as inescapable. Linking public and private, compulsion and release, the two reveal the inherent ambivalence of playing gender.

---

[15] As they fight over a copy of *Playboy*, Pajarito suggests that in the U.S., "hasta las reparten en los colegios" [they even distribute them in the schools], to which Cerdín replies: "con razón están así [. . .] llenos de degenerados" (16) [that's why they're like that, {. . .} filled with degenerates]. In *Disappearing Acts*, Taylor stresses the degree to which the military regime sought to define and repress sexuality and its representations.

CHAPTER 4

TORTURE ON STAGE

SCENES of staged violence bring into still sharper focus the dangers inherent in performance. The previous chapters have treated the potentially coercive effects of performance and the extent to which the enforced performance of social roles may be abusive. The play of gender in Sabina Berman's work, for example, illustrates the persistent tensions in even an unstable gendering. Performance figures have also been employed to illuminate abuses perpetrated through nontheatrical means: the official histories reexamined in plays such as Vicente Leñero's *Martirio de Morelos* or José Antonio Rial's *Bolívar* are revealed as constructed versions of events that at the moment of their occurrence were themselves bound up with contingency and representation. This chapter turns to the theatrical performance of physical abuse, in particular torture. Torture has been invoked in many of the plays already discussed: in the recalled justifications of Morelos's alleged betrayal, in the offstage battering of El Preso Bolívar or in the pain ritually inflicted by the protagonists of Mariela Romero's *El juego*. It is therefore appropriate to explore the issue of the theatrical representation of torture more fully.

Plays that question the established parameters of representation necessarily insert themselves into the process through which those definitions are negotiated. It is for this reason that the performance of gender and the representation of torture can be viewed together, for the theatricality of both relies on an audience fully indoctrinated into the "right" performance, an audience that must be aware of the performance without necessarily questioning either form or content. Again and again, the same excesses of theatricality merge as means and target of critique. Mario Benedetti's *Pedro y el Capitán* (Uruguay, 1979) [*Pedro and the Captain*], Eduardo Pavlovsky's *El señor Galíndez* (Argentina, 1973) [*Mr. Galíndez*], Griselda Gambaro's *El campo* (Argentina, 1967) [*The Camp*], and Ariel Dorfman's *La Muerte y la Doncella* (Chile, 1990) [*Death and the Maiden*] provide the framework for an examination of the theatrical performance of torture, the performance element in torture, and how the two are negotiated. These performances about violence reflect a construction of society in terms of spectacle. The plays also raise questions of visibility, of vulnerability, and of the ethics of representation. This investigation is not an attempt to explain torture per se, but rather to analyze the portrayal of torture in dramatic texts and the interrelations between the theatricality of the practice of torture and the means whereby torture is represented on stage. To stress the theatricality of torture is not to argue that torture is in any way unreal, but instead to emphasize the degree to which questions of spectacle and representation are part of its practice. The theatricality inherent in the political use of torture is exploited, reproduced, or questioned in theatrical representations "about" torture.

The plays analyzed here explore the theatricality of torture through elements such as role playing and spatial manipulation and through the transformation of a performance event into a stage for torture. *Pedro y el Capitán* traces the mutual disintegration of prisoner and interrogator through an extended exchange in which the roles of victim and victimizer become blurred. Benedetti's play outlines a number of elements common to the plays under consideration: the dynamics of interrogation, the insistent threats against the victim's private reality, and sexualized violence against women. *El señor Galíndez* presents an ambiguous, unreal space that is at once cellar and attic, locker room and operating theater. This undefined setting highlights the already troubled boundary between auditorium and stage, implies that torturers are no more readily recognizable than are their work spaces, and finally parallels the torture spectacle's blurring or obliteration of public/private distinctions. Gender-directed violence is another constant among the plays studied. In *El campo*, Emma's recital is a form of torture, a compelled performance as coercive in its impossibility as in its necessity. The use of "high culture" elements such as classical music in instances of torture highlights as well the vulnerability of performance, along with other art forms, to co-optation. *La Muerte y la Doncella* also underscores the potential linkages between elite, sanctioned performances–in this case, classical music–and systematic torture.[1] Dorfman's play explores how an individual–or a society–might assimilate a history of torture and move forward without reproducing the violence of the past.

Torture represents the extreme case of the coercion explored at different levels in earlier chapters. It also, in a number of countries from which the plays discussed are drawn, establishes the overarching societal version of the violence of which interpersonal relations present a microcosm. As a political tool, the spectacle of torture is projected in such a way as to silence dissent. The interwoven nature of horror and spectacle in the concrete scene of torture and in the projection of that scene onto a broader social screen make torture and its effects a logical choice for theatrical representation. At the same time, that choice creates an ethical dilemma for the artist. The difficulty lies in how to make theater *about* torture without recreating its dynamics, without parroting a regime's deliberate use of torture as spectacle. Artaud argued that "the image of a crime presented in the requisite theatrical conditions is something infinitely more terrible for the spirit than the same crime when actually committed" (85). In determining how to represent torture, the playwright faces a quandary: too "realistic" a portrayal may invite charges (possibly legitimate) of exploitation; a presentation that is not "realistic enough" is open to charges of evasion and sentimentality. In either case, the spectator, for whom the staged crime, according to Artaud, is the more terrible, is vulnerable not only to the cathartic terror Artaud seems to suggest but to the numbing, stupefying effects of the extratheatrical spectacle as well.

Placement and display, so central to the performance of gender, are, if anything, more crucial yet to the theatrics of torture. Questions of visibility and invisibility, and of who is allowed to see, arise in the differing use of hoods and blindfolds in Benedetti's and Pavlovsky's plays. The mask or hood is a fluid sign, associated, in different plays, with both torturer and victim. What seems impor-

---

[1] In a study of torture in ancient Greece, Page duBois observes: "So-called high culture–philosophical, forensic, civic discourses and practices–is of a piece from the very beginning, from classical antiquity, with the deliberate infliction of human suffering" (4).

tant is not whose face is hidden but the fact of hiding, the disparity of visual information between captor and captive, the control of sight. The hood gives the torturer anonymity while preserving his ability to see; the blindfold, by contrast, contributes to the dehumanization of the prisoner as a faceless, anonymous "package" while protecting the torturer's identity and also his (theatrical) space.[2] In *The Body in Pain*, Elaine Scarry asserts that torture "bestows visibility on the structure and enormity of what is usually private and incommunicable, contained within the boundaries of the sufferer's body. It then goes on to deny, to falsify, the reality of the very thing it has itself objectified by a perceptual shift which converts the vision of suffering into a wholly illusory but, to the torturers and the regime they represent, wholly convincing spectacle of power. The physical pain is so incontestably real that it seems to confer its quality of 'incontestable reality' on that power that has brought it into being" (27). The visibility bestowed by torture is itself problematic, for the practice of torture is routinely denied even as the open secret that torture is occurring is used to subjugate a population.[3] Yet it is the unseen spectacle, inescapable in its omnipresent invisibility, that produces the chilling effect of torture on the public at large. Scarry continues: "What assists the conversion of absolute pain into the fiction of absolute power is an obsessive, self-conscious display of agency" (27). This obsessive display has two audiences: the prisoner undergoing torture and the general public beyond the torture cell.

---

[2] In *The Politics of Cruelty*, Kate Millett argues that "Blindfolding is many things at once. For the one blindfolded, it is disorientation and vulnerability brought to a pitch of disability and dependence. One is physically helpless and psychologically intimidated. [. . .] Although those who are blindfolded can see nothing, they are absurdly visible: objects, marks of scorn and abuse. Each figure in the circle who abuses them remains invisible, protected against discovery and any possible prosecution" (233).

[3] Lawrence Weschler quotes Uruguayan psychoanalyst Marcelo Vignar on the prospect of a military amnesty: "This is such a sick little country [. . .]. All torn and twisted and broken, with so much of the brokenness concentrated around this notion of knowledge, of *knowing*: 'You can't possibly know what is was like.' 'We didn't know, we didn't realize.' The torturer's 'I know everything about you.' The victim's 'I don't even know what I said, what I did . . .' The torturer's 'Scream all you like, your resistance is completely futile, no one will ever know.' This point about no one's ever knowing was the very subject matter of the torturer's discourse, do you understand? That's what the torture was *all about*. That's why an amnesty will be so terrible, because it will perpetuate the torture itself" (171-72).

The plays I will examine in this chapter come from countries that experienced particularly brutal repression and widespread torture in the 1970s and 1980s: Chile, Argentina, and Uruguay. In this context, the spectacular politics of Argentina's "dirty war" offer a persuasive model of the theatrics of state violence. In his study of the "dirty war," Frank Graziano describes two particularly theatrical forms of military spectacle, the concrete staging of armed "confrontations" and what he terms the *"abstract* spectacle of atrocity" (73). The first of these employed the bodies of prisoners as props in the representation designed to condemn them publicly. Prisoners were carefully prepared for the drama in which they were to play an unchosen, unwilling role: "Days before they were to be shot, these prisoners received better food and were cleaned up and obliged to bathe, since it would have been difficult to explain to the public why 'extremists killed in shootouts' turned up with skinny, tortured, bearded, and ragged corpses" (Graziano 65). Similar scenarios are recorded in Alicia Partnoy's *The Little School*. She describes the fate of four *desaparecidos* with whom she was imprisoned: "after more than four months in detention, they were made to bathe and put on their own clothing; the guards gave Vasca back her bracelets and told them that they would be taken to jail. [. . .] I listened as they were injected with anesthesia–the guards joked about it and I could hear the deep and rhythmic breathing of those who are asleep." Soon afterward, "the two couples appeared in *La Nueva Provincia*, the daily newspaper of Bahía Blanca, as having been killed in a 'confrontation' with military forces" (124-25).[4] The fictitious "confrontations" provided a public explanation for disappearance: certain individuals "reappeared" as corpses appropriately costumed and positioned for public display. The reports of "confrontations" pointed to visible bodies as evidence that persons whose whereabouts were unknown would likely surface as guerrillas.

The "abstract spectacle" of the "dirty war" encompassed both the visible stagings of false "confrontations" and the invisible spectacle of absence occasioned by the growing number of the "disappeared." Certainly, the spectacle of state violence need not remain

---

[4] The case is that of Zulma "Vasca" Aracelli Izurieta, César Antonio "Braco" Giordano, María Elena Romero, and Gustavo Marcelo "Benja" Yoti. Partnoy lists several such instances in her appendix, "Cases of the Disappeared at the Little School."

abstract; public executions provide an instance in which an audience is invited to witness a spectacle at once cautionary and punitive. In addition, the "disappeared" were routinely seized in populated, public spaces. However, Graziano writes:

> the *abstract* spectacle of atrocity as evidenced in the Argentine 'dirty war' differs from spectacles staged in public view in that the rituals of torture, the doing and undoing of the crime on the victim's body, the cries of agony attesting to the generation of power and the restoration of truth, were all brought to bear without direct public witness and therefore engage their participant-observer audience not through graphic displays of atrocity but rather through *representation* of an absence (indexed by *desaparecidos*) whose presence was at once insisted and denied. The eerie, overwhelming silence of the victims–tortured but absent–was paralleled by that of the audience, terrorized by having 'witnessed' the abstract spectacle that the Junta at once staged and forebade. (73)

Diana Taylor argues that "military violence could have been relatively invisible, as the term *disappearance* suggests. The fact that it wasn't indicates that the population as a whole was the intended target, positioned by means of the spectacle. People had to deny what they saw and, by turning away, collude with the violence around them" (*Disappearing* 123). The obsessive display that Scarry describes corresponds to an equally obsessive silence: the consolidation of power relies on the display of visible absence, the gaps left by unseen *desaparecidos*. Moreover, by its silence, the audience is implicated in the ongoing spectacle.

The abstract spectacle translates the private experience of pain onto a public stage. Chapter 3 examined the traditional split of masculine and feminine, public and private space, and the implications of that division for the performance of gender. The public/private split is also relevant to plays about torture, at the level of the torture room, in the specific act of torture, and in the national spectacle torture underwrites. Paradoxically, the abstract spectacle of unacknowledged torture continues to rely on torture's public nature.[5] The erasure of public/private boundaries in the

---

[5] Approaching torture from the perspective of legal history, Edward Peters argues that torture invariably: "is torment inflicted by a public authority for ostensibly public purposes" (3).

generalized mechanics of torture and, more specifically, in Argentine "dirty war" violence is a recurring theme in discussions of the period.[6] A similar blurring of boundaries occurs in many of the plays reviewed in earlier chapters. The private violence of *El juego* not only reflects the women's repression at the hands of El Viejo but, in the scenarios of political imprisonment and social inequality they act out, reproduces the public violence of their society. In José Ignacio Cabrujas's *Acto cultural*, discussed in the next chapter, the blurring of public and private scripts contributes to the impossibility of performance. The ultimate obliteration of these frontiers is the recourse to intensely private, individual pain as the ground of a performative drama of authority designed to disperse an individual's anonymous, unacknowledged experience across an extended social field.

This is not to argue that the retention of a particular construct of public or private spaces is unambiguously benign. The previous chapter addressed the inequalities inherent in the rigid maintenance of arbitrary distinctions such as the gendering of public space as masculine, private space as feminine. Such divisions are not neutral: individual transgressions of those limits may be harshly punished. Nevertheless, it is significant that regimes loudly proclaiming their defense of traditional morality and of institutions such as "the family" were at the same time systematically undermining the family's security. The existing mythology of the family was appropriated as part and parcel of the "way of life" the military ostensibly undertook to protect. Yet Jean Franco contends that "one of the institutions that the military governments of Chile, Argentina and Uruguay were most concerned to destroy was the family as a region of refuge" ("Death" 13). Taylor writes that the "nocturnal raids on homes, the abduction of family members, the practice of raping and torturing loved ones in front of each other revealed the armed forces' uneasiness with the family as a separate space and organiza-

---

[6] As Taylor puts it, Gambaro's plays "reflect the intensification of annihilating violence as boundaries totally disappeared between private and public" (*Theatre* 120). Scarry also refers to the division of public and private, or the erasure of that division. She observes that the "dissolution of the boundary between inside and outside gives rise to [. . .] an almost obscene conflation of private and public. It brings with it all the solitude of absolute privacy with none of its safety, all the self-exposure of the utterly public with none of its possibility for camaraderie or shared experience. Artistic objectifications of pain often concentrate on this combination of isolation and exposure" (53).

tional unit. As the junta had warned, all the interior/private spaces were turned inside out" (*Disappearing* 88). The systematic attack on the family, cloaked as it was in a highly moralistic discourse, eliminated the home as safe house.[7] *Nunca Más* cites numerous examples of violence against the families of (alleged) subversives and of family members used as hostages. Franco maintains that, "In attacking the family, by torturing parents in front of children, by carrying off grandmothers or parents of militants, the military released powerful oppositional forces out of which emerged movements like those of the Mothers of the Plaza de Mayo and the Families and Relatives of the Disappeared in Chile. The strength of these movements lay not so much in the surprise element of women taking the initiative at a time of intense repression but more in their creative use of symbolism" ("Death" 13). In a context of heightened and cynical representations, such creative reclamations of common symbols became particularly necessary.

The recoding of public and private spaces is linked as well to the questions of visibility raised in the abstract spectacle or in the state's display of agency. Writing of the "dirty war," Taylor contends that in opposition to the "hidden, invisible interiority associated with subversion and femininity, the military represented itself as all surface, aggressively visible, identifiable in uniforms, ubiquitous, on parade for all the world to see. The spectacularity of their display of power indicates that the visual image was considered as important as the narrative in controlling their public's attention. Staging order was perceived as a way of making it happen" ("Spectacular" 21). The performative spectacle achieved the impression of power by acting as though that power were already in place. The aggressive visibility of the military defined its performative stagings. By com-

---

[7] In his discussion of dictatorship and redemocratization in Uruguayan literature, Jorge Ruffinelli observes the repetition of houses in the titles–and metaphorical evocations–of recent novels by women such as Alicia Migdal (*La casa de enfrente* [The house across the street]) and Mercedes Rein (*Casa vacía* [Empty house]). Ruffinelli asserts: "Esas 'casas' tienen obviamente el referente inmediato de un 'espacio' que la cultura patriarcal uruguaya le había reservado a la mujer, y el espacio que ella, por ende, debe analizar hasta sus últimas consecuencias, desmitificar, resemantizar en el imaginario (así como lo hace en la práctica cotidiana)" (56) [Those 'houses' obviously have the immediate referent of a 'space' that Uruguayan patriarchal culture had reserved for woman, and the space that she, therefore, must analyze up to its final consequences, demythify, re-semantize in the imaginary (as is done in everyday practice)].

parison, the unseen took on a dual significance encompassing both the secretive, nation-sapping "subversive" and the military's own hidden procedures. Taylor describes the gendering of political bodies under Argentine military rule in light of what she terms "the Patria/*puta* split," a shift that recast the dichotomy of public (whore) vs. private (virtuous) woman onto a pair of public women, the publicly held Motherland and the prostitute ("Spectacular" 26). Once made public in this sense, the Patria no longer represents the (private) virtues of the mother, because, as Taylor points out, it is the military men who have given birth to her, rather than the other way around. The Patria is stripped of "her" reproductive function to become a result of rather than a necessary condition for military dominance. This "demothering" of the Patria is then countered by the newly public actions of the Madres de la Plaza de Mayo, who used their supposed invisibility as homebound, private mothers to occupy a public stage. In a context of theatricalized politics, the Madres presented an alternative spectacle, one that recast the terms appropriated by the military spectacle to other ends.[8]

The links between public and private, visible and invisible, condition (and also motivate) the representation of torture. South African novelist J. M. Coetzee outlines two reasons for what he calls the "dark fascination" exerted by torture: "The first is that relations in the torture room provide a metaphor, bare and extreme, for relations between authoritarianism and its victims. [. . .] The fact that the torture room is a site of extreme human experience, accessible to no one save the participants, is a second reason why the novelist in particular should be fascinated by it" (363). The enclosure of the torture room establishes an absolute privacy that nevertheless tempts the imagination. Inside the torture room, there is a further contraction of accessibility. Scarry argues that "pain comes unsharably into our midst as at once that which cannot be denied and that which cannot be confirmed" (4). Theatrical representations of torture attempt to bridge this chasm of inexpressibility. At the same time, like other artistic representations, theatrical representations of torture are unconfirmable at yet another level, because the audience knows them to be "unreal."

Coetzee suggests that "in creating an obscenity, in enveloping it in mystery, the state unwittingly creates the preconditions for the

---

[8] Taylor discusses the Madres further in *Disappearing Acts*.

novel to set about its work of representation" (364). The fascination with torture comes to seem inevitable, inherent in the fiction-making process as much as in a specific sociopolitical context. Inevitable as it might be, however, this fascination remains troubling.[9] Coetzee defines the novelist's problem as "how to justify a concern with morally dubious people involved in a contemptible activity; how to find an appropriately minor place for the petty secrets of the security system; how to treat something that, in truth, because it is offered like the Gorgon's head to terrorize the populace and paralyze resistance, deserves to be ignored" (366). In short, how to represent the abstract spectacle without recreating its effects. The recurrence of theatrical imagery in discussions of torture, and its coincidence with the theatricality of violence in plays *about* torture, is striking. The specific scene of the torture chamber is projected into a theatrical spectacle for society at large–the "fifth participant" Taylor discusses,[10] the audience for the abstract spectacle defined by Graziano. Denunciatory theater, then, must recreate the spectacle of torture, this time *as* spectacle rather than as torture, but it must do so without recreating the numbing or terrifying effects of the spectacle the producers of actual torture seek from their audience.

As political spectacle, state-sponsored torture relies on certain fictions, notably the function of interrogation as a means of gathering information. According to Scarry, torture "consists of a primary physical act, the infliction of pain, and a primary verbal act, the interrogation. The verbal act, in turn, consists of two parts, 'the question' and 'the answer,' each with conventional connotations that wholly falsify it. 'The question' is mistakenly understood to be 'the motive'; 'the answer' is mistakenly understood to be 'the betrayal'" (35). Scarry's argument ignores the fact that torture may be an end

---

[9] Coetzee continues: "there is something tawdry about *following* the state in this way, making its vile mysteries the occasion of fantasy. For the writer the deeper problem is *not* to allow himself to be impaled on the dilemma proposed by the state, namely, either to ignore its obscenities or else to produce representations of them. The true challenge is: how not to play the game by the rules of the state, how to establish one's own authority, how to imagine torture and death on one's own terms" (364).

[10] Taylor writes: "Gambaro points to at least five participants involved in torture, all five caught up, in different ways, in its theatricality: the 'producer,' the victimizer, the victim, the victimized public, and the general public" (*Theatre* 133).

in itself, pain inflicted for the sake of inflicting pain.[11] Scarry's analysis is instructive, however, in its delineation of the formal properties of the confession. Although the conflation of torture and interrogation is an oversimplification, the relation of the two is useful in considering the retention of the formal interrogation in several of the plays examined here.

Ñacuñán Sáez observes that "everything seems to indicate that the typical torturer sincerely believes in his job as a means to investigate the truth. At the same time, however, he knows that the victim can be innocent and that the information that he gives is not always accurate. And yet, the contradiction seems not to affect the torturer. [. . .] Actually, it does not matter to him what the victim says; the only thing that matters is that he talk" (133). In opposition to Scarry's contention that pain carries the sufferer to a prelinguistic state, Sáez draws on a specific erroneous "confession" cited in *Nunca Más* to argue that "what makes Mirta Infrán's confession valuable for her torturers is that, *although it is not accurate*, it does make sense, it does convey a message, it does after all have a political effect. Pain has forced her to give concrete (but false) names, exact (but random) addresses, precise (but distorted) information. Her language has not regressed to a pre-coded, inarticulate, wild scream. On the contrary: it has proceeded to a point where its subjection to the code, its conformity with syntax, its artificiality, has allowed it to perpetuate itself, regardless of its accuracy" (138). Her speech, emptied of meaning, is treated as meaningful, its distorted precision producing the illusion of sense. Its artificiality, moreover, its repetition and excess, resemble the language of a performance piece, although it must be stressed again that this reduction is achieved through the infliction of real pain on a specific individual. Graziano maintains that the useless information gathered through the torture of nonmilitant prisoners "is rendered useful tautologically by being used *as though* it were valuable" (102). The process has two significant components: the prisoner must be made to talk, and the torturers must then appropriate the prisoner's voice to transmit their message.

---

[11] As Darius Rejali cautions, "just because torture was historically associated with confessions does not mean that this is the sole or even the main purpose of torture today" (3). In a similar manner, duBois suggests that "it may be that the function of torture today, rather than the production of truth, is still one of spectacle, of the production of broken bodies and psyches, both for local and international consumption" (155).

In recreating the interrogation scene, a drama may fall into the trap of repeating, unquestioningly, the state's justification of torture. This is to some degree the case in Benedetti's *Pedro y el Capitán*, a play that explicitly denounces torture yet tacitly accepts that interrogation is a means of gathering information. The condemnation, even by opponents of torture, of those who reveal information under duress bolsters the regime's self-congratulatory cycle.[12] The treatment of the title character in *Martirio de Morelos* as a victimized individual, and the subsequent controversial reception of Leñero's play as a betrayal of the great man, replays the dynamics of "betrayal" and "intelligence gathering" discussed by Scarry, Sáez, and Graziano. Objections to Leñero's depiction of Morelos as, in his words, "human" reflect the bias against the torture victim who "talks."

The four scenes of *Pedro y el Capitán* are performed on a set that resembles an interrogation room rather than a cell. Although his physical torture occurs offstage, Pedro enters each scene (or is forcibly shoved on stage) in progressively worsening states of physical breakdown. Even within the play's starkly limited framework, theatrical elements condition the characters' encounters. The use of pseudonyms by both characters introduces a note of role playing. Pedro bears a clandestine name, Rómulo, whereas the Captain's subterfuge consists in hiding behind a lower rank until Pedro informs him: "no me limito a conocer el nombre de tu mujer. También sé el tuyo. Y hasta tu alias. [. . .] Tu alias es el grado de capitán. Y vos sos coronel" (83-84; pt. 4) ["I not only know your

---

[12] Scarry notes that "there is not only among torturers but even among people appalled by acts of torture and sympathetic to those hurt, a covert disdain for confession" (29). She asserts that "While those who withstand torture without confessing should be honored, those who do confess are not dishonored by and should not be dishonored for their act" (330). Erminio Neglia, in contrast, writing of *Pedro y el Capitán*, sees in Pedro's resistance confirmation of the dictum that true heroes do not confess: "Pedro también traspasa el dolor y ya sabe que nadie le podrá sacar informaciones. De esto se desprende que existe un punto crítico durante el tormento en que el verdadero revolucionario se afirma como hombre y decide morir como tal en lugar de dejarse deshumanizar por la tortura" (94) [Pedro also transcends pain and thus knows that nobody can get information from him. From this one gathers that a critical point exists during the torture in which the true revolutionary affirms himself as a man and decides to die as such rather than allow himself to be dehumanized by torture]. Pedro differs from the majority of the *desaparecidos* Graziano discusses in that he is in fact portrayed as a militant and might actually have useful data to convey. Nevertheless, the dynamic whereby what the regime needs most is Pedro's speech, not a given utterance, remains in place.

wife's name. I know yours, too. I even know your alias. {. . .} Your alias is your rank, Captain. You're a Colonel" (50)]. Conscious role playing in the scene of torture is still more evident in the repeated invocation of the good cop/bad cop model, a recurrent motif in plays that deal with torture. In the final scene of *El avión negro* [The black airplane], "Las torturas," two characters designated Bueno and Malo discuss their roles in the day's work:

> BUENO: ¿A quién le toca hacer de bueno ahora?
> MALO: A vos . . . si recién hice yo . . . (Cossa 113)
>
> [GOOD GUY: Whose turn is it to be the good guy now?
> BAD GUY: Yours . . . I just went . . .]

The roles are arbitrary, distributed according to a twisted rendition of "fair play." Bueno's difficulty in sustaining his role–when he begins to lose control, Malo cautions him, "Sos el bueno, pará" ["you're the good one, stop"]–indicates how false the kindly pose of the good cop really is (117).[13] In Enrique Buenaventura's short play *La tortura*, by contrast, the suggestion is that the torturer's role, to the extent that it is a role, cannot be discarded. El Verdugo interrogates his wife about trivial details as though she were a prisoner and ultimately kills her. The detectives who discuss the case afterward lament the torturer's professional excesses but allow that the defense attorney will surely win acquittal: "Hará un formidable discurso sobre la infidelidad femenina" (111) [He will present a formidable discourse on female infidelity]. The situation presents yet another blurring of public/private space distinctions, as the torturer literally takes his work home with him. At the same time, his wife, relegated to her private space–a fact highlighted in his condemnation of her movements outside the home–is no longer safe even there. The links between violence against "subversives" and violence against women could hardly be clearer.

---

[13] The impossibility of giving the "right" answer to the interrogators–and, hence, the formal nature of the interrogation–are objectified in this play through the use of an inanimate doll to portray the prisoner. Because it is no longer physically performed or imitated on the human body but instead conveyed through the dismembering of the doll, the representation of pain is distanced. The turn-taking between Bueno and Malo also recalls the violent games discussed in chapter 2, in which the players alternate in the dominant position.

In Benedetti's play, El Capitán himself lays out the good cop/bad cop model for Pedro's edification; at this point, the tone of the questions for the first time becomes threatening: "A vos no tengo que explicarte las reglas del juego. Las sabés bien y hasta tengo entendido que reciben cursillos para enfrentar situaciones como esta que vivís ahora. ¿O no sabés que entre nosotros hay interrogadores 'malos,' casi bestiales, esos que son capaces de deshacer al detenido, y están también los 'buenos,' los que reciben al preso cuando viene cansado del castigo brutal, y lo van poco a poco ablandando?" (16; pt. 1) ["I don't have to explain the rules of the game to you. You know them very well and I even understand that you get training courses on how to face situations such as the very one you are in right now. Or don't you know that we have among us some vicious interrogators, almost bestial types, who are capable of real brutality. And then there are the human ones, those who comfort the prisoner when he's almost done in" (36-37)]. Although El Capitán insists on differentiating his role in Pedro's treatment from that of the "muchachos eléctricos" who wield the *picana*, Pedro rejects his rationalization: "el hecho de que usted no participe directamente en mi tortura, no garantiza que no lo odie, ni siquiera que lo odie menos" (27; pt. 2) ["just because you don't take a direct part in my torture doesn't guarantee that I don't hate you, nor even that I hate you less" (39)]. El Capitán justifies himself in terms closely tied to the formal requirements of interrogation and the manipulation of "usefulness" that makes interrogation an end in itself. He distances himself, however, from the actual torturers until Pedro calls his bluff: "Vos trabajaste de 'malo' y bastante tiempo, en un pasado no tan lejano. Te conocemos, capitán. O sea que tienen que hacer más espesas las capuchas. Siempre hay alguien que ve a alguien" (83; pt. 4) ["You worked as one of the 'bad guys' and for a long enough spell, and that wasn't so long ago either. We know you, Captain. You should make those hoods thicker. There's always somebody who sees you" (50)]. The use of an alias, or of a deceptively low rank, parallels the use of masks and blindfolds; in neither case is the seemingly hidden identity secure. The insecurity of identity establishes a certain equality between the play's protagonists. Stephen Gregory argues that El Capitán's self-differentiation "turns what is ostensibly a confrontation between the powerful and the powerless into a verbal encounter between two parties who, if not equal, occupy positions which are to some degree flexible"

(15). Indeed, it is the captain who "confesses" his weakness, while Pedro remains resolute. As was the case with Bueno and Malo in *El avión negro*, the distinctions are arbitrary, the roles reversible.

Pedro y el Capitán retains the importance of the confession in Pedro's refusal to speak, a refusal that ultimately destroys El Capitán and leaves Pedro, himself at death's door, the moral victor. Benedetti's structuring of the interrogation and his portrayal of El Capitán's need for justification through information represents a misreading of the interrogation's dynamics. Simply getting Pedro to talk ought to satisfy the "need" for information. Yet El Capitán insists: "la única forma de redimirme frente a los niños, es ser consciente de que por lo menos estoy consiguiendo el objetivo que nos han asignado: obtener información" (42; pt. 2) ["the only way I can face my children is to know that at least I am realizing the objective assigned to us, to get information" (42)]. Benedetti gives too much credence to the literal "intelligence" justification of interrogation at the same time that he gives too little to the possibility that the torturer might believe in what he does.[14] Gregory contends that "Pedro only has to deal with an agent of repression already willing to lay down his arms" (24). The Captain's self-disgust is a foregone conclusion, as Pedro's moral superiority clearly gives him the psychological edge. The near reversal of roles is initiated by El Capitán who, in his eagerness to elicit a response, allows Pedro to question

---

[14] In his analysis of Benedetti's treatment of the figure of the torturer in a number of works, Gregory asserts that "the image that Benedetti cannot, or will not imagine in the mirror is that of the torturer who does not see his job in purely interpersonal terms, who might justify it in the light of some collective good" (10). The captain does refer to the military's self-sacrifice in terms of a disagreeable necessity, one which must also elicit some admiration from Pedro and his fellow revolutionaries: "Nosotros no podemos dejar de apreciar en ustedes la pasión con que se entregan a una causa, cómo lo arriesgan todo por ella: desde el confort hasta la familia, desde el trabajo hasta la vida. [. . .] En compensación tengo la impresión de que ustedes también aprecian un poco la violencia que nos hacemos a nosotros mismos cuando tenemos que castigarlos, a veces hasta reventarlos, a ustedes que después de todo son nuestros compatriotas, y por añadidura compatriotas jóvenes. ¿Te parece poco sacrificio? También nosotros somos seres humanos" (15; pt. 1) ["We can't help admiring your passionate devotion to your cause, your readiness to risk everything for it: your personal comfort, your family, your work, even life itself. {. . .} As for you, I have the impression that you too have a certain healthy respect for our violent methods when we have to teach you a lesson–sometimes even going so far as to wipe you out completely–you who are after all our compatriots, and young compatriots besides. Don't you think all of this is a little hard on us, too? We're human too" (36)].

him. When El Capitán's asks, "¿Y cómo soy?" ["And what am I like?"] Pedro objects, "Pero es absurdo. Me mete en cana, hace que me revienten, y encima exige que le sirva de analista" (30; pt. 2) ["But this really is crazy! On top of everything else you expect me to be your analyst" (40)]. Although the moment is darkly comic, the scene affords other interpretations.[15] The entire process seems too easy. The audience, rather than being confronted with a credible scene of horror–or a persuasive interrogation–observes the self-congratulatory image of the victim who, despite his apparent vulnerability, continues to hold all the cards.

That the interrogator's capacity to interpret Pedro's speech–or lack of it–is to some degree visual is made clear in the second scene when he removes Pedro's hood with the words, "Quiero que veas y que yo pueda ver cómo ves" (26; pt. 2) ["I want you to be able to see and I want to be able to see how you react" (39)]. The invisibility of Pedro's face, the impenetrability accorded him by the hood, hampers the Captain's ability to interpret the information he allegedly requires. In the third scene, Pedro, again hooded and now covered with blood, is forcibly placed on the chair and begins to emit confused, ambiguous sounds that only with the removal of the hood are revealed as laughter. The source of his laughter: "en plena sesión de picana, sobrevino el apagón, ese mismo apagón que previó su maldito coronel" (49) ["in the middle of the electric prod

---

[15] Gregory argues that Benedetti's play, "in order to demonstrate the superiority of humanitarian empathy [. . .] finds itself having to manipulate the relationship of torturer and tortured into an extended session between therapist and patient, thus betraying the reality of what it purports to interpret by turning it into something else" (2). Luys Díez argues that "la obra fracasa por la artificialidad del lenguaje, especialmente en boca del capitán. Todo resulta demasiado literario para ser convincente y no lo suficientemente irreal para que, como parábola del horror (estilo Genet o Arrabal), sea aceptable al espectador" (74) [the work fails because of the artificiality of the language, especially that of the Captain. Everything is too literary to be convincing and not unreal enough that, as a parable of horror (in Genet or Arrabal's style), it is acceptable to the spectator]. Ruffinelli concludes: "Tanto como dos individuos concretos, estos personajes asumen una representación: la de una parte del Uruguay castigada hasta la ignominia y que sin embargo opta por el silencio y la muerte como últimos reductos de dignidad, y otra parte degradada por sus propias funciones, bestial pero moralmente débil porque su única fuerza reside en la destrucción del prójimo" (47) [As two concrete individuals, these characters become representative of one part of Uruguay punished to the point of ignominy that nevertheless opts for silence and death as the last refuges of dignity; and another part degraded by its own functions, bestial but morally weak because its only strength lies in the destruction of its fellow man].

session the power failed; that same blackout that your damned colonel mentioned" (43)]. The torturers, disoriented by the loss of their technological superiority, are forced to suspend the session. Although there are numerous options for the exercise of brute force without electricity, Pedro notes that "a oscuras no puede saberse cuando el tipo no da más. El doctor precisa buena iluminación para diagnosticar la proximidad del paro cardiaco" (49; pt. 3) ["Even the doctor needs a good light to tell how close a person is to heart failure" (43)]. While the prisoners remain indisputably in the torturers' power, this moment of disarray affords a brief opportunity to fight back. The graphic description of another prisoner's torture is counterbalanced by her (temporarily) successful resistance: "estaba aquella muchacha con la picana en la vagina, y cuando vino el apagón no sé cómo les pudo dar una patada" (49; pt. 3) [there was that girl with the electric prod in her vagina and when the power failed, I don't know how, but she managed to give them a kick].[16] The darkness that the hooded prisoner experiences is transferred to the torturers, and the ability to see, which they previously controlled, is denied.

The blackout scene presents one of a cluster of references to violence against women. In keeping with the sexualization of violence frequently associated with torture, El Capitán threatens to rape Pedro's wife while he watches, a threat that corresponds to the military attack on the family discussed by Jean Franco. El Capitán, in turn, is highly defensive when Pedro mentions his family. El Capitán's sadistic sexuality is revealed when he confesses an ability to perform sexually with his wife only by recalling his arousal during the torture of a young woman the day before. The sexual violence against women finds a parallel in the repeated references to the imminent or recent destruction of Pedro's testicles. The captain's sadism belies his claim of being "el bueno" and further highlights Pedro's moral superiority.

The description of the blackout also begins to move away from the realistic tone of the protagonists' earlier interactions: "a partir de este momento y durante casi toda la escena, Pedro dará la impresión de alguien que delira, o quizá, de alguien que simula estar delirando" (49; pt. 3) ["Beginning at this moment and during al-

---

[16] I have modified the published translation here to retain the mention of the young woman's brief resistance.

most the whole scene, PEDRO will give the impression of someone hysterical or perhaps someone who is pretending to be hysterical" (43)]. The ambiguity of his performance extends to the question of whether it is in fact a performance. When El Capitán cautions, "No te hagas el delirante. Conmigo no va ese teatro" ["Don't pretend you're delirious. I don't fall for theatrics"], Pedro replies: "No es teatro, capitán. Estoy muerto" (52; pt. 3) ["I'm not an actor, Captain. I'm dead" (44)]. Frustrated by Pedro's insistent use of figurative language, by his inability to determine the "reality" of Pedro's attitudes, El Capitán points out that his pain can be prolonged, perhaps indefinitely. Used to being the only one "on stage," the one who in any event distributes the scripts, El Capitán is ill prepared to respond to Pedro's unexpected performance.

Alternately, Pedro's silence may be read in terms of "insilio," an Uruguayan coinage to that denotes internal exile. Carina Perelli describes "inxilio" as "exilio dentro de las propias fronteras, de ese nuevo relacionamiento con un orden vivido como externo, pero al que, por el mero hecho de obedecer, se hace funcionar y, en última instancia, se termina por legitimar" (90) [exile within one's own borders, a new relationship to an order lived as external but which, through the very act of obedience, one allows to function and, finally, ends up legitimating]. [17] Jorge Ruffinelli writes, "Durante doce

---

[17] Moreover, "El inxilio es algo más que la mera privatización de actividades consideradas inherentes a la esfera pública. Es una mística, parte de la 'mística del miedo', resultante de la visión que introyectan los sujetos acerca de la peligrosidad potencial no sólo de entablar relaciones significativas con 'otros', sino de entrar simplemente en contacto con ellos" (Perelli 90) [Inxile is something more than the mere privatization of activities that are considered inherent to the public sphere. It is a mysticism, part of the "mysticism of fear," resulting from the vision that individual subjects absorb concerning the potential danger not only of establishing significant relations with "others," but also of simply entering in contact with them]. Weschler relates a portion of an informal discussion among Uruguayans about life under the military regime: "'They had informants everywhere,' another guest explained, 'or anyway made you think they did. All the phones were bugged, or might as well have been'" (90). Bugged or not, the populace began to behave as though it were under continual surveillance. According to María Rosa Olivera-Williams, "Los que se quedaron en el país sufriendo el terror de un sistema arbitrario habían sido expulsados de su comunidad –en el caso de los escritores– de lectores, de críticos, de editoriales, de materiales, ya que todo o casi todo, en un primer momento, entraba en el peligroso límite de lo censurable, de lo condenable. Así se acuñó en el Uruguay el neologismo 'insilio' o 'inxilio' para referirse a la situación de 'marginación' de la cultura producida en el país" (71) [Those who stayed in the country suffering the terror of an arbitrary system had been expelled from their community–in the case of the writers–of readers, of critics, of publishers, of materi-

años, y con la excepción del 'canto popular' que entró en auge hacia los ochenta, el Uruguay sufrió un 'apagón' cultural. Ese apagón cultural se llamó también insilio, una forma de resistencia que consistió de hecho en no escribir, en no hablar, y también en no colaborar con el régimen" (42) [For twelve years, and with the exception of the "popular song" that thrived in the eighties, Uruguay suffered a cultural "blackout." The cultural blackout was also called inxile, a form of resistance that in fact consisted of not writing, not speaking and also not collaborating with the regime]. Pedro's refusal to speak parallels the noncooperation of the inxile. The insidious silence of self-censorship and internal exile presents yet another ambiguous means of resistance, analogous, in some ways, to a performance that remains implicated in the relations it seeks to contest. The refusal to speak or write that characterizes *insilio* attempts to make of an absence–the absence of publications, of literature, of visible, readable text–a statement louder than the thundering pronouncements of the regime. The discussion of feigned paralysis in chapter 2 addressed the use of silence as resistance, one of the "tretas del débil," the feints of the weak. The isolation of the victim–the unshareability of pain to which Scarry points, the "no one will ever know" underscored by Vignar–might also be a form of *insilio*, a forced retreat into one's innermost recesses even as that interiority is denied in the attempt to turn the victim inside out. But the isolation is reinforced through the insistence that no one will ever know. The notion of *insilio* as self-silencing turns the silence *imposed* by dictatorship into an active resistance, silence as protest.

The torture space and its bleeding into "normal" space are central to Pavlovsky's *El señor Galíndez*. The setting of the play is initially ambiguous, unidentified. In their introduction to the published version, Pavlovsky and director Jaime Kogan describe the deliberate instability with which the scene is defined, an uncertainty intended to heighten the spectator's awareness that torture can occur anywhere. Pavlovsky and Kogan describe the stage design in terms of the aesthetic problem of how to "resolver escenográfi-

---

als, since at the beginning everything or almost everything was within the dangerous limit of the censorable, the condemnable. This is how the neologism "inxile" was coined in Uruguay to refer to the situation of "marginalization" of culture produced inside the country].

camente lo que todos sabíamos (los espectadores también): en nuestro país se tortura en muchos 'lugares.' En 'ámbitos' muy diferentes 'profesionalmente' adecuados a esos fines" (11) [resolve scenographically what we all knew (the audience included): torture occurs in many "places" in our country. In very different "surroundings," "professionally" adjusted to these ends]. The uncertainty of the setting is significant not only because it underscores the variety of spaces used for torture and the unreliability of apparently safe, "normal" settings but because that same unreliability suggests that the torturer is no more automatically recognizable than is the torture room. When the borders of the stage are erased, the audience is doubly implicated in the performance of torture, either as passive bystander or as potential victim.

The unnamed work Beto and Pepe share (and are to teach Eduardo) is only gradually revealed to be systematic torture. The men are dependent on the disembodied instructions of Galíndez, who never appears on stage and who communicates with them solely by telephone. For the audience, his voice is inferred from the protagonists' actions rather than being heard.[18] Beto and Pepe's primary activity is waiting for instructions. Between jobs, Galíndez sends two women, announced as "dos paquetes" [two packages], to help them pass the time (37).[19] In keeping with the Patria/*puta* split, the women Galíndez sends are prostitutes: Coca and La Negra. The pairing is completed in the person of Doña Sara, the middle-aged, quasi-mother figure who keeps house for Beto and Pepe. In her unblinking acceptance of the men's brutality and her participation in the manipulation of Eduardo, Doña Sara may be viewed as part of the militarized Patria, the mother no longer a source of refuge, nor capable of reproduction, but brought into being–given birth to–by the needs of Galíndez. Coca and La Negra are treated as expendable, objectified not solely in sexual terms but as "paquetes," playthings with which the men may do as they will.

---

[18] Galíndez also has a textual presence, in the form of a manual written by him and read aloud by Eduardo.

[19] Graziano notes the practice of "referring to prisoners selected for execution as 'packages.' In further development of 'package' poetics, detention center personnel sometimes tied red ribbons around prisoners' necks to identify them for the task forces that carried out their 'transfer' (execution)" (104). *Nunca Más* concludes, with reference to a particular burial: "the way they were buried–naked and with a number from one to five painted on their chests with yellow paint–gives the impression that the dead bodies were treated as bundles, objects or animals, rubbish thrown on a tip" (218).

The episode with the two women mimes a scene of torture, preparing the ground for the ritualized brutality averted only by yet another call. The implications of the three men's actions are clear, carried out with a precision that grimly echoes the rhythms of a surgical theater.[20] Beto explains their work in terms directly in line with the abstract spectacle. He instructs Eduardo: "por cada trabajo bien hecho hay mil tipos paralizados de miedo. Nosotros actuamos por irradiación" (47) [for every job well-done a thousand guys are paralyzed with fear. We work by irradiation]. Visibility and surgery were linked in *Pedro y el Capitán* as well, in the recognition that, during the blackout, the doctor was unable to determine the prisoner's breaking point, unable to reliably preserve the victim for a subsequent session. The theater audience, too, watches from a distance, occupying the same room, perhaps, but not precisely the same space as the actors on stage. The boundaries between stage and spectacle are more thoroughly eradicated in Gambaro's *Información para extranjeros*, treated in the next chapter, in which the audience is placed physically on stage with the performers, jostled by the actors, within striking distance of the violent vignettes. On a conventional stage, relations of visibility are more straightforward. The performers, isolated on the lighted stage, are also, in a manner of speaking, hooded: blinded by the footlights so that the audience becomes a scarcely visible blur. Seated in the dark, the audience enjoys the luxury of seeing without being seen, peeking through the hidden, but here acknowledged, window.

Although Eduardo is also tormented and beaten by his instructors, it is the nude body of Coca that graphically describes the ground of torture and reveals the true function of the previously ambiguous space. At the invitation of Pepe and Beto, "Eduardo le marca a Coca zonas del cuerpo que deben interpretarse como zonas

---

[20] Graziano states that "torture rooms were denominated *quirófanos*" (79) and observes that "The signifier *quirófano* assigned by the repressors to the 'clandestine' torture rooms thus contributed to the poetics of the hidden spectacle's disclosure: A window–such as those along the ceilings of operating theaters–opened into the 'clandestine' torture sessions to make them accessible to the implied audience" (80). Other connotations of the term, as Graziano notes, include the implied inversions of surgical practice and the military phrase "theater of operations." In a similar vein, Taylor writes: "I've come to think of the Dirty War as a theatre of operations, for the expression emphasizes the theatricality, the medicalization, and the violence of the operation exercised simultaneously on social space and human bodies" (*Disappearing* 96).

neurálgicas. Beto la tiene sujeta a La Negra, que trata de zafarse y grita histéricamente. Cuando Eduardo termina de marcarla a Coca, Pepe toma un sifón y la moja totalmente. Esta grita y llora. Está desesperada. Pepe saca de la caja una picana. La enchufa. Se ven las chispas" (45) [Eduardo marks areas on Coca's body that should be interpreted as neurological zones. Beto holds La Negra as she tries to break loose and screams hysterically. When Eduardo has finished marking Coca, Pepe takes a siphon and wets her completely. She screams and cries. She is desperate. Pepe takes a prod from the box. He plugs it in. We see the sparks]. Because loud music masks the actors' voices, the cries of Coca and La Negra are seen rather than heard. Similarly, the telephone that interrupts Eduardo as he vacillates over accepting the *picana* is first visible in the actors' sudden stillness, then audible as the music diminishes. By rendering the women's cries inaudible, the scene reproduces the silence of the abstract spectacle, obliterating crucial sensory evidence of what is manifestly taking place. The audience cannot remain unaware of the import of the action, although the women's cries, evident in their visible physical attitudes, are not corroborated aurally. The spectator is invited to disbelieve her senses or to question the ease with which the inaudible is glossed as unspoken, the invisible as unreal.

The treatment of Coca and La Negra, however, is more than a *mime* of torture. Although the women are released "unharmed," the action establishes a parallel with mock executions, in which the prisoner is subjected to the immediate threat of death and then "spared." The entire episode is a torture of Coca, a scene of abuse dramatically and visibly represented on stage. Coca is subjected to the torture known as "showing the instruments" and to a variation on the "mock execution" in the form of a "mock torture session."[21] Her friend looks on helplessly, an unwilling but immobilized observer. The spectator also sees the instruments, so that the torturer's violence may be understood as directed toward the audience as well–the audience in the theater and the audience as stand-in for the implied audience of the *quirófano*.

When Eduardo departs with the women, Beto and Pepe begin another practiced ritual, rearranging the furniture and costuming

---

[21] Scarry states that "testimony given by torture victims from many different countries almost inevitably includes descriptions of being made to stare at the weapon with which they were about to be hurt" (27).

themselves in smocks and rubber gloves. Beto inspects and replaces a series of medical instruments, leaving out only "una especie de elemento fálico de metal muy grande" (46) [a very large phallic object made of metal]. Again, the action is accomplished without words.[22] Eduardo, disconcerted upon reentering the transformed scene, is reassured by Pepe: "No te asustés. Es la rutina" (47) [Don't be afraid. It's routine]. Finally the two put on their hoods. However, yet another call from Galíndez freezes the action before Beto and Pepe can complete their routine. This time, the pair's growing paranoia casts uncertainty on the authenticity of the call.

To the extent that they are teaching Eduardo, indicating that the role is not natural but learned, Beto and Pepe are aware of performing. Much is made of the torturer's occupation as just another job. Pepe assures Eduardo that it is steady work and angrily rejects Beto's reminder that his previous excess killed a prisoner with the outburst: "¡Yo soy un profesional! ¡He dedicado mi vida a este laburo!" (49) [I'm a professional! I have dedicated my life to this work!]. But the torturers also describe their work, and their rapport, in musical terms: laughing, just before putting on his hood, Pepe informs Eduardo, "tocamos la misma melodía" (47) [we play the same tune]. Later, *picana* in hand, Eduardo expresses his own ambition: "algún día aprenderé a tocar mi propia melodía" (50) [one day I'll learn to play my own tune]. If the *picana* is the instrument, the prisoner's body provides the ground on which it resonates. Playing his own melody, Eduardo will reproduce the spectacle of torture through which the victim's voice is made to mouth the precepts of the powerful. The individual focus of the image–Eduardo will play *his own* melody–belies the suggestion that the torturers are themselves victims, caught in a network of oppression beyond their control. Though they are at the mercy of Galíndez's arbitrary instructions, it is the individual voice of the torturer that initially overtakes the victim.

The ultimate cancellation of the anticipated session is put in question with Eduardo's final line: "Sí, señor Galíndez" (51). As Albuquerque notes, "The 'apagón' that accompanies Eduardo's resolute greeting of the repressive figure not only reveals his readiness

---

[22] According to Jacqueline Bixler, "In a world governed by closure, censorship, and repression, torture is an unmentionable reality, the conveyance of which relies not on words but on these non-verbal forms of expression" ("Toward" 68).

to join the brutal practice but also anticipates the enormous suffering he is to impose directly or indirectly on others" (108-09). The blackout, a brief occasion for resistance in *Pedro y el Capitán*, here becomes another index of the threat only temporarily relegated to the wings. The sudden darkness corresponds as well to the traditional opening of a concert or theatrical performance, the first step toward Eduardo's personal melody. Nora Eidelberg concludes that "Toda la pieza ha sido una preparación, y, en parte, una retardación para este momento: la ceremonia que se frustra" ("La ritualización" 36) [The whole play has been a preparation, and, in part, a delaying of this moment: the ceremony that fails]. The audience is left with a sense of mingled expectation and frustration–the ordeal is temporarily canceled but looms close in Eduardo's ready agreement to Galíndez's undisclosed instructions. It is possible that the postponement of the final episode mitigates the audience's early discomfort at seeing the weapons. The interruption also offers the possibility of decompression, revoking the threat to the spectator's personal security implicit in the use of an undefined space. As an interrupted torture, the preparatory ritual is to some degree a non-performance, setting the stage for an action that never takes place; the type of unrealized performance suggested in this scene will be discussed more fully in the next chapter. Here, however, it is important to note that, while the full-blown, "official" torture session is never represented, torture does not remain entirely offstage. Taylor maintains that "Pavlovsky reproduces and aestheticizes the violence against women without challenging or even addressing the phenomenon" (*Disappearing* 179). Moreover, and this is a critical point, "the play focuses events so that political torture (which is not depicted onstage) is considered real and important, while the torture of naked women (which is depicted onstage) is not the 'real' thing and is hardly worth noting" (*Disappearing* 181). To view the play primarily in terms of frustration or postponement is to pass over–to obliterate, to disappear–the naked, suffering woman whose body the torturers abuse and then discard, and over (or through) whose inaudible screams they speak to one another.

The piano concert of Griselda Gambaro's *El campo* provides the most notable example of performance as violence. With its SS uniforms and suggestively named director, *El campo* calls on recent history even as it prefigures Argentina's "dirty war." Gambaro's play highlights the interplay of performance and abuse and the way in which gender oppression may be mediated through performance. The three main characters, Martín, Franco, and Emma, all participate in role playing and deliberate dramatization. Martín, newly contracted bookkeeper at an unidentified organization, plays the spectator suspending disbelief so thoroughly that he himself is caught in the trap he pretends to ignore. Martín is welcomed upon arrival by Franco, whose costume, a mainstay of theatrical performance, is presented as purposely, perhaps inevitably misleading. Franco's polished SS uniform clashes with his young, almost good-natured face. He recognizes the negative reactions his uniform invites, yet insists, "es una manía inofensiva" (169; 1.1) ["It's a harmless little quirk" (58)]. Through technological interference–intercoms, canned music–and deceptive "explanations," Franco orchestrates Martín's perception of his surroundings. Franco is a theatrical director as well, critiquing Emma's behavior "como un director de escena" (182; 1.2) ["like a theater director" (72)]. Emma, her appearance unmistakably that of a concentration camp inmate, is caught between Franco's demands that she perform and Martín's ineffectual and inconsistent efforts on her behalf. As an unrealized performance, Emma's concert may be classed with the nonperformances of chapter 5. Here I want to focus on the mechanism of public performance as ritual humiliation and on the ties between this specific instance of individual abuse and the foregrounding of the links between torture and performance.

Although Emma participates in the attempted seduction of Martín–Franco's so-called attempt to make him more comfortable in the face of threats to leave–hers is in all respects a forced performance. She enters "empujada con violencia, virtualmente arrojada sobre la escena" (173; 1.2) ["Emma lurches in as though she had been pushed" (62)]. Despite her shaved head, ragged smock, and the livid wound on her right palm, "hace un visible esfuerzo, como si empezara a actuar, y avanza con un ademán de bienvenida" (173; 1.2) ["She makes a terrible effort, as though she were about to act a role. She advances like a hostess welcoming a guest" (62)]. The stage directions stress that her gestures are in complete disaccord with her appearance. Contrasting with her bald head and gray clothing, her wounded hand is the only note of color. The concert is also a dodge intended to deflect Martín's attention from the reality around him. As such, it is yet another flippant gloss of the sort

Franco offers when questioned about anguished screams or troubling smells. When Martín observes "un olor asqueroso. ¿Por qué no lo impiden? Parece carne quemada" (170; 1.1) ["Stinks! Why don't you forbid it? Smells of burnt meat" (59)], Franco explains the smell as that of a cat or dog caught in the burning garbage and attributes it to the cruelty of children. In addition to Franco's immediate deflection of attention and responsibility, it is significant that Martín invites such rationalizations, asking why the smell is not controlled or eliminated, eager to ensure his own comfort rather than pressing for a truthful explanation.

The obvious artificiality of Emma's and Franco's performances underscores the unreliability of theatrical representation. However, the motives behind and the effects of their performances are quite different. Franco performs for personal gratification. Emma's, by contrast, is a forced performance, a distinction that becomes clearer in the piano recital but that is already evident in the visible effort she makes to "act" for Martín despite her horrifying, degraded appearance and physical discomfort. Franco's self-consciousness is different, as is his greater, though not absolute, ability to sustain a role. Eugene Moretta describes Emma and Martín as victims who "bear within themselves the agonizing and ultimately devastating contradiction between a reality experienced in the flesh and a quite opposite one summoned into existence by the playing of parts" ("Spanish" 23). Scarry states that it is the nature of pain to be verbally inexpressible. The playing of parts, then, may be understood not solely as a mask hiding the felt reality from view but as an attempt, however inadequate, to externalize that reality *for* view. The contradictory performances point up the impossibility of representation in this context: Emma's pain is ultimately unshareable. The overwhelming nature of Franco's spectacular power is evident in the inescapable performances imposed on his victims, who are unable to avoid playing their assigned roles in his scenarios.

It is not unambiguously clear that Emma ever *was* a concert pianist outside the camp, only that within its confines she replays a hideous parody of the celebrated artist.[23] Her fragile pose as pianist

---

[23] Linda Zee contends that Emma "by clinging to her past as a concert pianist, implies that she still harbors a shred of optimism" (605). However, Emma's attachment to that past is motivated as much by Franco's goading as by her own optimism.

is nevertheless Emma's most stable identity. When Martín asks her simply who she is, Emma "hace un gran esfuerzo para contestar, trata de recordar, inútilmente" (175; 1.2) ["making a great effort to answer him, trying to remember, but in vain" (63)]. She asks instead for a mirror in order to retouch her makeup. The reinforcement of her image is denied–Martín has no mirror to lend–and Emma makes do with his handkerchief, giving her face an erasive scrub before absentmindedly leaving the cloth on the table. These attempts at improving her image and so perhaps approaching or retrieving an identity pass quickly. Emma's speech is free associative, her attention wanders, her efforts at seducing Martín are wavering and uneven, just as her intimations of the camp's horror move in and out of focus, in and out of Martín's awareness.

Emma's inability to recall Martín's name or to remember a simple question, even for a few moments, produces an inverted scene of interrogation. Martín's increasingly agitated attempts to learn who branded Emma's arm bring on a frightened response: "Le digo cualquier nombre, ¿se conforma?" (178; 1.2) ["I'll give you a name, and then you'll be satisfied. Any name!" (67)]. Unable to remember a name, she again assumes her party manners and offers to sign a photograph. The offer of a name, any name, repeats the exchange between torturer and victim in which the victim's terrified, desperate attempt to say anything that will stop the pain only points up the insignificance of the earlier question, important for its form but not its content. Already in this first encounter the relation between Emma and Martín is ambiguous: she responds to the compassionate outsider who ought to be able to save her as yet another tormentor. Her instinctive fear will ultimately be justified when Martín's passivity and refusal to believe the clear evidence of his senses–the screams, the stench of burning flesh–lead to his and Emma's recapture after a false, stage-managed escape.

Jean Franco argues that Emma's recital is the state's gift to her for seducing Martín ("Self-Destructing" 110). While I concur with Franco's analysis of the potential pitfalls in the selection of performance as liberating metaphor, I disagree with her characterization of Emma's recital as "gift." Not only has Emma failed to seduce Martín, a failure that undermines the motivation for such a reward, but the concert itself is a complex ordeal, combining physical pain and ritual humiliation in a coerced performance that ultimately, like the nonperformances I discuss in the next chapter, cannot be realized. The piano is broken, and Emma is forced to supply the melody with her own broken voice, all the while tormented by the itch and consumed with violent, surreptitious scratching. Emma faces multiple audiences within the play, all of them, with the partial exception of Martín, hostile. Following an interruption from the prisoners who make up the audience and a word in her ear from Franco, Emma "simula tocar el piano con gestos ampulosos y tararea la gran polonesa de Chopin" (194; 1.3) ["playing with grand gestures while she imitates with her voice Chopin's 'Polonaise'" (83)]. Nevertheless, during her second piece, "el SS, cabeza de fila, hace una señal a los presos y éstos comienzan a cantar, a boca cerrada y suavemente al principio, pero van aumentando el volumen con la evidente intención de cubrir la voz de Emma. Ella alza la voz también, pero a pesar de sus esfuerzos, cada vez más desesperados, el coro de los presos termina por sepultar su voz. A una señal dada por el SS, los presos cesan de cantar bruscamente. Emma sigue simulando la ejecución, pero aunque abre la boca, sólo se escucha un hilo de su voz enronquecida" (194; 1.3) ["At a given sign from the Gestapo officer at the head of the bench, the prisoners begin to sing, or rather to hum, softly at first, and then louder, with the obvious intent of drowning out Emma's voice. Emma becomes louder, but in spite of her efforts, which are ever more desperate, the chorus of prisoners drowns her out. At another sign from the Gestapo officer, the prisoners cease suddenly. Emma continues with her performance, but even though her mouth is wide open, all we hear is the frayed thread of her hoarse voice" (83)]. Emma's voice, thoroughly appropriated by Franco, shudders forth not music but evidence of her own abjection. Franco's performance moves seamlessly between good-natured cheerleader and brutal tormentor. The theater audience, finally, observing both Emma's performance and its reception within the play, must consider the conditions of performance that it underwrites with its ticket purchases and approving presence.

Taylor stresses that in the concert, "the torment involves splitting Emma in two, rupturing her sexual identity: the ideal woman is gracious, talented, frivolous, and beautiful; the real Emma is a failed woman, clumsy, ugly, and painful to watch" (*Theatre* 130). Such gender-specific abuse has already been observed in *El señor Galíndez* and *Pedro y el Capitán*. The concert, framed by the character of Franco as in part an element of Martín's seduction–not only a sexual seduction but the seduction of his disbelief–is predicated on Emma's battered femininity, decked out with ridiculous wig and ragged train, and at the same time undermined by her inadequate gender performance. Nevertheless, the focus on Emma, rather than on the overall mechanism of the recital, may be misplaced. As Taylor observes, "The entire spectacle focuses not so much on the degradation of Emma as on Franco degrading Emma" (*Theatre* 131). Franco's performance, in fact, is the more effective performative: taking on the multiple roles of director, stage manager, and impresario, he creates, from a jarring display of pain and humiliation, a cultural event.

Tamara Holzapfel asserts that "*El campo* is clearly an allegory about the pressures exerted by political dictatorships on the arts" (11). Yet the degrading or coercive potential of performance spreads beyond the neatly demarcated stage of Emma's disastrous recital to the self-conscious theatricality of Franco's self-display and to Martín's energetic suspension of disbelief, his choice to behave as a spectator insistently discounting the reality of the spectacle he observes. Moretta concludes that in *El campo*, "performance emerges as a basically oppressive, debilitating activity. Placed at the service of all that is sinister and malevolent in human life, it confuses man's efforts to recognize and confront evil" ("Spanish" 24).[24] Culture, like the torture victim's own voice, is transformed into yet another agent of repression, an agent specifically designed to hide, to erase reality *through* its very visibility as culture or art. The abstract spec-

---

[24] He suggests that Martín "llega a ser el pasivo espectador de una comedia de engaños que dirige Franco y en que actúa Emma. El papel de ella–en una especie de teatro dentro del teatro–consiste en utilizar los elementos de la alta cultura–música clásica, el discurso refinado–esencialmente para crear una realidad falsa y artificial que oculte la verdad horrorosa del campo de concentración. De este modo, parece decirnos Griselda Gambaro, se perpetúa la tiranía: convirtiendo en cómplices a sus propias víctimas, concediéndoles acceso únicamente a esa 'cultura' que en sus manos será, perversamente, un instrumento de disimulo, un arma en defensa del orden que las esclaviza" ("Reflexiones" 144) [becomes the passive spectator in a comedy of deception that Franco directs and in which Emma acts. Her role–in a sort of play within the play–consists of using the elements of high culture–classical music, refined discourse–essentially to create a false and artificial reality that hides the horrifying truth of the concentration camp. In this way, Griselda Gambaro seems to tell us, tyranny is perpetuated: converting its own victims into accomplices, conceding them access solely to that "culture" that in their hands will perversely become an instrument of dissimulation, a weapon in defense of the order that enslaves them].

tacle is complemented by the concrete spectacle, not only in the form of spurious "confrontations" with illusory terrorists but on the decorous stages of high culture.

Classical music and the concert hall are again touchstones in Ariel Dorfman's *La Muerte y la Doncella*, written after the return of (limited) democracy in Chile. The play is a postdictatorship attempt to address the coexistence of unpunished torturers and their victims and the perhaps inevitable meetings of the two. Dorfman's play depicts the forced confession of Roberto Miranda, an alleged rapist recognized only by his voice when he unexpectedly arrives at his victim's house late at night after meeting her husband on the road. Rather than the initial abuse, the play presents the torture victim's reprisal. Following sessions of torture, Paulina had been seen by a doctor who resuscitated her for the next assault and himself raped her repeatedly, all the while playing Schubert's "Death and the Maiden." Several recurrent elements are already in evidence: violence against women, the complicity of members of the medical profession along with the co-optation of medical imagery, the interlacing of "high culture" and violation.[25]

Fifteen years after her imprisonment, Paulina's husband Gerardo has been named to a commission that will investigate a limited category of the past regime's crimes. Dorfman describes the Rettig Commission, on which the commission in the play is modeled, as one that "would investigate the crimes of the dictatorship that had ended in death or its presumption, but which would neither name the perpetrators nor judge them" (*Death* 76). The commission further resonates with the limited prosecution and subsequent amnesty of Argentina's dirty warriors, as well as with Uruguay's amnesty law and efforts to overturn it through referendum. As Paulina asks, "por qué tengo que ser yo la que se sacrifica ¿eh?, yo

---

[25] On the participation of physicians in torture, and efforts by the Chilean Medical Association to address such abuses, see Eric Stover, *The Open Secret: Torture and the Medical Profession in Chile*. For further discussion of the sexual torture of women, see Ximena Bunster, "Tortura de presas políticas: Una forma de esclavitud sexual" [Torture of female political prisoners: A form of sexual slavery] and Lea Fletcher, "La tortura genéricamente específica (la violación) ejercida contra mujeres en la última dictadura militar y su representación en la literatura argentina" [The gender specific torture (rape) exercised against women during the last military dictatorship and its representation in Argentine literature].

la que tengo que morderme la lengua, siempre nosotros los que hacemos las concesiones cuando hay que conceder, ¿por qué, por qué?" (79; 3.1) ["And why does it always have to be people like me who have to sacrifice, why are we always the ones who have to make concessions when something has to be conceded, why always me who has to bite her tongue, why?" (68)]. Although the action occurs within a private house, part of the play's conflict centers on whether memories must remain private, whether it is possible (for a survivor or a society) to turn over a new leaf and move forward without a more public reprisal against the torturers, or at least public recognition of the crimes committed. The tension between public and private is evident in the Commission's charge to determine the truth of the cases it is assigned but not to release the names of the assassins.

In her confrontation with Roberto, Paulina reverses the earlier scene of torture. Now she is the one who wields the gun, who demands that her prisoner confess to crimes he may not have committed. Undeterred by the possibility that Roberto is innocent as he claims, Paulina resorts to many of the tactics of her torturers. The good cop/bad cop routine is invoked as Roberto accuses Gerardo of playing the "bueno" to Paulina's "mala." Display of the weapons may be aural as well as visual; to Gerardo's request to speak with her in private, Paulina replies: "No veo por qué tenemos que hablar a espaldas del Doctor Miranda. Ellos discutían todo en mi presencia" (48; 2.1) ["Why? The doctor used to discuss everything in my presence, they–" (35)]. Dorfman notes that the original production in Santiago had casting problems: "We had to change the male actors two or three times. [. . .] I think they found it very difficult in a macho culture such as Chile's to be abused like this on stage by a woman" (Rohter 32). Much of the play's violence is framed in sexual terms. Paulina describes to Gerardo her initial wish to rape Roberto in retaliation for her own suffering and considers enlisting her husband or a broom handle for the task. She settles for a confession, however, and much of the play's ambiguity (Miranda's identity is never explicitly decided) revolves around the accuracy and authenticity of the document the doctor finally signs. Gerardo is torn between his commitment to legal resolutions and his obligations to his wife; he shrinks from having to hear the details. Roberto accuses him: "el que me va a matar eres tú, es lo que haría cualquier hombre bien nacido, al que le hubieran violado la mujer, es lo que yo haría si me hubieran violado a mi mujer . . . así que dejémonos de farsas. Te cortaría las huevas" (61-62; 2.2) ["And once I've confessed, you're the one, not her, you're the one who's going to kill me, it's what any man would do, any real man, if they'd raped his wife, it's what I would do if somebody had raped my wife. Cut your balls off" (49)]. The reflexive construction ("si me hubieran violado a mi mujer"), lost in the English translation, makes Paulina's rape as much a crime against her husband as against her, and Gerardo is almost goaded into action. The interpretation of Paulina's rape as in some measure a crime against Gerardo recalls El Capitán's threats against Pedro's wife in Benedetti's play. Alternately, like the "paquetes" passed between torturers in *El señor Galíndez*, Paulina is a token of exchange more than an assaulted individual. The casting difficulties Dorfman describes further suggest that Paulina's aggressive reprisal is shocking not so much because it may be misdirected as for its regendering of the roles of victim and victimizer.

Discussions of the Broadway production return repeatedly to the question of whether or not the play is political. Larry Rohter quotes director Mike Nichols: "'it turns out it is not a political play at all,' Mr. Nichols said from New York. 'It's a thriller about the intimate lives of three people and the ways in which their sexual natures are intertwined.' He added: 'I can't see this as a political play in any way, and I consider that a plus. God preserve us all from a true political play'" (32). Benedict Nightingale cites Nichols's later elaboration of his statement that the play is not political: "This was my point: a political play is all about a thesis. *Death and the Maiden* is about human nature and the sickening ways people abuse power. Nobody ever said that *Hamlet* was about the government of Denmark changing three times in rapid succession" (34). Politics, of course, is not limited to governmental succession, and the abuse of power is eminently political. Nichols also speaks within a U.S. context in which "political," attached to a work of art, is frequently more insult than adjective. In Latin America, however, the line between political and nonpolitical art is not so absolute. Indeed, in a context of state terror in which all space, public or private, is subject to military domination, and in which any perceived opposition is classed as "subversive," such a distinction is untenable. To view the play solely in terms of "intertwined sexual natures" is to once again elide the centrality of the woman who has been raped and to accept the torturer's interpretation; as Taylor stresses, the "sexualization of the ordeal is the torturer's doing, not the victim's" (*Disappearing* 154).[26] Dorfman himself insists that the play is political, "not because it is a propaganda piece, not because the violence done to the protagonist is the result of state terror, but primarily because it demands of the country that it examine its own complicity in the events happening on stage; it lodges the tragedy of the protagonist in the fractures and failings of society" ("Playwright's" 4). Nichols relates the play to recent events in the U.S.: "It's the Clarence Thomas hearing, the William Kennedy Smith trial, the Tyson trial" (Rohter 32). The events Nichols lists, certainly spectacles and certainly political–what else could the Thomas hearings be?–also center around the truth or falseness of a woman's claims of sexual harassment or rape. *Death and the Maiden*, however, never questions whether or not Paulina was raped. The uncertainty lies, instead, in whether she has correctly identified her assailant and, beyond that, whether her personal retaliation is just.

The play's final scene, set in a concert hall, uses a giant mirror that occupies the stage to confront the audience with an image of itself. When Paulina and Gerardo enter, they sit facing the mirror, their backs to the audience although their reflected faces are visible. The audience of Dorfman's play is doubled, not only in the mirror reflection but through sound effects that supply the noise of scattered coughs, rattled programs, and people shifting in their seats. While the theatrical audience may attempt to avoid producing the telltale sounds of fidgeting, sounds that inescapably reveal the physical presence of the audience as a group of sentient and hence vulnerable bodies, the soundtrack foregrounds that presence, that vulnerability, and redirects the audience's attention toward itself. Following an intermission during which Gerardo chats with imaginary audience members, Roberto enters, lighted in a ghostly way that leaves his reality in question. As "Death and the Maiden" is played, he and Paulina look at each other, briefly, deliberately, before the lights go down. With the placement of the actors among the spectators the audience is implicated in the rite whereby Paulina meets her captor's image in public and must keep her eyes trained on the

---

[26] In Roman Polanski's 1994 film, only Paulina, played by Sigourney Weaver, is presented partially clothed. We see her breasts, but the men remained covered. Even when Paulina takes Roberto to the bathroom, she unzips his fly but the camera cuts away before any skin is revealed.

stage as though nothing were wrong. Whatever the outcome of her confrontation with Roberto, the society she moves through–the audience of the concert and of the play–holds in store further painful and dangerous encounters.

Simply making violence visible is not sufficient to eliminate it and may in fact exacerbate the problem. Marguerite Feitlowitz describes her immediate reaction to the performance of Eduardo Pavlovsky's *Paso de dos*, a theatrical production of his previously published script, *Voces*, as "a kind of shell shock after so much violence. And then revulsion at the aestheticized brutality and exhibitionism" ("Dance" 64).[27] Writing of the same production, Taylor concludes that "Under the political guise of denouncing victimization and the 'dirty war,' the play carries out a systematic assault on the feminine; the female body is destroyed through violence; the voice vanishes into a metaphor for victimization, hovering at the outer limits of the military discourse" ("Spectacular" 33).[28] The character of the torturer presents yet another problem of representational ethics. Gregory views much of Benedetti's work as revealing "a need to believe (and convince readers) that torturers are somehow both different and lesser human beings than the rest of us" (14). The portrayal of the torturer as other-than-human glosses over the persistent blurring of categories, the even more horrifying possibility that a torturer, rather than being a monster, might regard himself as a dedicated civil servant, much like Beto in *El señor*

---

[27] Feitlowitz's article includes interviews with Laura Yusem, who directed the production, and Pavlovsky and his wife Susana Evans, who played the roles of HE and SHE respectively. Feitlowitz notes that "all of the artists involved insist that *Paso de dos* is a feminist work" ("Dance" 64). Feitlowitz, by contrast, argues that "I felt that the setup effectively made us complicit with HE. There we are, in a dark, constricted space, passively watching and listening as yet another torturer tells us his story. Passively watching highly eroticized murder" ("Dance" 65).

[28] Taylor extends Coetzee's concern with the ethical obligations of the novelist to those of the critic: "More difficult to overcome, however, is what I perceive as the trap laid out for those who would critique such representations of violence. Am I not opening myself to the very charges I bring against Pavlovsky? Can I help but reproduce the violence against women by describing the performance? Is silence, as in the play, the truly heroic response? Again, I feel I have to speak back to the performance, even at the risk of falling into the trap. Rather than add to the violence, my intention is to illuminate that which must be suppressed or repressed–her pain and her extermination–in the performance/text/master narrative in order for the triumphalist reading to work" ("Spectacular" 35).

Galíndez, talking to his daughter on the telephone and studying accounting with an eye to future opportunities. At the same time, the torturer may be portrayed as too human, so that audience sympathy and attention are displaced. Taylor insists that in Gambaro's theater, the "theatrical aura of the victimizers," far from being merely absurd or symbolic, is designed to demonstrate that "the theatricality of the victimizers is *real*; victimization could not continue without it. Victimizers, however theatrical, do not represent something else, such as the 'human condition'; they are not make-believe 'bad-guys' that delight audiences. They kill people. But it is precisely our inability to credit the reality behind their theatricality that allows extermination to continue" (*Theatre* 100). This emphasis on the *reality* of the theatrical or spectacular victimizer is as significant to the internal dynamics of many plays as to their contextual interpretations. The self-serving dramatizations of Bolívar-as-myth orchestrated by the camp personnel in *Bolívar* mask the torture of the prisoners collectively and, specifically, the poet whose task has been to write the script for the spectacle intended ultimately to celebrate, and reinforce, his own victimization. Emma's piano recital in *El campo* is an actual source and scene of pain even as it represents the predicament of the artist under a repressive regime.

The role of the audience in legitimizing torture is inescapable. Graziano asserts that the military's "staged terrorism, choreographed before and marketed after the spectacle, was structured by considerations of public reception rather than by strategies of enemy elimination. The dead 'terrorists' generated by mock battles mediated a discourse between the Junta and the public. Here the military's maneuvers were distanced from theater proper only by the forced participation of some of the players and by the use of bullets in place of blanks. The illusion of power generated by the spectacle was dependent on an imaginary enemy whose pain was real" (65-66). Indeed, as Scarry indicates, it was the reality of that pain that sustained the spectacle. The use of real bullets made the staged violence a sort of live-action snuff film, with primarily political rather than sexual intent. The audience, inescapably called into service as witness, became another forced participant, another victim of the carefully packaged violence designed to forestall its resistance. The audience's enabling complicity is essential to the effectiveness of the abstract spectacle of torture. The innocent bystander unwittingly caught up in events or ignoring (consciously or unconsciously) evidence of oppression is a necessary component of the representation. Audience complicity is also inherent in theatrical performance, as the audience agrees to observe the action presented on stage. Theatrical spectatorship is not innocent, in that a deliberate choice has been made to view this show, this stage.

Self-reflexive theater multiplies the audiences the performer must face, so that the perils of visibility shift. An audience trained not to intervene, to look the other way on the street or, in the theater, to accept whatever happens as part of the act, offers little protection to the performer. The audiences of the prisoners' performance in *Bolívar* range from the hostile vigilance of the guards to the uncertain sympathies of the spectators watching Rial's play. In *El campo*, Emma, too, faces numerous audiences: Franco, Martín, SS guards, other prisoners, and finally the theatrical audience. Plays like Gambaro's *Información para extranjeros* that deliberately undermine the line between player and spectator draw the audience into a degree of identification with the performers–who, after all, appear at times to be fellow spectators–without necessarily eliminating the audience's stubborn, persistent recollection that the action represented is "only" a play, unreal, and so ultimately safe.[29] This is not to advocate a theater that would in fact physically attack the audience but to point out the limits of transfer between the theater and extratheatrical reality. To the extent that the spectator feels assaulted by the performance and identifies, in that sense of danger, with the jeopardized performer, this identification may or may not silence, outside the theater, the destructive, self-justifying rationalizations that reinforce oppression. The theatricality of torture is not accidental.[30] Theatricalized real-world violence calls up the accustomed response to a stage representation, dulling audience reactions or limiting the likelihood of active measures.

It is possible that the almost choric insistence of a number of critics that scenes of violence are stronger if not actually staged cor-

---

[29] *Información para extranjeros* will be discussed more fully in the next chapter, in which the conflation of theater and world and the drawing-in of the audience is complemented by an increasing degree of stymied or denied performance and the theater of torture gives way to a paralyzing nonperformance.

[30] Taylor argues that "the theatricality of torture, then, tries to make violence 'safe' for the audience. [. . .] But it also converts people into a 'safe' audience, one that will not interfere or disrupt the show" ("Violent" 169).

responds to a fear of the exploitative potential of improperly staged violence.[31] An excess of violence also carries with it a potential numbing effect. At the same time, the preference for offstage violence reported rather than seen has a long history, going back to the Greek theater. Taylor suggests that "torture, abductions and other scenes of atrocity frighten us away from seeing and recognizing them by appealing to ways of seeing that we, consciously or unconsciously, associate with *bad* seeing, perversion, voyeurism, and transgression" (*Theatre* 141). The reluctance to look that Taylor describes can be avoided if the atrocity never appears on stage. Furthermore, if the violence occurs offstage, the audience is spared the discomfort of "seeing the weapons." Yet the refusal to show violence or torture also sidesteps the possibility that the audience will too readily rationalize or assimilate such images.

Rather than elect a strict either/or division, a play may present a judicious mix of staged, narrated, and implied or threatened violence. In *El campo*, for instance, the audience is bombarded with both. In addition to the psychological humiliation Emma suffers during the concert, Franco pours an irritating liquid on her wounded hand, and Martín is beaten by the SS guards. However, the final act of violence, the branding of Martín, is suggested rather than realized: the play closes as El Funcionario approaches Martín with a red-hot iron; the final sound is Emma's whimper. Similarly, in *El señor Galíndez* violence occurs on stage in the treatment of Coca and La Negra and in Beto and Pepe's beating of Eduardo. In *La*

---

[31] Albuquerque suggests that "the impact on the audience may be greater when no torture is actually carried out, and the strong impression of violence is elicited by the mere view of the portentous setting as a whole" (200). Elsewhere he writes: "the evocation of the horrors of the torture is considerably more powerful when actual torture is not seen on stage, as in *Pedro y el Capitán*, *El señor Galíndez*, *Milagre na cela*, and *Fábrica de chocolate*" (228). Eidelberg says of the frustrated ceremony of *El señor Galíndez*: "El impacto en el espectador es más traumático que si se hubiese elaborado en la escena la tortura" ("La ritualización" 36) [The impact on the spectator is more traumatic than if the torture had been staged]. As I have indicated, however, actual torture *is* visible in *El señor Galíndez*. Gregory, far from arguing that violence is necessarily more effective offstage, writes of *Pedro y el Capitán*: "Instead of being a central element in the action, the violence practised on him always takes place off-stage (a nebulous elsewhere) and merely becomes part of the backdrop against which there unfolds a quite different drama" (15). Similarly, Holzapfel suggests that in Gambaro's plays "through concrete representation on stage of cruel and violent situations a direct visceral response is evoked from the audience" (11).

Muerte y la Doncella, the relatively mild binding and gagging suffered by Roberto is offset by Paulina's narrative of electric shock and multiple rapes. Through the combination of hidden and represented violence, the audience's reluctance to look is both appeased and overridden. The tension of viewing horrifying subjugation is mitigated through the withholding of portions of the spectacle, yet, lest the unseen become too unthreatening–out of sight, out of mind–violence remains insistently present on stage.

Whether it occurs at the national or the auditorium level, the spectacle of atrocity requires an audience for its realization. The situation of the audience becomes increasingly untenable as it is implicated in both the atrocity its passivity tacitly approves and the awareness or recognition necessary in order to counteract the overwhelming spectacle with oppositional action. The interaction of theatrical stage and spectator reproduces on a smaller scale the relations of spectacle and audience that obtain in society at large. It is thus possible that a stage representation of torture can be in its way as coercive as the state-sponsored spectacle, silencing the audience with its own spectacle-induced paralysis. The visible, fraudulent power achieved through torture is a direct result of the deliberate theatricality of oppression. The theatrical performance of atrocity, then, is particularly vexed, in danger of reproducing the coercive mechanisms of political spectacle derived from pain that it aims to denounce.

CHAPTER 5

NOTHING'S HAPPENING: PERFORMANCE
AS COERCION

IN contrast to plays that present identity as a construct of ritualized violence dramatically performed, the plays discussed in this chapter foreground the fact of performance rather than the particular role enacted or the oppressive imposition of such roles. Isaac Chocrón's *La revolución* (Venezuela, 1971) [The revolution], Griselda Gambaro's *El despojamiento* (Argentina, 1974) [The striptease],[1] Sabina Berman's *Esta no es una obra de teatro* (Mexico, 1975) [This is not a work of theater], and José Ignacio Cabrujas's *Acto cultural* (Venezuela, 1976) [Cultural ceremony] are all structured around narratives of unrealized performance. These plays are characterized by a lack of action. The case of Gambaro's *Información para extranjeros* (1973) [*Information for Foreigners*] is rather different, but here, too, the image of a play that is not quite performed becomes important. Unlike plays such as José Triana's *La noche de los asesinos*, these texts do not depict a self-contained set of rituals meant at some level to stand in for the outside world. The play within the play is a stage event so demarcated, and it is not left to the spectator/reader to identify the stage-like quality of the play's interior action. Performance becomes coercive as it is both de-

---

[1] As Sharon Magnarelli has pointed out, "despojamiento" bears many connotations, including robbery and dispossession; moreover, etymologically, "*despojar* derives from the Latin *spoliare*, to strip the hide or the skin from an animal" ("Acting" 11). Magnarelli therefore translates the title as "The Dispossession." Both aspects–striptease and dispossession–are fundamental to the interpretation of the play, which manipulates conventions of feminine behavior to reveal, as Magnarelli puts it, that "femininity itself is theatre" while at the same time stymieing the realization of that performance and with it the audience's expectation of or desire for a titillating striptease ("Acting" 14).

manded and denied. Nonperformance returns me to the image of the blue leper as that which exceeds the performance space, that which cannot be fully assimilated into any interpretive model. For all their disquieting, often violent content, these performances remain curiously empty, incomplete. The players are explicitly before an audience and, once there, regale the audience with nothing less (or more) than their inability to perform: there is a performance but not a performance *of* anything; what *is* performed is a clearly inadequate substitute for what *should* be performed, and the performance becomes an enforced nonperformance, the representation of a negation.[2]

These plays mark an outward progression from the pre-performances of *Esta no es una obra de teatro* and *El despojamiento*, monologues in which the impossibility of performance is figured by an examination or audition, to the plays that cannot be performed in *Acto cultural* and *La revolución*, and finally to the move beyond the theater in *Información*, which the playwright's notes suggest be staged in a large house of several stories and in which the scenes may be produced in any order, so long as the groups of spectators weaving independently through the house meet for the final episode. This shift also traces a change in the performers' constitution as actors: from student actor, to washed-up professional, to amateur, to the actor as audience member, a change that reflects the convergence of a highly theatricalized space with an insistent suggestion of nontheatrical "reality." The performances are increasingly concerned with a world beyond the stage, and the impossibility of realizing the assigned performances seems to carry with it the implication that action must necessarily take place outside the theater, or at least outside the context of a play. The self-consciousness of these plays carries over into a self-criticism of the dramatic medium itself, a suggestion that "mere" theater cannot affect the outside world, cannot contain or represent action, cannot even achieve its own purposes. Still, this implicit rejection of theater occurs within dramatic texts, so that the rejection is at best partial.[3]

---

[2] In its way, of course, so is *La noche de los asesinos*: a performance of a performance that is never to take place.

[3] The selection of plays is representative rather than exhaustive. Other plays in which coerced, resisted, or stymied performance is significant include Gambaro's *El campo* and Rial's *Bolívar*, discussed in earlier chapters, Jorge Díaz's *El cepillo de dientes*, and Luis Rafael Sánchez's *Farsa del amor compradito*, in which characters

These are plays about unperformed plays, about the terror of a nonperformance in which the performer's body becomes the site of coercion as the impossible performance coyly promised at the beginning is teased out. The strategies of nonperformance, the insistence that nothing is happening, and the reshaping of individual and cultural identity as functions of performance seem to reflect a profound ambivalence about theater and about the world outside the theater. Strategies of nonperformance include the pre-performance of *Esta no es una obra de teatro* and *El despojamiento*, in which performance is limited to the provisional context of the audition; the plea for guidelines, either from the director or from other actor-characters; and the attempt to assure the audience that the lack of action is only temporary. These strategies serve to demonstrate the impossibility of performance and also to involve the audience in the (absent) spectacle.⁴ The emphasis on problems of performance also contributes to the self-reflexive turn of these plays, as the (im)possibilities of theater are explored. The performers are coerced into performing inadequate or inappropriate roles, and the most determined resistance to those roles may be finally reincorporated into the prevailing order as though the disruptions were simply variations on a preestablished theme. Nonperformance, rather than freeing the players from the need to perform, becomes itself a performance, one emptied to the extent that only "performance itself" remains, but a performance nonetheless.

Even within a theatrical context—or as represented within a dramatic text—performance is not an unambiguously liberating force, nor does it provide guaranteed access to a space "beyond" the text. Anthony Kubiak has suggested that "theatre is not merely a means by which social behavior is engineered, it is the *site* of violence, the locus of terror's emergence as myth, law, religion, economy, gender, class or race, either *in* the theatre, or in culture *as* a theatricality that paradoxically precedes culture" (4-5). In the plays discussed

---

resist their prescribed roles and the audience is ultimately informed that "esta obra no acaba así" (109) [the play does not end this way]. The alternate, never realized scenarios of Osvaldo Dragún's *El amasijo*, although rehearsed by characters who are not explicitly actors, are also similar to the nonperformances discussed here.

⁴ The absent spectacle in turn recalls the "abstract spectacle" of state terror discussed in chapter 4, although the dynamic of audience involvement in the endlessly promised yet deferred spectacle of nonperformance does not reproduce all of the coercive intent of the abstract spectacle as a means of terrorizing the general public.

here, not only the theater but the performer, and in some cases the performance, becomes the site of violence. Kubiak also emphasizes the unrepresentability of terror, arguing that "when terror and pain assume signification, they assume meaning [. . .]. When terror moves into signifying systems it is consequently transformed into terrorism" (38). Represented in the theater, then, terror becomes terrorism, a violence that may be directed against the characters or, at least intellectually, against the spectator. The potential for terrorism in theatrical representations of torture, and the danger that such representations would reproduce rather than denounce such practices, was discussed in the previous chapter. The unrepresentable terror Kubiak describes may insinuate itself into the gaps between performer and role, actor and audience. In these plays, there is the suggestion that the representation cannot be realized at all, which implies that terror might reside in the unperformed text itself. At the same time, rather than simply being that which cannot be represented, terror here becomes the inability to represent, the fact of nonperformance. Paradoxically, this terror of nonperformance is personified by characters trapped within a situation in which performance is as inescapable as it is impossible.

Marvin Carlson proposes that "the concept of the supplement, as theorized by Derrida, provides a new way of thinking about several of the key paradoxes which bedevil theories of performance as illustration, translation, or fulfillment," so that neither performance nor dramatic text is privileged as ultimately authoritative or independent ("Theatrical" 9). Carlson's suggestion is echoed by David George's assertion that "the actor-character 'binary' is–really–a *polarity* of performer and role in which it is not the disappearance of one in(to) the other which is experienced but the creative dynamism of their interplay" ("On Ambiguity" 80). In both arguments, it is the connection or tension between text and performance, performer and role, that is most revealing. According to Derrida, "the supplement adds itself, it is a surplus, a plenitude enriching another plenitude, the *fullest measure* of presence," while, at the same time, the supplement "adds only to replace" so that "its place is assigned in the structure by the mark of an emptiness" (144-45). The supplement is both superfluous and necessary, adding to what is already complete, yet, in that addition, revealing an incompleteness. Derrida's allusion to the "dangerousness" of the supplement is also suggestive as applied to performance, particularly to a construction of performance as at least potentially coercive–dangerous both to the performer as sentient being and to the unstable self the actor struggles to make real. The danger of performance as supplement lies in its inescapability and its not-so-hidden power: the liberating escape from textual control is at the same time the violence of nonperformance.

Nonperformance undermines the authority of the text as well as the unity of the actor's role. Eugene Moretta emphasizes the degree to which the dramatic text "often summons into being a life whose inner dynamic is itself shown to be a *performance* of one kind or another" ("Spanish" 5). Role playing may take a variety of forms, from the consciously assumed theatrical persona to the unacknowledged adoption of culturally imposed behavioral norms. In the plays I will discuss here, role playing is not simply a means of escape from a harsh present reality or an attempt to reach an "authentic" inner self. Role playing becomes an inescapable fact of life at the same time that the roles themselves become increasingly undefined, the role being obliterated in favor of performance. Michael Vanden Heuvel contends that "performance deconstructs authorial power and its illusion of Presence, and disperses its quanta of energies among the performers and the spectator as a potential source of a deferred, hypothetical and immanent power. Performance is therefore initially the displacement of Presence, or power, and the affirmation of Absence and powerlessness" (5). "Affirmation" seems inaccurate applied to plays in which performance is the site (or source) of powerlessness rather than its celebration. However, the performances attempted in *La revolución* and *Acto cultural*, continually straying from the text that implicitly precedes them, decenter that text, creating a new space between author and spectator. The coercive aspect of the performance lies in part in the actors' inability to escape that mediating space, to exist other than as the axis on which the interplay of performer and role is negotiated.

The self-reflexive foregrounding of performance demands attention both of and to the audience, as well as to what is (not) happening on stage. The spectator's role in validating a performance constrains the actor, even as the audience may be kept in line through the process of witnessing troubling or violent events. Just as the text is not a given, the audience, too, must be constructed. As Herbert Blau argues, the audience "does not exist before the play but is *initiated* or *precipitated* by it; it is not an entity to begin with but a consciousness constructed" (*Audience* 25). George suggests that, in the actor-audience relationship, "the spectator complements the work of the performers by the *act* of relating" ("On Ambiguity" 80). In these plays, however, the act of relating seems to have broken down, and the traditional exchange between performer and role, and between actor and audience, is frustrated.

Perhaps because of the social contexts in which these plays are situated, the performance experience suggested does not partake of the joyousness that Vanden Heuvel describes but instead has more in common with the deconstruction of reality that Diana Taylor attributes to terrorism. In all five plays, the refrain "nothing's happening" is repeated in endless permutations: "aquí no pasa nada," "no pasó nada," "no ha pasado nada" [nothing's happening here, nothing happened, nothing has happened]. The insistence, within a theatrical context, that nothing is happening necessarily foregrounds the fact of nonperformance. The refrain describes the nonperformance in which the characters are trapped and also the world outside the theater, echoing the comforting voice of denial which renders state violence invisible. The refrain is an index of absence, of disappearance. "No pasa nada" is the necessary complement to the repeated "por algo será" [there must be a reason] that served to shift blame onto the *desaparecidos* while offering the passive onlooker the comfort of a spurious "explanation." Taylor observes that "the general public does in fact become complicitous and guilty, denying the gruesome reality it knows to be true" (*Theatre* 144). Without wholly preventing the transformation into terrorism that Kubiak describes, the general public maintains terror's position at the margin. This staging of terrorism is particularly evident in *Información*, with its scenes of torture and kidnapping. The audience, brought into being by the performance, also makes the performance possible through the "act of relating" that George emphasizes, either struggling to "make room for these performative acts [of terrorism] within our canon of the admissible" or, through its denials, sustaining the invisible, offstage scene of terror (Taylor, *Theatre* 143).

Esta no es una obra de teatro portrays Félix's struggle to pass an acting examination; his performance consists of throwing out any tidbit from his repertoire that might please his (invisible, unspeaking) professor. The collection, *Teatro de Sabina Berman*, contains two versions of the monologue, as well as a note emphasizing that the original was never intended for performance: "fue escrita originalmente como teatro para ser leído exclusivamente" (301) [it was originally written as theater only to be read]. The text is defined from the start as unrepresentable, making it an unperformable play about an impossible (for different reasons) performance.[5] As the narrative preface reveals, Félix is one of three students, the first of whom leaves the stage in tears as the second goes in search of a costume, excusing himself, he tells the narrator, "porque iba a vestirme para entrar en personaje" (304) [because I was going to get dressed in order to get into character]. Félix is left alone, "a punto de invocar a Dios" [about to invoke God], already preceded by the unrealized performances of his peers (304). The narrative prologue itself establishes a context of deferral: the narrator promises that at future date "escribiré de lo que me surgieron aquellos camerinos sin nadie, de los fantasmas con que los poblé, de las invisibles divas gordas, desnudas a no ser por los collares de rubíes que herían sus gargantas" (303) [I will write about what emerged from those empty dressing rooms, about the ghosts with which I populated them, about the fat prima donnas, nude but for the ruby necklaces that hurt their necks]. The narrative of Félix's experience, moreover, is inexact, distorted by memory, "apenas tan aproximada a lo que sucedió como puede ser una rememoración" (305) [only as close to what happened as a memory can be].

Not yet a certified actor, Félix is forced to invent the role that will gain him admittance to the stage. The inadequacy of all prior texts is highlighted as the numerous passages he has memorized evaporate, leaving him to repeat again and again, "revisa tus textos, mono idiota, revísalos" (305) [review your lines, stupid monkey, review them]. His career is one of "promesa frustrada" [frustrated promise] though he is eager enough to leap on the optimistic phrase: "gracias por lo de promesa. Nunca me dijiste que era una promesa" (309) [thank you for that about promise. You never told

---

[5] A number of performances, as well as Abraham Oceransky's incorporation of the text as an acting examination, led Berman to reconsider. The second version is described as "más apta para la representación escénica, menos anecdótica, formada como unidad" (301) [more appropriate for staging, less anecdotal, formed as a unity]. The primary difference is in the omission, in the later text, of the narrative introduction of *Esta no es una obra de teatro*. For the purposes of this study, the earlier version, with its stage history of initially unintended performance, is more relevant, suggesting as it does the paradoxical simultaneity of the insistent need to perform that which cannot be performed or represented.

me it was a promise]. The theater becomes a ridiculous enterprise as he proposes the portrayal of a bear whose "conflicto dramático es que es un oso polar que quedó dormido y a su alrededor, envolviéndolo, se formó un iceberg" (308) [dramatic conflict is that he is a polar bear that fell asleep and an iceberg formed around him]. Félix views the theater as ultimately degrading, an ambivalence suggested in his proposed shift from playing dogs on stage to running an obedience school: "puedo siempre dedicarme a los perros. Dentro del teatro, digo. O fuera. Poner una tienda de perros. No, mejor una escuela de perros" (309) [I can always work with dogs. Inside the theater, I mean. Or outside. I could have a dog store. Or even better, a dog school].[6] Félix's tenuous relation to the theater is expressed in his questioning of theatrical norms and his hostility to the theorists who have left him unable to face his present ordeal: "Malditos teóricos, ¿de qué sirven? Ven a mi memoria Stanislavsky. Grotowsky. ¿Artaud? Vacío" (305) [Cursed theoreticians. What are they good for? Come into my memory, Stanislavsky. Grotowsky. Artaud? Nothing]. The empty theater in which Félix finds himself substantially corresponds to Grotowski's "poor theater," which, in Timothy Wiles's summary, "is stripped of any element not deemed essential to the theater event, which for Grotowski consists of the confrontation between actor and audience," here, between actor and professor (114). Yet even that confrontation is undermined. Unable to elicit a response, Félix has no proof that his audience is still present. Without an audience, the hypothetical roles he proposes erode still further. The confrontation is reduced to a struggle between Félix and the demand that he perform, while the performer-role axis is destabilized because the role is never fully defined.

El despojamiento presents the paralyzed performer as the site of degradation, depicting a woman awaiting an audition that never occurs. Her paralysis is not feigned; instead, the woman gradually cedes her mobility to the youth's unspoken demands and her own rationalizations of her treatment. Despite instances of physical affront–the youth tears off her earring–the coercion the woman experiences is largely psychological, the product of her dialogue with

---

[6] Inevitably, this actor whose forte is playing dogs on stage recalls the protagonist of the last of Dragún's *Historias para ser contadas*, "El hombre que se convirtió en perro."

the imagined reactions of those in charge of the audition, the youth, and her husband/lover Pepe. Here, the performance does not represent coercion; the audition itself–or rather, the wait for the audition, the performance of the preparations which, the woman believes, will lead to the opportunity for a "real" performance–is coercive. The woman never auditions, is never photographed, indeed is never spoken to, and the overall experience is one of subtraction, as she is left with less and less confidence, less and less dignity, even as she is left also with less clothing and surrounded by less furniture. The apparent audience of her striptease, the youth, pays little attention, and the impossibility of representation never moves beyond the antechamber.

The stripping of the scene, not just of her body, suggests an equation between the two, and in stripping her of her pathetic costume, the youth strips her of her act. He also disassembles her, a process of which the woman is fully aware: as she attempts to explain his appropriation of one article of clothing after another, the woman wonders, "¿Pero por qué no vienen acá y me ven toda entera?" (175) [But why don't they come here and see all of me?]. The woman's entire representation is inadequate, as is suggested from the beginning with the description of her vain attempt at elegance and her worn, pathetic shoes. Even her movements are incomplete: she asks the youth how her snapshots have been received "con un gesto que no termina" (172) [with a gesture that she does not finish]. The woman is manifestly waiting to be assigned a role by the offstage director; her persona is not yet a "real" role but a vehicle toward such a part. Waiting for some sign, the woman imagines posing for pornographic still shots, a "performance" which would remain static, immobile. Again, the worst thing she can imagine is a form of "nothing's happening." This terrifying non-movement is developed further as she imagines herself the mirror to a younger, more attractive woman: "pondrán en la cama a una muchacha hermosa y yo . . . yo seré el espejo, el espejo adonde va a acabar todo" (181) [they will put a beautiful girl in the bed and I . . . I will be the mirror, the mirror where everything comes to an end]. The woman ends up stripping herself, removing her own skirt before the youth can tear it off. The final image is of the seated woman, legs spread, her smile petrified as she sobs for Pepe.

When she recalls Pepe's abuse, it too is constructed as a non-event: after the neighbors summoned the police following a particularly vicious beating, she told them: "aquí no pasó nada, me caí de la escalera" [nothing happened here, I fell down the stairs], a denial that corresponds, outside the theater, to the frequent dismissal of domestic violence (177). The invisibility accorded such ostensibly "private" violence is also evident in the public persona with which she attempts to overlay the evidence. Eyeing herself in the mirror, the woman reassures herself, "no se nota. Qué golpe me dio el desgraciado. Cosa de arruinarme" (174) [you can't tell. What a blow that jerk gave me. It could ruin me]. Her efforts at camouflage are ineffective, and she is left with the fear that the directors will think her poorly made-up. Becky Boling emphasizes the degree to which the woman performs for Pepe as well, arguing that "performance occurs on two levels: the woman is actress both to the young man who assaults her in the waiting room and to Pepe who abuses her in the bedroom" ("From Pin-Ups" 64). This spillover of performance from the theater to the domestic space not only clarifies the woman's position as object of desire in a phallocentric society, discussed by Boling, but parallels the construction of life as role playing or (non)performance in the other plays. The performance here is itself a node of self-generating violence.

The insistence that nothing is happening invites a consideration of what in fact counts as action, either at the level of admitting that incidents of torture do occur or on a less violent plane, granting the category "action" to the events of relatively unimportant lives. This is the case in Cabrujas's *Acto cultural*, the full title of which is *Acto cultural organizado por la Sociedad Louis Pasteur para el Fomento de las Artes, las Ciencias y las Industrias de San Rafael de Ejido con la presencia de la Honorable Junta Directiva y en la ocasión de celebrarse el quincuagésimo aniversario de la mencionada institución* [Cultural ceremony organized by the Louis Pasteur Society for the Encouragement of the Arts, Sciences and Industry of San Rafael de Ejido with the presence of the Honorable Executive Committee and on the occasion of celebration of the fiftieth anniversary of the aforementioned institution]. The play's inaction is framed as both a lack of performance and as a lack of material to perform. The play ostensibly to be presented, "Colón, Cristóbal, el Genovés Alucinado" [Columbus, Christopher, the Deluded Genoise] is interrupted by the Sociedad Pasteur's amateurish preparations, missed cues, and references to local history and gossip. The actors are unable to stay in character, and several threaten to walk out or suggest postponing the show. The motives behind these postponements range from simple frustration to Amadeo's bizarrely bleeding hands, a grotesque image treated with some confusion: Cosme mutters nervously, "Una emergencia . . . en fin, a cualquiera le pasa. Además, un milagro" [an emergency . . . well, it happens to everybody. Furthermore, a miracle], while Antonieta suggests, "Se podría pensar en la canonización" (21; 1) [One could think of canonization]. The situation of *Acto cultural* is doubly coercive in that the necessary yet impossible performance is based on an effectively absent script. During his opening speech, Amadeo rambles confusedly about what he had planned to say without reading the actual speech. Later, Cosme, as prompter, is unable to find the required page and appears on stage to complain, "¡No hay página veintisiete!" (60; 1) [There is no page twenty-seven!]. Even the ending of the play is unstable. After Antonieta describes a missing scene, Amadeo informs her, "Esa nunca se escribió. Se presintió pero nunca se escribió" (99; 2) [That was never written. There was a premonition of it but it was never written]. All of these incidents reveal a script both absent and unreliable, imagined by the players but unavailable to them on stage.

The blank pages of the script translate into a stage devoid of action. Following one interruption, Cosme assures Francisco Xavier: "continuamos y no ha pasado nada" (49; 1) [we continue and nothing has happened]. When Cosme rejects the entire enterprise, Amadeo reassures him: "no va a pasar nada, Cosme. ¡Tú y tus temores!" (72-73; 2) [Nothing will happen, Cosme. You and your fears!]. The impossibility of performance is tied to the function of the play itself, a self-aggrandizing pageant put on by a small-town cultural society. Written by one of their own, the play must mediate between the Sociedad Pasteur and the lengthy list of dignitaries to whom it is addressed. The stage becomes a space of negotiation between individual performances–or attempted performances–rather than an effective means of presenting the highbrow self-portraits the Junta Directiva would like to create. The nonperformance of the "acto cultural" inadvertently reveals a more authentic "cultural ceremony," that of a group of disaffected, marginalized players unsuccessfully attempting to claim the roles that, in Moretta's terms, might confer a "stable sense of self" ("Spanish" 7). The Sociedad's audience, identified in tedious detail yet resolutely silent, is as problematic as the disappearing script. Purificación's insistent query,

"¿Estás ahí, mamá?" [Are you there, mama?] is one index of the performers' isolation (22; 1). The final enumeration of invited guests, each name answered by Cosme's implacable "absent," replaces the welcoming roll call that began the evening with a catalogue of absence.

The dramatic reenactment of Columbus's life reveals the lack of both contemporary and historical action, so that the problem of inaction is not limited to players unable to perform but reflects the status of backwaters like San Rafael. As Kirsten Nigro notes, "Columbus' story becomes a tale of domestic woes and little private triumphs" ("History" 42). In contrast to the attempted bombast of *Bolívar*'s interior play, the pageant staged by the Sociedad Pasteur presents a domesticated Columbus surrounded by poorly executed, quasi-mythical tableaux. Indeed, Columbus's story runs a poor second to Amadeo's: rejecting Cosme's efforts to get him back on track, Amadeo says of Columbus, "Él descubre el continente al final y la tenacidad triunfa. Soy yo quien no triunfa y por eso creo que el cuento de Lucrecia es mucho más interesante" (45; 1) [he discovers the continent at the end and tenacity triumphs. I am the one who does not triumph and that's why I think the story of Lucretia is much more interesting]. The play is self-consciously anachronistic, as Amadeo, playing the role of Columbus, describes his dream of America and admits: "sé que no debo decir América, pero como son las dos de la mañana, puedo permitirme una premonición" (35; 1) [I know I should not say America, but since it's two in the morning, I can allow myself a premonition]. Amadeo forgets his lines and begins to repeat, like a broken record, while Cosme gives him his cue with ever greater insistence: "Y te vas. [. . .] Y se marcha. [. . .] Te marchas simplemente" (43; 1) [And you go. {. . .} And he leaves. {. . .} You simply leave]. Caught in the unchanging routine of San Rafael, Amadeo can neither complete his lines nor escape the pedantic role that has overtaken his life: "después de veinte años nadie me escucha porque suponen que digo una conferencia . . . Ni siquiera las frases más banales . . ." (44; 1) [after twenty years nobody listens to me because they think I'm giving a lecture . . . Not even the most banal phrases . . .]. Amadeo's nonperformance of his stage role mirrors a life so thoroughly dominated by performance–by the very role he struggles with on stage, Presidente de la Sociedad–that he is unable to greet an acquaintance without the other expecting a tedious lecture. Amadeo is never able to fulfill his role adequately, or to select freely the role he will be playing. His existence is thus an ongoing, and coercive, nonperformance.

The theater's practical potential is made clear as several characters explain, in no uncertain terms, what they hope to get out of the performance and the Sociedad. Openly mixing sexual imagery and praise of the theater, the widowed Herminia exults: "¡Qué bello el teatro! [. . .] El arte, mi amor, que te llena, que te invade y tú ahí sintiendo y estrujándote como si fuera un hombre, un macho" (23; 1) [Theater is so beautiful! {. . .} Art, my love, that fills you, that invades you and you feeling it and being squeezed as if it were a man, a male]. As a way to fill the time since her husband's death, the Sociedad's staged recitations are better than nothing. Recalling her fifteen-year membership, Antonieta also describes the Sociedad and its spectacles as a substitute for some unattainable happiness: "Estar aquí podía parecerse a una alternativa. Era, por lo menos, no estar en otra parte, y ya eso es mucho" (53; 1) [Being here could seem like an alternative. It was, at least, not being somewhere else, and that's already a lot]. While not a satisfying performance of a unified role, this ceremonial affair is at least a different space than that of everyday existence. Here, however, that everyday space invades the ostensibly protected theater, and one after another the members of the Sociedad slip out of character to describe their lives. "Nothing will happen" may be reassuring to the individual who fears things might go terribly wrong, even as it is a source of desperation to the playwright threatened with no script or to the audience bored without a spectacle. Yet, whether or not anything happens on stage, as the only show in town the Acto Cultural becomes an event by default.

The most extended treatment of the stage as a space of inaction occurs in Chocrón's *La revolución*, in which Gabriel, an aging transvestite, refuses to perform the role of Miss Susy that Eloy, "mesonero de tercera categoría" [third-rate waiter], promises the audience. Gabriel's promised yet deferred transvestism represents the resolution to a negotiation between performer and role that is never realized in a unified fashion. Thus, his proposed performance occupies a position analogous to the one that Marjorie Garber attributes to transvestism as a third term between genders. The play cannot go on because the actors can no longer (or are no longer willing to) play their parts. As Nigro argues, "this prelude to the performance-as-advertised is in itself an explosive theatrical event, a kind of triple insurgence against the sexual, artistic and political codes of a society ruled by the mighty money market" ("Triple Insurgence" 48).[7] Discussing the audience's supposed purpose in coming to the theater, Gabriel asks: "¿A qué vinieron? ¿A buscar ambiente o a ver si pasa algo?" [Why did you come? To find atmosphere or to see if something would happen?] and insists: "A ver si pasa algo, ¿no es verdad? ¡Porque allá afuera no está pasando nada! [. . .] Y a lo mejor aquí, conmigo, puede que tengan el presentimiento de que . . . algo . . . todavía. . . puede pasar" [To see if something would happen, right? Because outside, nothing is happening! {. . .} And probably here, with me, you have the feeling that . . . something . . . still . . . can happen]. Later he admits: "aquí no pasa nada. [. . .] A lo mejor lo único que pasa soy yo. Y creo que 'paso' porque viene gente a verme. [. . .] Yo, tú, esto, formamos un acontecimiento en un lugar donde ya no ocurre ningún verdadero acontecimiento" (26; pt. 1) [nothing's happening here. {. . .} The only thing that happens here is me. And I think I "happen"/"pass" because people come to see me. {. . .} I, you, this—we form an event in a place where no real event any longer occurs]. The term "passing" resonates with Gabriel's transvestite performance as well: in drag, he passes for a woman; on stage, he passes for action. This sense of Gabriel's ability to pass contrasts with Eloy's closer identification with the audience. Gabriel's transvestism, only briefly and incompletely visible on stage, confronts the audience with its implicitly prurient interest in the promised spectacle. Eloy, by contrast, assures the spectators, "Yo me parezco a ustedes. O por lo menos me parezco más que él" (73; pt. 2) [I resemble you. Or at least more than he does]. Yet audience sympathy is contested, as when Gabriel demands of Eloy, "¿Cómo sabes que están de tu parte?" (50; pt. 1) [How do you know they're on your side?]. Both protagonists alternately confront and seduce the spectator; each in turn differentiates himself from the audience—risking, in the process, audience hostility—and courts the public's goodwill.

---

[7] Nigro stresses *La revolución*'s critique of a capitalist consumer culture in which all interpersonal relations are reduced to monetary transactions. While this aspect of Chocrón's play is certainly important, I would argue that the critique of role playing goes beyond the economic level and that Gabriel's resistance is ultimately less successful, less affirmative, than Nigro suggests.

The audience is also directly confronted with the lack of action, as Eloy invites the spectators to blame Gabriel for their displeasure: "si alguno de ustedes tiene alguna queja sobre lo que ha pasado, o más probablemente sobre lo que ha dejado de pasar, diríjansela a este personaje semidesnudo, maloliente, triste cómico" (61; pt. 2) [if any of you has any complaint about what has happened, or more probably about what has failed to happen, speak to this half-naked, smelly, tragicomic character]. Like the "acto cultural," Gabriel's threadbare show offers the audience its only hope of witnessing an event, however inadequate. Yet in a place where real events are no longer possible, "acontecimiento" [event, happening] becomes ironic, a performance or representation of a performance that, if it occurred, would be only a pseudo-event. The performer's dependence on the audience–he happens only if people come to see him–highlights his constricted options: trapped on a stage that will disappear if the audience fails to show. The audience then must bear some responsibility for the spectacle, whatever it becomes. *La revolución* illustrates the paradoxical insistence that although nothing is happening, on stage or off, each person must have both role and audience all the same. Gabriel "happens" because he is observed, yet the audience is present only because it hopes something will happen, some event which will offer an escape from the static world "out there." Inaction is an issue not only of performance but of interpretation, a weighing of what counts as "real" action just as the "real" performance initially promised is displaced by a nonperformance that, failing to conform to accepted definitions, becomes, in Eloy's words, "lo que ha dejado de pasar."

Moretta contends that "if we regard *La Revolución* as performance within a performance, we must further appreciate the fact that the play itself subsumes two distinct notions of what performance should be and do. In opposition to the kind of unacknowledged action through which Eloy seeks to deny his being and leave his audience in undisturbed complacency, we witness Gabriel's unabashedly fervent involvement in a role to which he gives himself freely and completely" ("Spanish" 27). Yet, Gabriel never fully gives himself to a role. He remembers days in which he was able to do so, but the play is concerned precisely with his *inability* either to invest himself in the part at hand or to locate an alternative. According to Moretta, "a certain kind of posing conceded to be fictitious nevertheless serves as a means whereby the individual at least begins to gain an awareness of the possibility of living a truly authentic life" ("Spanish" 24). However, this "authentic" life remains theatrical, as evidenced by Gabriel's emphasis on role playing in all circumstances.

Nigro argues that "Gabriel breaks down [the] boundary between fiction and reality by being himself rather than a created character," and she continues, in a footnote: "obviously Gabriel *himself* is a created stage figure, but the important point here is that he refuses to refract that character even further solely for the delight of his patrons" ("Triple Insurgence" 51). Even as "himself," Gabriel remains highly conscious that to live is to play a role and that the presence of an audience is what makes the role possible. The stress on role playing both elicits and comments upon the audience's complicity in the humiliating process. The suggestion that all people, in and out of theater, are playing roles places the spectator on a level with the actor already presented as the site of coercion. When an infuriated Eloy demands: "¿Qué quieres que haga? ¿Que haga tu papel?" [What do you want me to do? Play your part?] Gabriel responds: "Que hagas un papel. Que asumas un papel. Que te conviertas en un papel. Eso es estar vivo" (46; pt. 1) [That you take a role. Play a part. That you become a character. That is being alive]. In keeping with the play's emphasis on incomplete or blocked performance, the nature of the proposed role remains unclear. Gabriel insists: "sé que no soy ejemplo ni bueno ni malo. Soy otra cosa. [. . .] Por eso vienen a verme" (50; pt. 1) [I know that I'm neither a good nor a bad example. I am something else. {. . .} That's why they come see me]. The spectacle is that which is different, which does not suggest behavior to be imitated or shunned, which is, quite simply, "something else."

The insistence of inaction and the refrain "nothing's happening" are also evident in Gambaro's *Información para extranjeros*. Highlighting the complicity of both the audience following the guide through *Información* and the extratheatrical audience in need of information, El Hombre assures La Muchacha of scene 3, an evident torture victim, "no te pasará nada. Hay mucha gente. Nos miran" (72) ["Nothing will happen to you. There are lots of people. They're watching us" (73)]. The audience's ethical obligation is to prevent violence by bearing witness. This obligation, however, is undercut by the force of theatrical conventions that demand audience passivity. Following an offstage gunshot implicitly linked to the young woman, the guide repeats "aquí ya no pasa nada" ["It's over"] with evident disappointment, leading his group out of the room as he offers his own judgment of the spectacle: "Soy antiguo. Prefiero otra cosa" (114) ["I'm old-fashioned. I prefer something else" (115)].[8] What was reassurance is now complaint; like the non-performance woven throughout these plays, the lack of action is both trap and release. *Información* replicates within the theater the terrors of the extratheatrical abstract spectacle whereby the audience is both assaulted with horrific information and enjoined to disbelieve. The audience also directly subsidizes this spectacle and is not allowed to forget its collaboration.[9]

Gambaro's play combines the realistic staging of scenes of torture with an unstable frame of shifting spaces and unidentified characters. As the audience is guided from one scene to the next, the reality displayed is at once jarringly clear and deliberately blurred. The audience is also in the scene: actors planted in the audience are abducted; in the narrow passageways, spectators must inevitably brush up against members of the cast.[10] The overlay of a seemingly innocuous space and a torture cell observed in Eduardo Pavlovsky's *El señor Galíndez* becomes even more effective when the spectator must recognize as the torturer's domain the rooms she concretely occupies. In scene 13 a young woman is killed by an apparent member of the audience: "Silenciosamente, un personaje mezclado con el público, se acerca a la Muchacha. Le pone la mano sobre la boca y la nariz. La Muchacha opone una resistencia muda y desesperada. Muere. El hombre la acuesta con suavidad. La cubre

---

[8] Although the script emphasizes that the scenes may be performed in any order and the separation of the spectators into multiple groups assures that no two groups will observe the same sequence of scenes, the presentation of multiple scenes centered on the same characters, most notably the group dealing with the young woman of scene 3, introduces an element of narrative continuity, though subtle and repeatedly undercut.

[9] Explicit reference to the audience's payment for the show also occurs in *La revolución* when Gabriel demands payment from Eloy up front and ostentatiously counts his take.

[10] Gambaro's setting recalls Artaud, who writes of the stage: "We abolish the stage and the auditorium and replace them by a single site, without partition or barrier of any kind, which will become the theater of the action. A direct communication will be re-established between the spectator and the spectacle, between the actor and the spectator, from the fact that the spectator, placed in the middle of the action, is engulfed and physically affected by it. This envelopment results, in part, from the very configuration of the room itself" (96).

con la sábana. Se aparta y se mezcla con el público, como un espectador más" (106) ["Silently, a character mixed in with the audience goes up to the GIRL. He puts his hand over her mouth and nose. The GIRL offers desperate, mute resistance. She dies. The man gently lays her out, covers her with the sheet. Then he moves off and mixes in with the crowd, like one more spectator" (107)]. The series of scenes centered on the young woman recently subjected to the *submarino*, the immersion in filthy water almost to the point of drowning, brings together the themes of voyeurism, audience complicity, and sexualized violence against women. The guide leads his charges into a darkened room, directing them toward chairs and calling for "preferencia para las señoras" (72; sc. 3) ["Ladies first" (72)] when faced with a shortage of seats. Seating the women establishes a visual parallel between the female spectators and the young woman, dripping wet, seated in the center of the room. She is handed a gun, and more than once it is suggested that, given her lack of boyfriend, she may as well end it all. In scene 7, the guide gives the young woman an insolent pat, then worries aloud about the delicate sensibilities of the ladies, attempting to obstruct their view of certain wall paintings. Throughout the scenes in which she appears, the spectators are repeatedly invited to view the young woman and her surroundings yet urged to ignore the evidence of torture her words and her abject appearance present. *Información* stages a constant negotiation between the displayed and the hidden, the recognized and the inferred.

The evident critique of an audience able to witness scenes of brutality passively presents a particularly complex trap for the theater audience of *Información*, aware that the scenes are fictitious (staged by actors although often based on verifiable fact) yet repeatedly invited to view the scenes as real. Short of leaving the theater mid-play, the audience's only available response is to become part of the general public whose respect for authority "can lead innocent bystanders to become indirect and even direct participants in torture" (Taylor, *Theatre* 137). The guide's harassment of the young woman further implicates the audience because it is *their* guide–essentially, their employee, their surrogate–who is committing the abuse. Moreover, the guide's authority is in direct proportion to the audience's docility. The spectator's complicity may also permit the coercion or manipulation of the audience itself. Rosalea Postma's study of *Información* emphasizes the role of an audience inescapably drawn into the space of performance, so that "the lack of distance between the spectator and the action becomes a physical threat. Under normal circumstances, a spectator in a theatre can open a door and escape, but the spectator in *Información* is not free to leave" (38). Although an introductory note insists that the audience will never be forced to participate in the action, the planting of actors in the crowd and the necessity of following the guide from one room to another, acquiescing to his directions as to where to stand or sit, occasion a confusion of audience and performer, a confrontation in which the coercion of performance is to some degree realized on the body of the spectator as well as that of the actors.[11] Nothing is happening in part because this *is* "only" a play, yet to accept that is to accept one's role as bystander.

In several of these plays, the audience's alleged impatience is used as a threat to keep other characters in line, underscoring the performers' dependence on outside validation. In *Acto cultural*, the action is frequently interrupted with the assurance, directed toward the audience, that the real show will soon be underway. Similarly, Eloy insists "enseguida comenzamos" [we'll start right away], although Gabriel never performs the show both he and Eloy continually promise (11; pt. 1). *Información* also tempts the audience with offers of a better entertainment, as the guide encourages his charges: "No todo el espectáculo es así. Espero" (86; sc. 5) ["The whole show's not like this. I hope" (87)]. In scene 2, the guide knocks on a closed door, saying: "traigo un grupo de espectadores. Están ansiosos" ["I've brought a group of spectators. And they're getting anxious"], to which the voice behind the door replies: "estoy ensayando" (71; sc. 2) ["I'm rehearsing" (72)]. The openly expressed need to placate the audience forces upon the spectators an awareness that their presence makes possible the theater event.[12]

The self-reflexivity at the heart of performance is highlighted as

---

[11] Indeed, the play's violence may be too much for the audience–or the actors–so that nonperformance extends beyond that represented *in* the text to the impossibility of staging the play as a whole. Taylor concludes that Gambaro's "depictions of atrocity are violent–too violent to stage the play as it was written" and adds, tellingly, "Gambaro herself resists the idea of producing the play, realizing perhaps that the violence of the period provoked her to respond with violence" (*Disappearing* 133).

[12] The audience's constitutive role is noted perhaps most openly in the Prologue to Dragún's *Historias* with the admission, "Nosotros existimos porque existen ustedes" (56) [We exist because you exist].

theatrical norms are undermined through confrontation with the audience or by the actors' inability to stay in character. Strategies of nonperformance are employed as a means of filling the gaps left by the silent director or the unreadable text. Thus, the woman of *El despojamiento* supplies her own "direction," explaining the youth's peremptory treatment in terms that reflect her construction of the absent directors' wishes. Elsewhere, characters plead openly for guidance, as when Félix demands of his professor: "¿Qué quieres que te haga?" (306) [What do you want me to do for you?], or, more directly: "dame una orden" (307) [give me an order]. The role to be performed is always in process, a product of multiple directors, multiple scripts, and guidelines may come from the implied audience or from other performers. In *Acto cultural*, the Junta Directiva counsels Amadeo, "no te exaltes" [don't get carried away] after he loses himself in his introductory speech (20; pt. 1). The first guide of *Información* eagerly follows the recommendation of another that he hurry to catch the show that is about to begin. Lacking direction, performers take on provisional roles in tacit recognition of the need to fill *some* role. Because the performers are unable to sustain these roles, all of the plays under discussion reflect a persistent moving in and out of character. Boling argues that the woman in *El despojamiento* "bears meaning but cannot create it" ("From Pin-Ups" 63). This is similar to Josette Féral's contention that "performance is the absence of meaning" and that "performance does not aim at *a* meaning, but rather *makes* meaning insofar as it works right in those extremely blurred junctures out of which the subject eventually emerges" (173). The somewhat contradictory conflation of an absence of meaning with the making of meaning is nevertheless helpful in assessing the role of performance in these plays in which individual performers bear but do not create meaning, playing roles which are only provisional.

These are explicitly plays about plays and playing, and even *Información* stresses its existence as theater, as not "real." Nigro emphasizes the distinction between *La revolución*'s two audiences, the imaginary one eager for Miss Susy's advertised performance and the audience of Chocrón's play, for whom "what does *not* happen constitutes a complex performance whose self-reflective nature works to undermine the same artistic codes to which it refers" ("Triple Insurgence" 51). George's view that performance is an act of relating, rather than the authoritative imposition of a particular interpretation, also describes these endlessly tentative, circular performances. Similarly, Boling argues that *El despojamiento* "achieves a self-reflective level by foregrounding 'performance' within the drama." Moreover, "the device of the play-within-the-play gives way to 'representation' or 'performance' itself" ("From Pin-Ups" 59). The foregrounding of "performance itself" implies that it is not a representation *of* anything, that the axis George describes is no longer anchored. Yet from its position as supplement, the text (or the play within the play) reveals "performance itself" as both complete and ultimately lacking.

While these plays begin with a suggestion of the impossibility of representation, as they incorporate historical narratives (including current events) they insist on an opening for social engagement through a continually stymied medium. In the progression from a pre- to a posttheatrical focus, there are in fact two trajectories, that of the performer and that of the material performed and its orientation. The not-yet actor of *Esta no es una obra de teatro* becomes the washed-up, no longer viable professional of *El despojamiento* and *La revolución*, only to be replaced by the amateur actors of *Acto cultural*. In *Información*, the deliberate mixing of actor and audience questions the very position–role–designated "actor." At the same time, the focus of the plays becomes more openly concerned with issues outside the theater, although even *Esta no es una obra de teatro* situates the text within a geographical context, as Félix discards imported theory with the question: "¿cómo voy a ser actor si el teatro lo inventaron del otro lado del mundo?" (307) [how am I going to be an actor if theater was invented on the other side of the world?]. The element of extratheatrical reference is stronger in both *La revolución* and *Acto cultural*. Gabriel's recourse to violence is framed as an attempt to affect not only the theater audience but the world outside: "esa revolución dentro de mí ha sido provocada por la revolución allá afuera" (70-71; pt. 2) [this revolution inside of me has been provoked by the revolution out there]. The Sociedad Pasteur's use of historical material, deformed or newly imagined, insists on an extratheatrical context. The characters are continually referring to outside concerns, such as Amadeo's repetition of the circumstances under which he found his wife "en brazos del Secretario del Partido Liberal" (46; 1) [in the arms of the Liberal Party Secretary]. His revelations are nothing new: as Cosme notes: "lo sabe todo San Rafael" (46; 1) [all of San Rafael already knows].

This invasion of the stage by local gossip situates the theater within a specific community and emphasizes the social nature of the medium, at the same time underscoring both the inescapable repetition that colors the individual lives portrayed–even the gossip is old news–and the sense of "no first time" that Blau sees as characteristic of performance.

Información suggests the most complex move outward by forcibly blurring distinctions between performance (as representation, as unreal, as imitation) and experienced reality. *Información* also presents a maximum coercion of both audience and performer, demanding that the audience question and discard the comforting escape, "it's only a play." At the same time, the theatricality of the representation is emphasized, with the guide's reference to a particular scene needing "por lo menos . . . un mes más de ensayos" (86; sc. 5) ["They need at least another month of rehearsal" (87)] or his comment: "Grotowsky decía: A mayor distanciamiento físico, mayor proximidad espiritual. ¡Qué macana! ¡Participen sin miedo, señoras y señores!" (115; sc. 15) ["Grotowsky used to say: The more physical distance, the more spiritual closeness. What nonsense! Don't be afraid to join in, ladies and gentlemen!" (116)]. The guide's repeated attempts to view the couple in need of additional practice also contributes to the image of a play that is never performed. Stage directions such as "El Hombre cae. Visiblemente, aplasta una bombita con sangre" (111; sc. 14) ["The MAN falls. His blood is obviously fake" (113)] add to the metatheatrical effect. Still, these self-reflexive turns are interspersed with documentary announcements declaimed by the guide "con tono profesional, seco y rápido" ["in a professional tone, dry and rapid"] and introduced with the words: "Explicación: para extranjeros" (92; sc. 9) ["Explanation: For Foreigners" (93)]. As Taylor points out, "the information the Guide reads out is verifiable, accessible both to the audience in the house and to the reading public inside and outside Argentina" (*Theatre* 135).[13] Verifiable historical information is recreated on stage in a highly theatricalized manner. In the case of the Milgram experiment reenacted in scene 4, overt theatricality includes

---

[13] Gambaro's title evokes the extraction of "information" under torture, a process in which the recipient of that information–in this case, the theater audience–is necessarily implicated. Just as the audience's complicity makes the spectacle possible, the audience's need to know (and to look) gives the information a purpose. The guide's explanations also recall Franco's spurious rationalizations in *El campo*.

the Alumno's rhyming speech and his parrot-like voice, and the guide's asides to the audience suggesting that none of the action to be observed is real. Taylor describes the experiment as one in which "the pseudoscientific trappings of the process veil the fact that it actually tests an individual's capacity for inflicting pain and even death on a stranger at the command of an 'expert'" (*Theatre* 137-38). The repetitions of performance suggest a parallel with the laboratory issue of reproducibility—and the superficial experiment is in fact concerned with repetition, in the form of the "learner's" ability to recall the word pairs read out by the "teacher." [14]

The invitation to misapprehend the boundaries between stage and reality is also evident in the rehearsal of *Othello* in scene 17. The actors, in rehearsal clothes, are interrupted by a police officer in Elizabethan costume. The officer, however, is the outsider. He attacks the first actor for his supposed murder of the two women until a second actor "a su pesar, en papel" ["In spite of himself, in character"] responds "¡Quitadle la espada!" (118) ["Wrench his sword from him" (120)]. The scene, closed with the guide's dismissive "Un poco confuso el desarrollo, ¿no?" ["A bit confusing, the way that happened, don't you think?"] is followed by another explanation: "6 de agosto de 1971. La policía irrumpe en una casa antigua, con muchas habitaciones como ésta, en la ciudad de Santa Fe. En una de las habitaciones se descubrió 800 gramos de trotyl. Dicen. Detenidos un periodista y tres integrantes del Grupo de Teatro 67" (119) ["August 6, 1971. The police burst into an old house with many rooms, like this one, in the city of Santa Fe. In one

---

[14] According to Stanley Milgram, "In the basic experimental design, two people come to a psychology laboratory to take part in a study of memory and learning. One of them is designated as a 'teacher' and the other as a 'learner.' The experimenter explains that the study is concerned with the effects of punishment on learning. The learner is conducted into a room, seated in a kind of miniature electric chair [. . .]. He is told that he will be read lists of simple word pairs, and that he will then be tested on his ability to remember the second word of a pair when he hears the first one again. Whenever he makes an error, he will receive electric shocks of increasing intensity. [. . .] The learner, or victim, is actually an actor who receives no shock at all. The point of the experiment is to see how far a person will proceed in a concrete and measurable situation in which he is ordered to inflict increasing pain on a protesting victim" ("Perils" 643-44). Milgram writes: "Before the experiments, I sought predictions about the outcome from various kinds of people—psychiatrists, college sophomores, middle-class adults, graduate students and faculty in the behavioral sciences. With remarkable similarity, they predicted that virtually all subjects would refuse to obey the experimenter. [. . .] These predictions were unequivocally wrong" ("Perils" 645).

of the rooms they find eight hundred grams of trotyl. They say. One journalist and three members of the Grupo 67 theater are arrested" (121)]. The obliteration of spatial definitions implied by the reference to "una casa como ésta" once again implicates the audience in the action. Similar blends of reality and caricature accompany the interweaving of enactment and explanation throughout the play. Dick Gerdes argues that Gambaro's choice of the word "chronicle" in the subtitle "implies a present-day history, newspaper records and nightly news accounts" (12). The word "chronicle" carries yet another meaning: the historical echo of the "cronistas de Indias" recording the discovery and colonization reenacted in *Acto cultural*. Gambaro's subtitle positions the play not only within a context of world events but within the Latin American reality evoked in the opening lines of the play by the guide's reference to "nuestro estilo de vida: argentino, occidental y cristiano" (70) ["our way of life: Argentine, Western, and Christian" (71)]. This combination of highly theatrical, stylized scenes with verifiable historical material further disrupts the illusory border between inside and outside the theater already destabilized by the confusion of actor and audience.

The portrayal of societies which demand that individuals perform in order to exist becomes part of a critique of a system in which the individual is devalued, reduced to subemployment (or pre-performance) or to being the object of an audience's voyeuristic pleasure. Both *La revolución* and *El despojamiento* depict the plight of aging performers, suggesting that the theater is one more institution that tosses people aside when they cease to be useful, an exploitative aspect of theater emphasized by both Nigro and Boling. The woman in *El despojamiento*, like the women in *Información* and *Acto cultural* (or Lupe in *El eterno femenino*), finds herself trapped in a double layer of role playing which combines the performance required of all members of society with the particular "feminine" roles demanded of her. The repetitive claim that nothing is happening also implies an extratheatrical reality somehow arrested or stagnating, perhaps evoking a lack of political or social change. The construction of historical knowledge as performance in *Acto cultural* calls into question the relation between past and present; each one redefines or reinvents the other, and both a present and a past in which nothing happens are discounted. If nothing happens within received historical narratives, they must be replaced with the minutiae of everyday life, the details of cooking and nightmares incorporated into the Sociedad Pasteur's reinvention of Columbus.

At the end of *La revolución*, Gabriel is wounded by his own wild rifle fire. Dragging him from the stage, Eloy begs: "por favor, señores, salgan rapidito. Aquí no ha pasado nada. Esto es parte del espectáculo" (79; pt. 2) [please, gentlemen, leave quickly. Nothing has happened here. This is part of the spectacle]. If to live is to assume a role, the rapidly exiting audience is in a position analogous to that of the actors on stage. Yet the (scarcely credible) insistence that everything was planned, that the bleeding Gabriel is part of the spectacle, closes the circle in which the nonperformance of the assigned dramatic text is both the performer's experience of coercion and his or her only available role. Nonperformance becomes a means of approaching a terror that otherwise remains locked outside representation. Nevertheless, like a photographic negative, or like a nonperformance taking the place of the promised "acto cultural," this unrepresentable terror is not entirely absent or invisible. Kubiak's contention that "the history of theatre's filiation with psychic and political terror is the perfect twin of terror's own history as politics" suggests a connection between the interior theatrical worlds of the plays discussed and their larger political implications, including the degree to which the "isolation" of the "interior" of the theater is only apparent (2). Yet this questioning of theater's relation to society, a questioning of the very possibility of a play, takes place through dramatic plots explicitly concerned with stage performances. The search for "something else" haunts both actor and audience, and the spectacle retains its coercive power and its fascination.

Conclusion

DISPLACEMENT, REPLAY

THE search for "something else" that bottoms out in nonperformance, the coercive demand that an impossible performance be repeatedly undertaken regardless of its cost to performer and audience, displaces, if only partially, the struggle to perform appropriately the gender roles, ritual games, and historical truths examined in the course of this study. For instance, Lupita's sequence of quickly discarded roles in Castellanos's *El eterno femenino* anticipates the lack of role that paralyzes the woman of Gambaro's *El despojamiento*. In nonperformance, performance becomes most clearly an irreducible figure, as the plays continually rehearse the impossible. Nonperformance is perhaps the logical result of the attempt to create, in the theater, a spectacle about torture that will not reproduce the parameters of the oppressors' torture spectacle. If Anthony Kubiak is correct that representation transforms terror into terrorism, then an invocation of terror, stopping just short of representation, logically calls for an unrealized performance. However, the foregrounding of coercive performance should not be interpreted as a rejection of the theatrical medium. After all, theater here is not only the target but the means of critique. Nonetheless, the move beyond the theater space in plays such as Gambaro's *Información para extranjeros* invites a consideration of performance in a broader context, the displacement of performance onto stages defined according to different criteria.

Coercion in performance takes a variety of shapes. There is the coercion of the individual constrained to inhabit a humiliating role that ultimately negates his identity, as in *Esta no es una obra de teatro*. Coercion and violence may also touch the performer more directly, most clearly in the explicitly coerced performances of the prisoners in Rial's *Bolívar* or in Ana I's demand that Ana II drag herself across the floor to the wheelchair in Romero's *El juego*. The placement and display of gender performances are replayed in the endless recitation of the attempted text and ultimately displaced through the paralysis of nonperformance. What began with a questioning of historical narrative becomes a story without content, a performance that stands only for itself.

Henry Sayre's formulation of performance as "the single occurrence of a repeatable and preexistent text or score" (91) resonates with the performances depicted in these plays, themselves texts that prefigure potential stagings. Any given performance is necessarily singular, because it cannot be exactly reproduced or repeated. Yet the demand for repetition is constant, already present in the theater's conditions of realization. The genre's intrinsic reliance on repetition is evident in the convention of the script itself, in the work of rehearsal, in the multiple performances that make up a show's run. The repetition of performance is also evident within the plays, in the traps of gender, in the need to placate the audience, and in the shows that never move beyond rehearsal. Plays such as *El juego*, Cabrujas's *Acto cultural*, Navajas's *La agonía del difunto*, and Berman's *Esta no es una obra de teatro* and *El suplicio del placer* foreground repetitive narrations and the negotiations surrounding them, the powerful connections between control of the story and control of the game, between reenactment and interpretation, flashback and memory. The endless repetitions, both evident and implied, point back to the "no first time" observed by Herbert Blau as inherent to the nature of performance ("Universals" 171). The dependence on historical narrative in history plays and the concomitant need to retell, to tell again more accurately, more complexly are two manifestations of the need to address such repetition.

The text, constituted in performance, is always the rewriting of a prior text, the retelling of an earlier dream. One means whereby coercion enters the performance is through the instability of the text, its vulnerability to control or deformation by rival performers and receivers. Coercion is also evident in the desperation of the performer left textless, speechless, on an expanding stage with no possibility of escape. Yet while the destabilization of the text is clear, the priority of performance over text is not. The ongoing struggle to *re*stabilize the scripts suggests that any liberation from the script remains highly problematic. Authority is in no way absent from these performances, but it *is* constantly disputed. The "consumption" of the text in performance, the loving cannibalism Gambaro proposes, renders the self-consuming nature of cannibalism, even of criticism, as well as Castellanos's ironic self-condemnation in *El eterno femenino*. Text and performance mutually undermine and enable one another, and the performer is as often caught between the two–the impossible text and the imperative performance–as freed by the ludic contingency of the event.

Although performance demands the concrete placement of the actor's body, the demarcation of a stage, however provisional or undefined, is also a process of displacement. Offstage reality is displaced (at least temporarily) by the staged representation and is at the same time displaced *onto* the stage in the form of sets and decorations depicting a restaurant, a stifling apartment, a camp. Questions of displacement have been a continuing theme in this study. In Leñero's *Martirio de Morelos*, official histories are displaced by documentary theater. Torres Molina's *. . . Y a otra cosa mariposa* utilizes Pajarito's transvestism as an icon of displaced femininity. In Benedetti's *Pedro y el Capitán*, the interrogation room stands in for the offstage torture cell; in *Acto cultural*, the petty rivalries of San Rafael are rewritten across the history of Columbus's voyage. More than simply a means to substitute one narrative for another, displacement, like foregrounding, is a spatial image. These performances mark the renegotiation of spatial definitions, destabilizing the clear separation of theater and "reality" in order to redistribute the figurative charge of the space denoted as "stage" across a broader field. The boundaries and definitions of public and private spaces are repeatedly undercut, blurred, reappropriated: through the workings of military strategy, for example, or among women forced to perform in private or willing to risk performance on a public platform. Alternately, individuals may claim–demand–the right to perform in public. The privacy of the audience is also invaded, particularly in the ambiguous spaces of Pavlovsky's *El señor Galíndez* or in *Información para extranjeros*, in which the audience is first forced to recognize the stage as unidentifiable and then obliged to occupy the stage alongside the actors.

It is their focus on performance that allows these plays to address an extratheatrical reality. Stage representations about performance replay societal structures of theatricality. Through parody, satire, imitation, or simply by making certain processes visible (as in documentary theater), performance undermines dominant orders, but it also, in its very coming into being, repeats those patterns. Thus, the violence between players in *El juego* reproduces the violence that Ana I and Ana II experience outside their imaginary world. Performance is seen as the only available, but a nevertheless inadequate, strategy of resistance. However, resistance is inevitably mediated by the use of performance to elude performance. Because of performance's entanglement in the fabric of oppression, of state-sponsored spectacles and regulated gendering, to reshape performance is necessarily to work with the oppressors' tools. Within the plays, performance represents the characters' most immediate obligation (clear when the characters are explicitly performers, as in Chocrón's *La revolución*, but evident elsewhere as well) and the characters' only avenue of escape. Performance is also a way of understanding oppressive structures, such as official history and the theatrics of state terrorism.

Traps inherent in the attempt to redirect performance as a strategy of resistance include the vulnerability of feigned passivity and the potential dangers contained within the text, as in the case of the physical subjugation of the Muchacha of *Información para extranjeros* or Coca in *El señor Galíndez*. In becoming visible, the performer becomes vulnerable. Even Boal's invisible theater must be visible to an audience, if not as pre-scripted theater, then as social interaction. The most obvious vulnerability is the danger of abduction, torture, and disappearance, a danger clearly invoked in *Información*. For women especially, there is the more generalized danger of making an untoward spectacle of oneself. But the dangers of visibility extend to a more global vulnerability, that of exposure. Exposure differs from display in its greater implication of danger and coercion, as contrasted with display's connotations of a certain pride of presentation. The negative image that is nonperformance, once exposed, reveals a double exposure that leaves the performer trapped and visible on stage, going through the motions of an empty performance that is nonetheless obligatory.

The performer's vulnerability is evident at multiple levels. The protagonist of *El despojamiento* subjects herself to abuse in the search for work. The actors rehearsing *Othello* in *Información* are abducted by the police. The poet of *Bolívar* writes at gunpoint, and El Preso Bolívar is unchained only when he takes the stage. In

Gambaro's *El campo*, Emma is physically assaulted and forced to "play" a dysfunctional piano. All of this violence relies on the exposure of the performer, as if the displacements realized through performance–displacements of official history, of unified gender identity, of the *galanes* put off by the false mustache in Berman's "Uno," and the reality of the camp that Martín refuses to acknowledge–rely on the body of the actor to effect that shift, to serve as bridge between one version and another. The act of relating between performer and role expands into an act of relating between spectator and historical record or between an absent script and the need to perform.

The necessity of repetition also recalls the layering of theatrical metaphors and scientific discourse. The Milgram experiment discussed with reference to its reenactment in *Información* is already a highly structured drama, a play in which one subject acts–dissembles–in order to flush out the obedience of the unsuspecting "teacher." Milgram writes that "An element of theatrical staging was needed to set the proper conditions for observing the behavior, and technical illusions were freely employed" (*Obedience* 193). (Appropriately enough, experiments are commonly said to be "performed," or alternately "conducted," a term that bears its own performance resonances.) As with any properly designed experiment, Milgram's was reproduced, and the experiments were carried out at several times and places.[1] Gambaro's recreation of the experiment confronts the audience with its own potential for obedience, a potential for complicity with authority that is reinforced by the guide's dismissal of the experiment's reality.

In depicting a theatricalized society, the plays necessarily address the theatrical audience's role as part of the audience represented by the public at large. Within the plays, the general public appears in the form of the women in the beauty parlor enforcing Lupita's wedding day costuming or the wealthy woman unmoved by Ana I's paralysis. The implied public outside the auditorium is also the audience for the "abstract spectacle," an audience whose awareness of that spectacle is at once demanded and denied. The plays' observers are therefore doubly spectators: openly, willingly viewing the plays on stage and inescapably witnessing the offstage

---

[1] Originally conducted at Yale, the experiments were repeated in Princeton, Munich, Rome, South Africa, and Australia (Milgram, "Perils" 645).

spectacles alluded to through images of enforced performance or political posturing. The clearest identification of on and offstage theatricality perhaps occurs in the history play, in which both the past events recreated and the methods of their recording and recall are described in theatrical terms. Yet the identification of social spectacle and theatrical stage is not limited to the machinations of officials who appropriate histories such as those of Morelos or La Malinche. The Madres de la Plaza de Mayo are a clear instance in which a supposedly given gender performance–the assumption that mothers are quiet, self-sacrificing, safely enclosed within their private homes–is turned on its ear to produce both a revised performance and a retelling of the absent story of the *desaparecidos* whose reappearance the mothers demand.

The concern with performance may be displaced still further off stage, onto paratheatrical representations such as those involved in spiritist healing cults and traditional fiestas. The dramatic critique of the historian's performance finds an echo in Ruth Behar's critique of the anthropologist's performance as theater audience as well as recorder of *historias*. In *Translated Woman*, Behar describes a Mexican healing cult in which Chencha, a woman, plays the role of Pancho Villa. Chencha's masculine appearance contributes to her performance: "It may well be that the stereotyped gender casting of 'real life' left Chencha with little choice but to play a male lead in the theater of spiritism; yet her performances, both in real life and in spiritism, seem to turn both womanliness and manliness into masquerades, in which there truly is no difference between the genuinely gendered identity and the mask" (Behar 316). Behar argues that, "plotting herself, with a vengeance, into a national narrative of male heroism, dominance, violence, and coercion, she is writing herself out of the masochistic marianismo narratives of the suffering Virgin and the treacherous woman archetype. And she is writing herself back into national epic history by reenacting that history and appropriating that history as performance and as healing" (315). The performance described by Behar represents an instance of performance outside theatrical boundaries, a displacement of historical theater, and an intriguing instance of cross-dressing. The "masochistic narratives" Chencha's representation rejects include the models offered for Lupita's inspection in *El eterno femenino*, the endless renderings of the treacherous translator and the passive mistress of the home. Chencha's recreation of Pancho

Villa may be read alongside the reinterpretations of other mythical figures, such as La Malinche in Berman's *Águila o sol*, but with a difference: the spectator's participation in Chencha's performance is both more active than that of the typical theater audience and differently nuanced. Chencha's public pays handsomely not for an aesthetic or entertainment experience (though elements of both enter the spectacle) but for cures that will liberate the sufferer from illness or from the evil designs of others. Behar concludes that "As Chencha's theater of cruelty and healing takes account of the terror and submission of revolutionary history, patriarchy is reproduced ironically, making Pancho Villa a twentieth-century Saint Michael, a key defender of women in their daily battles against the dragon of male domination" (317). The spiritist's theater is both historical and performative: through the assumption of the historical role, Chencha makes herself healer. The theater is transformed into a performance that combines historical revision with spiritual cure.[2]

What María Escudero terms the "género fiesta" [fiesta genre] presents another displacement, or replacement, of performance. Here the blue leper steps off the stage and into the street. Both of the images that frame my study–the blue leper of the high school play and the Mama Negra of Latacunga–are connected to the commemoration of local patron saints, each a distinct apparition of the Virgin. The (ambiguously) feminine figures of their performances thus echo, however distantly, the smiling, ethereal images of the female icons paraded through town. As in performance more generally, the normative and the transgressive are present simultaneously. The fiesta of La Mama Negra has two versions. The one performed in September is sponsored by local market vendors and coincides with the feast day of the Virgen de la Merced. A second performance in November commemorates Latacunga's independence. In September 1994, when I observed the procession in Latacunga, I found that many of my middle-class Ecuadorian acquaintances either were aware only of the November event or tended to value the

---

[2] Behar also addresses the question of the audience's level of historical awareness when she writes: "Of the history I need to recover for my own understanding, how much is implicit as social knowledge and how much is knowledge irrelevant to Chencha, Esperanza, and other participants in the cult? [. . .] Esperanza, for example, knows little more about Villa than that he was a general of great valor during the Revolution. And yet an experiential history of Villa is embedded within the cult, and it is what makes its magic and its healing effective" (308).

later procession much more highly, as the "real" fiesta, "la de la gente bien, digamos, la gente blanca" [that of the fine people, that is, the whites], as one man informed me. The November fiesta appears to draw a larger number of tourists, many of them Ecuadorians, and is visibly bound up with local politics and status hierarchies, so that a video documenting the event includes lengthy speeches from the various actors acknowledging the great honor they feel in representing the festival's protagonists and lauding the dignitaries of the town. The September procession, by contrast, is far more popular in feel, with greater participation by the indigenous and mestizo communities.[3] The procession offers suggestive images of an offstage theatricality, one that combines audience participation, select transvestism, healing, and latent historical narrative in an overarching performance. Escudero sees the fundamental theme of the fiesta as the "renovación anual del encuentro entre pueblos y naciones" [the annual renewal of the encounter between peoples and nations], and she concludes: "La Mama Negra es realmente una forma dramática, al margen de las definiciones occidentales" (22) [The Mama Negra is really a dramatic form, at the margin of Western definitions].[4] Repetition remains key–yearly repetition, repetition of the dance steps, the multiplication of the Mama Negra.

Although its origins are disputed, the procession combines pre-Hispanic, Hispanic, and African elements. Escudero has suggested a historical aspect to the procession, a narrative lurking behind the mythological characters and the puzzling figure of La Mama Negra: "la conmocionante narración contiene cierta búsqueda de explicación desde el presente de hechos del pasado, es decir, se narra la historia" (21) [the moving narrative contains a sort of search for an explanation of events of the past from the vantage point of the present, that is to say, history is narrated]. The various originary myths

---

[3] I would like to express my thanks to María Escudero and friends, who took me to see the Mama Negra, and to Marco Padilla, who located the video.

[4] The recourse to the image of the Mama Negra in a dramatic text by Iván Toledo and Raúl Arias, *Luces y espejos en la oscuridad*, which treats, in a highly theatricalized manner, portions of the life of Eugenio Espejo, illustrates the circulation of material between stage and extratheatrical reality. An important figure within the play is Mama Blanca, described in the stage directions as the inverse, in black and white, of Latacunga's Mama Negra. She plays a variety of roles: narrator, representative of the people of Quito, colonial taskmaster. Unlike the Mama Negra, Mama Blanca is played by a woman.

used to explain the fiesta incorporate several violent histories, including the Virgin's shielding of the city from certain destruction and the local presence of escaped slaves. However, the procession's narrative remains more implicit than overt, closer to the "experiential history" Behar cites than to any objective comprehension of past events. What becomes most apparent to the observer of the procession is the repetition, a repetition of bands, of multiplying dancers, of Ashangas bent under the weight of liquor bottles and roast pigs. Even La Mama Negra is multiplied. The September 1994 procession boasted two performers, one of whom changed costume, so that the effect was of three figures: one in a yellow cape near the beginning of the parade, one in orange somewhere midway through, and one in blue toward the end. The Virgin is almost an afterthought, her image pulled by a John Deere tractor and flanked by military cadets, a small sign announcing the homage of her devotees from Quito.

The fiesta offers two images of transvestism, both male to female. Most visibly, La Mama Negra is played by a man. Escudero finds in the cross-dressed Mama Negra evidence for the fiesta's African roots and argues that the procession has its origins in Yoruba traditions brought inland by escaped or shipwrecked African slaves, so that the procession becomes a historical narrative of their flight and incorporation into the community: "la Mama Negra está representada por un hombre, escogido por 'ser buena gente' [. . .]. Una de las figuras del rito yoruba es bisexual y tiene hijos gemelos" (21-22) [the Mama Negra is performed by a man, chosen for 'being a good person' {. . .}. One of the figures of the Yoruba ritual is bisexual and has twin children].[5] La Mama Negra, wearing a glossy, deep black mask and holding aloft a doll, is a large, festive, brightly colored character who interacts with festival onlookers by throwing water into the crowd. The second example of cross-dressing is that of the Camisonas. Masked, wigged, and decked in long, embroidered smocks, these figures clear the path of the procession, dance with the spectators, and also pass out sweets. Paulo de Carvalho-Neto describes the Camisonas as "terribles hombres enmascarados de mujer, que infunden miedo al público porque lo persigue,

---

[5] Alternative explanations of the fiesta's origins include the commemoration of the Virgin's protection of the city from a volcanic eruption during the colonial period and a syncretic recuperation of pre-Columbian traditions.

obligándolo a alejarse, a fin de abrir cancha para los yumbos, el Rey, la Capitanía y los demás personajes del auto. Si no fuera por las Camisonas, no se podría representar" (63) [terrible men masked as women who instill fear in the audience because they pursue them and force them to move away to make room for the *yumbos*, the King, the Captain, and the other characters of the procession. If it were not for the Camisonas, they would not be able to perform]. According to Escudero, the Camisonas "se dedican a divertir, y a poner en ridículo a los hombres, preferentemente mestizos. Los tocan, los acarician, les dicen frases de cuño popular" (22) [are dedicated to fun, and to ridiculing men, preferably mestizos. They touch them, caress them, and make coarse remarks]. As transgressive figures, the Camisonas are at once hostile and playful. The Camisonas' regulatory function is to defend the borders of the "stage," so that the audience, always invited and obliged to participate, nevertheless will not interfere in the performance. By enforcing the free space of the procession, the Camisonas make representation possible.

To a degree, the possibility of representation requires the coercion of the public in addition to its participation: the audience must be whipped into shape for the procession to advance.[6] The audience is inevitably involved in the fiesta, crowding the stage of the city's narrow streets until the Camisonas remove them to the sidelines or, rather, push the sidelines back so that the procession can pass. (The necessary herding of the audience also recalls the criticisms by Gambaro and others of sheep-like bystanders only too willing to remain passive.) Individual requests for healing represent another instance of audience participation. Healing is incorporated into the procession through the work of the Huacos, masked sorcerers whose role presents "un mixto de teatro y verdad" [a mixture of theater and truth] in which children suffering from *espanto*—"una enfermedad que se produce espontáneamente, por haber el niño visto algo raro, quedando con fisonomía de asustado" [a sickness that is produced spontaneously because of the child having seen something strange, that leaves it with an expression of fear]–are cured (Carvalho-Neto 26). In a more playful mode, the audience participates through the consumption of *champuz* and

---

[6] The fiesta, too, has on and offstage sectors: the Camisonas' internal regulatory role is mirrored by the transit police stopping traffic at parade-route intersections.

other, stronger, beverages and by eating the candies the Camisonas distribute and dodging the water thrown by the Mama Negra.

The interplay of coercion and transgression is personified in the regulatory yet ludic figure of the Camisona whose activity makes possible the performance. The audience's central role, in turn, is visible in the frightened face of the child suffering from *espanto*, whose fear might reasonably spring from the figures in the spectacle but whose illness can be recognized and cured during the performance. The annual repetition, and the doubling and tripling within the procession of both the central figures and the traditional brass bands and groups of costumed dancers, replays the implicit history behind the fiesta (whatever one may take that to be) and the imperative of performance: to do it again, as if for the first time. Or, because a first performance remains impossible, to do it again, only better, to retrace the path of last year's parade, reincarnate Pancho Villa, reinvent the individual identity that is constituted in performance through the telling and retelling of slightly varied, always vaguely familiar *historias*.

Performance is at once familiar and strange, a replaying of what the spectator already knows in a form that may be scarcely recognizable. The coercive force of performance, affecting both actor and spectator, is inescapable. Yet the demand for repetition and displacement is also an invitation: to move offstage, rewrite the script, perform elsewhere. The possibility of freedom or transformation finally resides in the spectator's recognition that performance is not limited to the clearly bordered stage. If scientific observation is dependent upon the observer, the endless variations on a theme that performance both offers and demands open the door to a shifting of control. It is not performance but the understanding of performance that offers hope. Natalie Schmitt's suggestion that performance (and imaginative play) are "more rewardingly analyzed as perceptions of reality rather than as imitations of reality" is again helpful ("Theatre" 230). Performance is not a way to elude power but a way to understand it. And, perhaps, to exercise it. Performance can only be successfully transformed into a means of resistance if audience complicity is engaged on the side of the performer. On and off the stage, performance weaves, weft-like and inseparable, in and out of the negotiations that are gender and history, coercion and play.

WORKS CITED

Abel, Lionel. *Metatheatre*. New York: Hill and Wang, 1963.
Adoum, Jorge Enrique. *El sol bajo las patas de los caballos*. *Conjunto* 14 (1972): 43-85.
Ahern, Maureen, ed. and intro. *A Rosario Castellanos Reader: An Anthology of Her Poetry, Short Fiction, Essays, and Drama*. Austin: U of Texas P, 1988.
Albuquerque, Severino João. *Violent Acts. A Study of Contemporary Latin American Theatre*. Detroit: Wayne State UP, 1991.
Aponte, Barbara Bockus. "Estrategias dramáticas del feminismo en *El eterno femenino* de Rosario Castellanos." *Latin American Theatre Review* 20.2 (1987): 49-58.
Arenal, Electa. "This life within me won't keep still." *Reinventing the Americas: Comparative Studies of Literature of the United States and Spanish America*. Ed. Bell Gale Chevigny and Gari Laguardia. Cambridge: Cambridge UP, 1986. 158-202.
Artaud, Antonin. *The Theater and Its Double*. Trans. Mary Caroline Richards. New York: Grove, 1958.
Auslander, Philip. *From Acting to Performance: Essays in Modernism and Postmodernism*. London: Routledge, 1997.
Austin, Gayle. "Creating a Feminist Theatre Environment: The Feminist Theory Play." *Studies in the Literary Imagination* 24.2 (1991): 49-55.
Barker, Stephen. "'disorder of the lights perhaps an illusion.'" *Studies in the Literary Imagination* 24.2 (1991): 7-27.
Bateson, Gregory. "A Theory of Play and Fantasy." *Ritual, Play and Performance*. Ed. Richard Schechner and Mady Schuman. New York: Seabury, 1976. 67-73.
Behar, Ruth. *Translated Woman: Crossing the Border with Esperanza's Story*. Boston: Beacon, 1993.
Benedetti, Mario. *Pedro y el Capitán*. Mexico: Nueva Imagen, 1979. Translated by Freda Berberfall as *Pedro and the Captain*. *Modern International Drama* 19.1 (1985): 33-52.
Benston, Kimberly W. "Being There: Performance as Mise-en-Scène, Abscene, Obscene, and Other Scene." *PMLA* 107 (1992): 434-49.
Berman, Sabina. *Águila o sol. Teatro de Sabina Berman*. Mexico: Editores Mexicanos Unidos, 1985. 223-65.
———. *Entre Villa y una mujer desnuda. Muerte súbita. El suplicio del placer*. Mexico: Grupo Editorial Gaceta, 1994.

Berman, Sabina. *Esta no es una obra de teatro*. *Teatro de Sabina Berman*. Mexico: Editores Mexicanos Unidos, 1985. 300-11.

———. *El suplicio del placer*. *Teatro de Sabina Berman*. Mexico: Editores Mexicanos Unidos, 1985. 266-99.

Bissett, Judith I. "Constructing the Alternative Version: Vicente Leñero's Documentary and Historical Drama." *Latin American Theatre Review* 18.2 (1985): 71-78.

Bixler, Jacqueline Eyring. "For Women Only? The Theater of Susana Torres Molina." *Latin American Women Dramatists: Theater, Texts, and Theories*. Ed. Catherine Larson and Margarita Vargas. Bloomington: Indiana UP, 1998. 215-33.

———. "Games and Reality on the Latin American Stage." *Latin American Literary Review* 12.24 (1984): 22-35.

———. "Historical (Dis)authority in Leñero's *Martirio de Morelos*." *Gestos* 2 (1986): 87-97.

———. "Toward a Reconciliation of Text and Performance: How to 'Read' *El señor Galíndez*." *Gestos* 13 (1992): 65-77.

Blau, Herbert. *The Audience*. Baltimore: Johns Hopkins UP, 1990.

———. "Universals of Performance; or, Amortizing Play." *The Eye of Prey: Subversions of the Postmodern*. Bloomington: Indiana UP, 1987. 161-88.

Boal, Augusto. *Teatro del oprimido 1: Teoría y práctica*. Mexico: Nueva Imagen, 1980.

Boling, Becky. "From Pin-Ups to Striptease in Gambaro's *El despojamiento*." *Latin American Theatre Review* 20.2 (1987): 59-65.

———. "The Spectacle of the Other: Madness in *Falsa crónica de Juana la Loca*." *Gestos* 8 (1989): 87-97.

Bravo-Elizondo, Pedro. "La realidad latinoamericana y el teatro documental." *Texto Crítico* 14 (1979): 200-10.

Brewer, Mária Minich. "Performing Theory." *Theatre Journal* 37 (1985): 13-30.

Bruss, Elizabeth W. "The Game of Literature and Some Literary Games." *New Literary History* 9 (1977): 153-72.

Buenaventura, Enrique. "La dramaturgia en el Nuevo Teatro." *Conjunto* 59 (1984): 32-37.

———. *Teatro*. Havana: Casa de las Américas, 1980.

Bunster, Ximena. "Tortura de presas políticas: Una forma de esclavitud sexual." *Fem* 37 (1984-85): 43-45.

Burgess, Ronald D. *The New Dramatists of Mexico, 1967-1985*. Lexington: UP of Kentucky, 1991.

———. "Sabina Berman's Undone Threads." *Latin American Women Dramatists: Theater, Texts, and Theories*. Ed. Catherine Larson and Margarita Vargas. Bloomington: Indiana UP, 1998. 145-58.

Burns, Elizabeth. *Theatricality: A Study of Convention in the Theatre and in Social Life*. London: Longman, 1972.

Butler, Judith. *Gender Trouble: Feminism and the Subversion of Identity*. New York: Routledge, 1990.

———. "Performative Acts and Gender Constitution: An Essay in Phenomenology and Feminist Theory." *Performing Feminisms*. Ed. Sue-Ellen Case. Baltimore: Johns Hopkins UP, 1990. 270-82.

Cabrujas, José Ignacio. *Acto cultural*. Caracas: Monte Avila, 1976.

Carballido, Emilio. *Yo también hablo de la rosa*. *Nueve dramaturgos hispanoamericanos*. Vol. 3. Ed. Frank Dauster, Leon Lyday, and George Woodyard. Ottawa: Girol, 1979. 121-75. Translated by William I. Oliver as *I Too Speak of the Rose* in *The Modern Stage in Latin America: Six Plays*. Ed. George Woodyard. New York: E. P. Dutton, 1971. 289-331.

Carlson, Marvin. *Performance: A Critical Introduction.* London: Routledge, 1996.

———. "Theatrical Performance: Illustration, Translation, Fulfillment, or Supplement?" *Theatre Journal* 37 (1985): 5-11.

Carvalho-Neto, Paulo de. "Fiesta de la Mama Negra." *Revista del Folklore Ecuatoriano* 2 (1966): 5-82.

Case, Sue-Ellen. "Toward a Butch-Femme Aesthetic." *Making a Spectacle: Feminist Essays on Contemporary Women's Theatre.* Ed. Lynda Hart. Ann Arbor: U of Michigan P, 1989. 282-99.

Castañón, José Manuel, ed. *Bolívar y los poetas.* Caracas: Casuz Editores, 1976.

Castedo-Ellerman, Elena. "Feminism or Femineity? Six Women Writers Answer." *Américas* 30.10 (1978): 19-24.

Castellanos, Rosario. "A pesar de proponérselo." *El uso de la palabra.* Mexico: Excelsior, 1974. 269-72.

———. *El eterno femenino.* México: Fondo de Cultura Económica, 1975. Translated in Ahern.

———. "Kinsey Report." *Meditación en el umbral: antología poética.* México: Fondo de Cultura Económica, 1985. 204-08.

———. "La mujer y su imagen." *Mujer que sabe latín.* México: Fondo de Cultura Económica, 1992. 7-21. Translated in Ahern.

———. "Otra vez Sor Juana." *Juicios sumarios.* Veracruz: Cuadernos de la Facultad de Filosofía, Letras y Ciencias, 1966. 26-30. Translated in Ahern.

———. "La participación de la mujer mexicana en la educación formal." *Mujer que sabe latín.* México: Fondo de Cultura Económica, 1992. 21-41.

Castillo, Debra A. *Talking Back: Toward a Latin American Feminist Literary Criticism.* Ithaca: Cornell UP, 1992.

Castillo, Susana D. "*El juego*: texto dramático y montaje." *Latin American Theatre Review* 14.1 (1980): 25-33.

Chocrón, Isaac. *La revolución.* Caracas: Tiempo Nuevo, 1972.

Coetzee, J. M. "Into the Dark Chamber: The Writer and the South African State." *Doubling the Point: Essays and Interviews.* Cambridge: Harvard UP, 1992. 361-68.

Cohen-Cruz, Jan, ed. *Radical Street Performance: An International Anthology.* London: Routledge, 1998.

Cossa, Roberto, Germán Rozenmacher, Carlos Somigliana, and Ricardo Talesnik. *El avión negro. Tres obras de teatro.* Havana: Colección Premio Casa de las Américas, 1970. 7-123.

Costantino, Roselyn. "And She Wears it Well: Feminist and Cultural Debates in the Performance Art of Astrid Hadad." Forthcoming in *Latinas on Stage*, Third Woman Press.

Cypess, Sandra Messinger. "From Colonial Constructs to Feminist Figures: Re/visions by Mexican Women Dramatists." *Theatre Journal* 41 (1989): 492-504.

———. *La Malinche in Mexican Literature: From History to Myth.* Austin: U of Texas P, 1991.

Derrida, Jacques. *Of Grammatology.* Trans. Gayatri Chakravorty Spivak. Baltimore: Johns Hopkins UP, 1976.

Diamond, Elin. Introduction. *Performance and Cultural Politics.* Ed. Diamond. London: Routledge, 1996. 1-12.

Díaz, Jorge. *El cepillo de dientes. Nueve dramaturgos hispanoamericanos.* Vol. 3. Ed. Frank Dauster, Leon Lyday, and George Woodyard. Ottawa: Girol, 1979. 59-120.

Díez, Luys A. "Un festival para Nueva York: Teatro Popular Latinoamericano." *Latin American Theatre Review* 14.2 (1981): 71-77.

Dolan, Jill. "Geographies of Learning: Theatre Studies, Performance, and the 'Performative.'" *Theatre Journal* 45 (1993): 417-41.

Dorfman, Ariel. *Death and the Maiden*. New York: Penguin, 1992.
———. "*Death and the Maiden*: A Playwright's Perspective." *New York Times* 24 May 1992, sec. 2: 4.
———. *La Muerte y la Doncella. Teatro.* Vol. 1. Buenos Aires: Ediciones de la Flor, 1992.
Dragún, Osvaldo. *El amasijo. Nueve dramaturgos hispanoamericanos.* Vol. 1. Ed. Frank Dauster, Leon Lyday, and George Woodyard. Ottawa: Girol, 1979. 203-67.
———. *Historias para ser contadas. Teatro.* Buenos Aires: Pampa y Cielo, 1965. 55-85.
duBois, Page. *Torture and Truth.* New York: Routledge, 1991.
Eidelberg, Nora. "La ritualización de la violencia en cuatro obras teatrales hispanoamericanas." *Latin American Theatre Review* 13.1 (1979): 29-37.
———. "Susana Torres Molina, Destacada teatrista argentina." *Alba de América* 7.12-13 (1989): 391-93.
Elam, Keir. *The Semiotics of Theatre and Drama.* London: Methuen, 1980.
Escudero, María. "La Mama Negra de Ecuador." *Escenarios de dos mundos: Inventario teatral de Iberoamérica.* Vol 1. Madrid: Centro de Documentación Teatral, 1988. 4 vols. 18-22.
Feitlowitz, Marguerite. "Crisis, Terror, Disappearance: The Theater of Griselda Gambaro." *Information for Foreigners: Three Plays by Griselda Gambaro.* Ed. and trans. Marguerite Feitlowitz. Evanston: Northwestern UP, 1992. 1-11.
———. "A Dance of Death: Eduardo Pavlovsky's *Paso de dos.*" *The Drama Review* 35.2 (1991): 60-73.
Féral, Josette. "Performance and Theatricality: The Subject Demystified." Trans. Terese Lyons. *Modern Drama* 25.1 (1982): 170-81.
Fetterley, Judith. *The Resisting Reader: A Feminist Approach to American Fiction.* Bloomington: Indiana UP, 1978.
Fletcher, Lea. "La tortura genéricamente específica (la violación) ejercida contra mujeres en la última dictadura militar y su representación en la literatura argentina." *Fem* 16.109 (1992): 10-12.
Foley, Barbara. *Telling the Truth: The Theory and Practice of Documentary Fiction.* Ithaca: Cornell UP, 1986.
Foucault, Michel. *Discipline and Punish: The Birth of the Prison.* Trans. Alan Sheridan. New York: Vintage, 1995.
Franco, Jean. "Beyond Ethnocentrism: Gender, Power, and the Third-World Intelligentsia." *Marxism and the Interpretation of Culture.* Ed. Cary Nelson and Lawrence Grossberg. Urbana: U of Illinois P, 1988. 503-15.
———. "Death Camp Confessions and Resistance to Violence in Latin America." *Socialism and Democracy* 2 (1986): 5-17.
———. "Going Public: Reinhabiting the Private." *On Edge: The Crisis of Contemporary Latin American Culture.* Ed. George Yúdice, Jean Franco, and Juan Flores. Minneapolis: U of Minnesota P, 1992. 65-83.
———. "Self-Destructing Heroines." *The Minnesota Review* 22 (Spring 1984): 105-15.
Fuentes, Carlos. *Todos los gatos son pardos.* Mexico: Siglo Veintiuno, 1970.
Gambaro, Griselda. *El campo. Teatro.* Vol. 4. Buenos Aires: Ediciones de la Flor, 1990. 157-214. 6 vols. 1984-96. Translated by William I. Oliver as *The Camp* in *Voices of Change in the Spanish American Theater: An Anthology.* Ed and trans. William I. Oliver. Austin: U of Texas P, 1971. 47-103.
———. *El despojamiento. Teatro.* Vol. 3. Buenos Aires: Ediciones de la Flor, 1989. 169-81. 6 vols. 1984-96.
———. *El desatino. Teatro.* Vol. 4. Buenos Aires: Ediciones de la Flor, 1990. 59-106. 6 vols. 1984-96.

Gambaro, Griselda. "¿Es posible y deseable una dramaturgia específicamente femenina?" *Latin American Theatre Review* 13.2, Supplement (1980): 17-21.

———. *Información para extranjeros. Teatro*. Vol. 2. Buenos Aires: Ediciones de la Flor, 1987. 67-128. 6 vols. 1984-96. Translated by Marguerite Feitlowitz as *Information for Foreigners* in *Information for Foreigners: Three Plays by Griselda Gambaro*. Ed. and trans. Marguerite Feitlowitz. Evanston: Northwestern UP, 1992. 67-132.

———. "Respuestas al cuestionario." *Dramaturgas latinoamericanas contemporáneas*. Ed. Elba Andrade and Hilde F. Cramsie. Madrid: Verbum, 1991. 147-58.

———. "Voracidad o canibalismo amoroso." *Conjunto* 60 (1984): 61-63.

Garber, Marjorie. *Vested Interests: Cross-dressing and Cultural Anxiety*. New York: Routledge, 1992.

García, Luis Alberto. *I Took Panamá. Teatro colombiano contemporáneo*. Bogotá: Tres Culturas, 1985. 89-156.

George, David. "On Ambiguity: Towards a Post-Modern Performance Theory." *Theatre Research International* 14.1 (1989): 71-85.

———. "Performance as Paradigm: The Example of Bali." *Modern Drama* 35 (March 1992): 1-9.

Gerdes, Dick. "Recent Argentine Vanguard Theatre: Gambaro's *Información para extranjeros*." *Latin American Theatre Review* 11.2 (1978): 11-16.

Gladhart, Amalia. "Tragedia y metateatro en *Luces de bohemia*." *Hispanófila* 112 (1994): 11-25.

Gómez-Peña, Guillermo. "A Binational Performance Pilgrimage." *The Drama Review* 35.3 (1991): 22-45.

González, Patricia Helena. "Los juegos en 'La agonía del difunto.'" *El Café Literario* 5.28 (1982): 28-30.

Gorostiza, Carlos. *¿A qué jugamos?* Buenos Aires: Editorial Sudamericana, 1969.

Graham-Jones, Jean. "Myths, Masks, and Machismo: *Un trabajo fabuloso* by Ricardo Halac and . . . *y a otra cosa mariposa* by Susana Torres Molina." *Gestos* 20 (1995): 91-106.

Graziano, Frank. *Divine Violence: Spectacle, Psychosexuality, and Radical Christianity in the Argentine "Dirty War."* Boulder: Westview, 1992.

Gregory, Stephen W. G. *Humanist Ethics or Realist Aesthetics? Torture, Interrogation and Psychotherapy in Mario Benedetti*. Institute of Latin American Studies Occasional Paper 12. Victoria, Australia: La Trobe U, 1991.

Hart, Lynda. "Introduction: Performing Feminism." *Making a Spectacle: Feminist Essays on Contemporary Women's Theatre*. Ed. Lynda Hart. Ann Arbor: U of Michigan P, 1989. 1-21.

Heise, Ursula K. "Transvestism and the Stage Controversy in Spain and England, 1580-1680." *Theatre Journal* 44 (1992): 357-74.

Holzapfel, Tamara. "Griselda Gambaro's Theatre of the Absurd." *Latin American Theatre Review* 4.2 (1970): 5-11.

Huizinga, Johan. *Homo Ludens: A Study of the Play-Element in Culture*. Boston: Beacon, 1950.

Hutcheon, Linda. *The Politics of Postmodernism*. London: Routledge, 1989.

Inamoto, Kenji. "La mujer vestida de hombre en el teatro de Cervantes." *Cervantes* 12.2 (1992): 137-43.

Jones, Marion. "Actors and Repertory." *The Revels History of Drama in English*. John Loftis, Richard Southern, Marion Jones and A. H. Scouten. Vol. 5, 1660-1750. London: Methuen, 1976. 119-57.

Kintz, Linda. "The Space Where Speaking Bodies Evolve: Rosario Castellanos." *The Subject's Tragedy: Political Poetics, Feminist Theory, and Drama*. Ann Arbor: U of Michigan P, 1992. 239-73.

Kubiak, Anthony. *Stages of Terror: Terrorism, Ideology and Coercion as Theatre History*. Bloomington: Indiana UP, 1991.
Larson, Catherine. "Playwrights of Passage: Women and Game-Playing on the Stage." *Latin American Literary Review* 19.38 (1991): 77-89.
Leñero, Vicente. *Martirio de Morelos*. Mexico: Ariel y Seix Barral, 1981.
———. *La ruta crítica de Martirio de Morelos*. Mexico: Ediciones Océano, 1985.
León-Portilla, Miguel. *The Broken Spears: the Aztec Account of the Conquest of Mexico*. Trans. Lysander Kemp. Boston: Beacon, 1992.
Lichtblau, Myron I. "Desdoblamiento e inversión de papeles en *El juego* de Mariela Romero." *Studies in Honor of Gilberto Paolini*. Ed. Mercedes Vidal Tibbitts. Newark, Delaware: Juan de la Cuesta, 1996. 449-55.
Lindenberger, Herbert. *Historical Drama: The Relation of Literature and Reality*. Chicago: U of Chicago P, 1975.
Lispector, Clarice. "The Imitation of the Rose." *Family Ties*. Trans. Giovanni Pontiero. Austin: U of Texas P, 1990. 53-72.
Ludmer, Josefina. "Tretas del débil." *La sartén por el mango*. Ed. Patricia Elena González and Eliana Ortega. Río Piedras: Huracán, 1985. 47-54.
Magnarelli, Sharon. "Acting/Seeing Woman: Griselda Gambaro's *El despojamiento*." *Latin American Women's Writing: Feminist Readings in Theory and Crisis*. Ed. Anny Brooksbank Jones and Catherine Davies. Oxford: Oxford UP, 1996. 10-29.
———. "Contenido y forma en la obra de Maruxa Vilalta." *Plural: Revista Cultural de Excelsior* Sept. 1987: 77-78.
———. "Dramatic Irony and Lyricism in Historical Theatre: *El pobre Franz* and *Falsa crónica de Juana la Loca*." *Latin American Theatre Review* 22.2 (1989): 47-57.
La Mama Negra. Videotape. Serie: *Ecuador, País Turístico*. Quito: Dino Producciones, 1994.
Marqués, René. *Los soles truncos*. *Nueve dramaturgos hispanoamericanos*. Vol. 3. Ed. Frank Dauster, Leon Lyday, and George Woodyard. Ottawa: Girol, 1979. 7-58. Translated by Richard John Wiezell as *The Fanlights* in *The Modern Stage in Latin America: Six Plays*. Ed. George Woodyard. New York: E. P. Dutton, 1971. 1-41.
Márquez, Rosa Luisa. *Brincos y Saltos*. Cayey: Ediciones Cuicaloca/Colegio Universitario de Cayey, 1992.
Meléndez, Priscilla. "Co(s)mic Conquest in Sabina Berman's *Águila o sol*." *Perspectives on Contemporary Spanish American Theatre*. Ed. Frank Dauster. Lewisburg: Bucknell UP, 1996. 19-36.
———. "On Leñero's *Martirio de Morelos*: Reading the Empty Stage." *Gestos* 13 (1992): 51-64.
Mena, Karel. "Los juegos del poder." *Teatro venezolano contemporáneo: antología*. Coord. Orlando Rodríguez B. Madrid: Fondo de Cultura Económica, Sucursal España, 1991. 875-79.
Milgram, Stanley. *Obedience to Authority: An Experimental View*. New York: Harper and Row, 1974.
———. "The Perils of Obedience." *The Norton Reader: An Anthology of Expository Prose*. Ed. Arthur M. Eastman et al. New York: Norton, 1984. 642-54.
Millett, Kate. *The Politics of Cruelty: An Essay on the Literature of Political Imprisonment*. New York: Norton, 1994.
Mora, Gabriela. "Un diálogo entre feministas hispanoamericanas." *Cultural and Historical Grounding for Hispanic and Luso-Brazilian Feminist Literary Criticism*. Ed. Hernán Vidal. Minneapolis: Institute for the Study of Ideologies and Literature, 1989. 53-77.

Morello-Frosch, Marta. "El diálogo de la violencia en *Pedro y el Capitán* de Mario Benedetti." *Revista de Crítica Literaria Latinoamericana* 9.18 (1983): 87-96.
Moretta, Eugene L. "Reflexiones sobre la tiranía: tres obras del teatro argentino contemporáneo." *Revista Canadiense de Estudios Hispánicos* 7.1 (1982): 141-47.
———. "Spanish American Theatre of the 50's and 60's: Critical Perspectives on Role Playing." *Latin American Theatre Review* 13.2 (1980): 5-30.
Navajas, Esteban. *La agonía del difunto. Teatro colombiano contemporáneo: antología.* Coord. Fernando González Cajias. Madrid: Fondo de Cultura Económica, Sucursal España, 1992. 681-726.
Neglia, Erminio G. "El tema de la tortura en el teatro hispánico." *N/S* 8.16 (1983): 91-102.
Nightingale, Benedict. "*Death and the Maiden* Becomes a Tale of Two Cities." *New York Times* 10 May 1992, sec. 2: 14+.
Nigro, Kirsten F. "Breaking [it] up is [Not] Hard to Do: Writing Histories and Women Theatre Artists in Latin America." *Gestos* 14 (1992): 127-39.
———. "Entrevista a Vicente Leñero." *Latin American Theatre Review* 18.2 (1985): 79-82.
———. "History Grand and History Small in Recent Venezuelan Theatre: Rial's *Bolívar* and Cabrujas' *Acto cultural.*" *The Theatre Annual* 44 (1989-90): 37-46.
———. "Rosario Castellanos' Debunking of the *Eternal Feminine*." *Journal of Spanish Studies: Twentieth Century* 8.1-2 (1980): 89-102.
———. "A Triple Insurgence: Isaac Chocrón's *La revolución.*" *Rocky Mountain Review of Language and Literature* 35.1 (1981): 47-53.
Niño, Jairo Aníbal. *El sol subterráneo. Teatro colombiano contemporáneo.* Bogotá: Tres Culturas, 1985. 157-82.
Noakes, Susan. "On the Superficiality of Women." *The Comparative Perspective on Literature: Approaches to Theory and Practice.* Ed. Clayton Koelb and Susan Noakes. Ithaca: Cornell UP, 1988. 339-55.
Nunca Más: The Report of the Argentine National Commission on the Disappeared. Intro. Ronald Dworkin. New York: Farrar Straus Giroux, 1986.
Olivera-Williams, María Rosa. "La literatura uruguaya del proceso: Exilio e insilio, continuismo e invención." *Nuevo Texto Crítico* 5 (1990): 67-83.
Partnoy, Alicia. *The Little School: Tales of Disappearance and Survival in Argentina.* Trans. Alicia Partnoy with Lois Althey and Sandra Braunstein. Pittsburgh: Cleis Press, 1986.
Pavlovsky, Eduardo. *El señor Galíndez. Pablo.* Buenos Aires: Ediciones Búsqueda, 1986.
———. *Voces.* Buenos Aires: Ediciones Ayllu, 1989.
Perelli, Carina. "De la integración negativa a la herejía: identidades colectivas, actores y retóricas en torno a la enseñanza media en el Uruguay." *De mitos y memorias políticas: la represión, el miedo y después . . .* Carina Perelli and Juan Rial. Montevideo: Ediciones de la Banda Oriental, 1986. 87-116.
Peters, Edward. *Torture.* Oxford: Basil Blackwell, 1985.
Postma, Rosalea. "Space and Spectator in the Theatre of Griselda Gambaro: *Información para extranjeros.*" *Latin American Theatre Review* 14.1 (1980): 35-45.
Rejali, Darius M. *Torture and Modernity: Self, Society, and State in Modern Iran.* Boulder: Westview, 1994.
Reyes, Carlos José. "Teatro e historia." *Conjunto* 61-62 (1984): 146-56.
Rial, José Antonio. *Bolívar. Bolívar. Arcadio.* Caracas: Monte Avila, 1986. 9-64.
———. "Bolívar." *Conjunto* 53 (1982): 12-41.
Riding, Alan. *Distant Neighbors: A Portrait of the Mexicans.* New York: Vintage, 1986.
Rogers, Pat. "The Breeches Part." *Sexuality in Eighteenth-Century Britain.* Ed. Paul-Gabriel Boucé. Manchester: Manchester UP, 1982. 244-58.

Rohter, Larry. "Dorfman's 'Maiden' Cries Out." *New York Times* 8 Mar. 1992, sec. 2: 1+.
Romero, Mariela. *Esperando al italiano. Las risas de nuestras medusas: Teatro venezolano escrito por mujeres*. Ed. Susana Castillo. Caracas: Fundarte, 1992. 65-99.
——. *El juego. Teatro Venezolano*. Caracas: Monte Avila, 1982. 3: 75-112. Translated by Susan D. Castillo and Joseph Chrzanowski as *The Game* in *Contemporary Women Authors of Latin America: New Translations*. Ed. Doris Meyer and Margarite Fernández Olmos. Brooklyn: Brooklyn College P, 1983. 107-136.
——. *Rosa de la noche. Voces nuevas: Teatro*. Caracas: Centro de Estudios Latinoamericanos Rómulo Gallegos, 1982. 47-94.
——. *El vendedor*. Caracas: Fundarte, 1985.
Ruffinelli, Jorge. "Uruguay: dictadura y re-democratización: un informe sobre la literatura 1973-1989." *Nuevo Texto Crítico* 5 (1990): 37-66.
Sabido, Miguel. *Falsa crónica de Juana la Loca*. Mexico: Katún, 1985.
Sáez, Ñacuñán. "Torture: A Discourse on Practice." *Tatoo, Torture, Mutilation, and Adornment: The Denaturalization of the Body in Culture and Text*. Ed. Frances E. Mascia-Lees and Patricia Sharpe. Albany: State U of New York P, 1992. 126-44.
Sánchez, Luis Rafael. *Farsa del amor compradito*. Río Piedras: Editorial Cultural, 1976.
Sarduy, Severo. "Escritura/Travestismo." *Mundo Nuevo* 20 (Feb. 1968): 72-74. Translated by Alfred Mac Adam as "Writing/Transvestism." *Review* 9 (1973): 31-33.
Sayre, Henry. "Performance." *Critical Terms for Literary Study*. Ed. Frank Lentricchia and Thomas McLaughlin. Chicago: U of Chicago P, 1990. 91-104.
Scarry, Elaine. *The Body in Pain: The Making and Unmaking of the World*. Oxford: Oxford UP, 1985.
Schechner, Richard. *Essays on Performance Theory 1970-1976*. New York: Drama Book Specialists, 1977.
Schmidhuber, Guillermo. *Por las tierras de Colón*. Barcelona: Salvat, 1987.
Schmitt, Natalie Crohn. "Theatre and Children's Pretend Play." *Theatre Journal* 33 (1981): 213-30.
——. "Theorizing About Performance: Why Now?" *New Theatre Quarterly* 6.23 (1990): 231-34.
Schulz, Bernhardt Roland. "Travestismo como falsa liberación." *Revista de Estudios Hispánicos* 17-18 (1990-91): 217-23.
Seda, Laurietz. "El hábito no hace al monje: Travestismo, homosexualidad y lesbianismo en . . . *y a otra cosa mariposa* de Susana Torres Molina." *Latin American Theatre Review* 30.2 (1997): 103-14.
Senelick, Laurence. Introduction. *Gender in Performance: The Presentation of Difference in the Performing Arts*. Ed. Senelick. Hanover, NH: Tufts, 1992. ix-xx.
Shakespeare, William. *Macbeth*. Ed. G. K. Hunter. London: Penguin, 1967.
States, Bert O. "Performance as Metaphor." *Theatre Journal* 48.1 (1996): 1-26.
Stover, Eric. *The Open Secret: Torture and the Medical Profession in Chile*. Washington, D.C.: Committee on Scientific Freedom and Responsibility, American Association for the Advancement of Science, 1987.
Szurmuk, Mónica. "Lo femenino en *El eterno femenino* de Rosario Castellanos." *Mujer y literatura mexicana y chicana: culturas en contacto*. Vol. 2. Ed. Aralia López González, Amelia Malagamba, and Elena Urrutia. México: El Colegio de México, 1990. 37-47.
Taylor, Diana. *Disappearing Acts: Spectacles of Gender and Nationalism in Argentina's "Dirty War"*. Durham: Duke UP, 1997.
——. "Negotiating Performance." *Latin American Theatre Review* 26.2 (1993): 49-57.

Taylor, Diana. "Opening Remarks." *Negotiating Performance: Gender, Sexuality, and Theatricality in Latin/o America*. Ed. Diana Taylor and Juan Villegas. Durham: Duke UP, 1994. 1-16.

———. "Performing Gender: Las Madres de la Plaza de Mayo." *Negotiating Performance: Gender, Sexuality, and Theatricality in Latin/o America*. Ed. Diana Taylor and Juan Villegas. Durham: Duke UP, 1994. 275-305.

———. "Spectacular Bodies: Gender, Terror, and Argentina's 'Dirty War.'" *Gendering War Talk*. Ed. Miriam Cooke and Angela Woollacott. Princeton: Princeton UP, 1993. 20-40.

———. *Theatre of Crisis: Drama and Politics in Latin America*. Lexington: UP of Kentucky, 1991.

———. "Violent Displays: Griselda Gambaro and Argentina's Drama of Disappearance." *Information for Foreigners: Three Plays by Griselda Gambaro*. Ed. and trans. Marguerite Feitlowitz. Evanston: Northwestern UP, 1992. 161-75.

Tiello, Jaime, ed. *Los poetas a Bolívar*. Caracas: Instituto Venezolano de los Seguros Sociales, 1983.

Toledo Albornoz, Iván, and Raúl Arias. *Luces y espejos en la oscuridad. Teatro ecuatoriano*. Quito: Casa de la Cultura Ecuatoriana, 1991. 103-60.

Torres Molina, Susana. *Extraño juguete*. Buenos Aires: Apex, 1978.

———. *...Y a otra cosa mariposa*. Buenos Aires: Ediciones Búsqueda, 1988.

Triana, José. *La noche de los asesinos. Nueve dramaturgos hispanoamericanos*. Vol. 1. Ed. Frank Dauster, Leon Lyday, and George Woodyard. Ottawa: Girol, 1979. 133-201. Translated by Sebastian Doggart as *Night of the Assassins. Latin American Plays: New Drama from Argentina, Cuba, Mexico and Peru*. Ed. and trans. Sebastian Doggart. London: Nick Hern Books, 1996. 29-81.

Usigli, Rodolfo. *Corona de luz*. México: Fondo de Cultura Económica, 1965.

———. *El gesticulador: pieza para demagogos en tres actos*. Ed. Rex Edward Ballinger. New Jersey: Prentice-Hall, 1963.

Valenzuela, Luisa. "Cambio de armas." *Cambio de armas*. Hanover, NH: Ediciones del Norte, 1987. 111-46.

Valle-Inclán, Ramón del. *Luces de bohemia*. Ed. Alonso Zamora Vicente. Madrid: Espasa-Calpe, 1988. Translated by Anthony N. Zahareas and Gerald Gillespie as *Bohemian Lights*. Austin: U of Texas P, 1976.

Vanden Heuvel, Michael. *Performing Drama/Dramatizing Performance: Alternative Theater and the Dramatic Text*. Ann Arbor: U of Michigan P, 1991.

Versényi, Adam. *Theatre in Latin America: Religion, politics and culture from Cortés to the 1980s*. Cambridge: Cambridge UP, 1993.

Vilalta, Maruxa. *Pequeña historia de horror (y de amor desenfrenado)*. Mexico: Universidad Autónoma Metropolitana, 1986. Translated by Kirsten Nigro as *A Little Tale of Horror (And Unbridled Love)*. *Modern International Drama* 19.2 (1986): 25-60.

Weiss, Peter. "The Material and the Models: Notes Towards a Definition of Documentary Theatre." *Theatre Quarterly* 1 (1971): 41-43.

Weschler, Lawrence. *A Miracle, A Universe: Settling Accounts with Torturers*. New York: Pantheon, 1990.

White, Hayden. *The Content of the Form: Narrative Discourse and Historical Representation*. Baltimore: Johns Hopkins UP, 1987.

———. *Tropics of Discourse: Essays in Cultural Criticism*. Baltimore: Johns Hopkins UP, 1978.

Wiles, Timothy J. *The Theater Event: Modern Theories of Performance*. Chicago: U of Chicago P, 1980.

Worthen, W. B. "Drama, Performativity, and Performance." *PMLA* 113 (1998): 1093-1107.

Yarbro-Bejarano, Yvonne. *Feminism and the Honor Plays of Lope de Vega*. West Lafayette, Indiana: Purdue UP, 1994.

Zatlin, Phyllis. "Passivity and Immobility: Patterns of Inner Exile in Postwar Spanish Novels Written by Women." *Letras Femeninas* 14.1-2 (1988): 3-9.

Zee, Linda S. "*El campo, Los siameses, El señor Galíndez*: A Theatrical Manual of Torture." *RLA* 2 (1990): 604-08.

INDEX

Abel, Lionel, 133
Acto cultural (Cabrujas), 27, 63, 80, 160, 192-193, 196, 201-204, 211-212, 215, 218-219
Actor
   and audience, 20, 195, 197, 199, 212, 215-216
   and character, 64
   and role, 113, 196
   and spectator, 17, 19, 227
   coercion of, 207, 210
   female, 112-113, 115, 118-119, 143-145, 147-153
   imprisoned, 99
   presence of, 96
Adoum, Jorge Enrique, 30
Agonía del difunto, La (Navajas), 26, 76, 100, 106-109, 218
Águila o sol (Berman), 24, 26, 29, 49, 51, 58-65, 69, 71-74, 223
Ahern, Maureen, 127, 132
Albuquerque, Severino, 79-80, 86, 109, 176, 190
Aponte, Barbara, 127, 130
Arenal, Electa, 20
Argentina, 25, 27, 75, 77-78, 91, 111, 155, 158-162, 177, 183, 192, 213
Arias, Raúl, 30, 224
Artaud, Antonin, 15, 156, 199, 202
Audience
   absent, 199, 202
   active, 20-21
   and performance, 118
   as bystander, 21, 173, 188, 209-210, 226
   as victim, 173
   as voyeur, 215
   as witness, 17, 27, 110, 159, 188
   coercion of, 209, 213, 226
   complicity, 181, 188-189, 207-210, 213, 227
   confrontation of, 17, 42, 169, 186, 205-206, 208, 221
   constitution of, 13, 14, 126, 196-197
   discomfort, 177, 190-191
   distanced, 13, 20
   general public as, 14, 157, 175, 221
   hostile, 181, 205
   identification, 54, 72, 186, 189
   implication of, 27, 159, 173, 191, 209, 215
   knowledge, 30, 34-35, 38, 40, 91, 147, 162
   motivation, 205-206
   multiple, 125, 181, 189
   of torture, 163, 172-175, 188, 190, 207, 209
   participation, 210, 224, 226
   passivity, 17, 49, 207, 209
   performance of, 20
   placement, 174, 208, 219
   responsibility, 206-207
   role, 18, 21, 33, 147, 188, 209, 221, 227
   sympathy, 188, 205
   theatrical, 35-36, 49, 53, 181, 186, 189, 207, 209, 212-213, 221-223
   vigilance of, 58
   vulnerability of, 186
Auslander, Philip, 17, 20

Austin, Gayle, 129, 143
Authority
  absent, 82, 97
  and performance, 44, 160, 219
  displacement of, 18, 22, 28
  historical, 26, 40, 42, 45, 73
  in games, 80
  of documents, 35, 40
  of narrator, 69
  of text, 18, 21-22, 27, 45-46, 196
  resistance to, 21, 28
  respect for, 209, 221
  undermining of, 73

Barker, Stephen, 20
Bateson, Gregory, 83
Behar, Ruth, 222-223, 225
Benedetti, Mario, 168, 187
  Pedro y el Capitán, 27, 155-156, 165-172, 174, 177, 181, 185, 190
Benston, Kimberly, 19
Berman, Sabina, 13, 134, 154
  Águila o sol, 24, 26, 29, 49, 51, 58-65, 69, 71-74, 223
  El suplicio del placer, 12, 27, 111, 116, 119, 123, 135-142, 145-146, 150, 152, 218, 221
  Esta no es una obra de teatro, 27, 192-194, 197-199, 212, 217-218
Bissett, Judith, 47
Bixler, Jacqueline, 31, 35-36, 42, 46, 54, 59, 77, 79, 81, 84, 142, 144-145, 176
Blau, Herbert, 18, 22, 196, 213, 218
Boal, Augusto, 20-21, 25, 220
Body
  as canvas, 93
  as signifier, 17
  female, 99, 115, 120, 145, 174, 177, 187
  of actor, 15, 219, 221
  of performer, 17, 194
  of prisoner, 158, 176
  of spectator, 13, 186, 210
  of victim, 157, 159
  political, 162
Boling, Becky, 67, 72, 201, 211-212, 215
Bolívar (Rial), 16, 26, 29-30, 32, 41, 47-58, 64, 68, 70, 73, 80, 99, 154, 188-189, 193, 203, 218, 220
Bravo-Elizondo, Pedro, 33
Brecht, Bertolt, 20, 74
Breeches role, 118-119, 151

Brewer, Mária, 28, 32
Bruss, Elizabeth, 82, 84
Buenaventura, Enrique, 23, 25, 79, 166
Bunster, Ximena, 183
Burgess, Ronald, 62, 137-139
Burns, Elizabeth, 22
Bustamante, Maris, 16
Butler, Judith, 111, 116-117, 123, 139, 144

Cabrujas, José Ignacio
  Acto cultural, 27, 63, 80, 160, 192-193, 196, 201-204, 211-212, 215, 218-219
  Campo, El (Gambaro), 27, 47, 73, 79, 120-121, 155, 177-183, 188-190, 193, 213, 221
Carballido, Emilio, 20
Carlson, Marvin, 15, 195
Carvalho-Neto, Paulo de, 225-226
Case, Sue-Ellen, 138, 144
Castedo-Ellerman, Elena, 121
Castellanos, Rosario, 13, 60, 72, 116, 123, 139
  "A pesar de proponérselo," 133-134
  "Jornada de la soltera," 132
  "Kinsey Report," 133
  "La mujer y su imagen," 128-129
  "La participación de la mujer mexicana en la educación formal," 128-129, 131
  "Otra vez Sor Juana," 61, 130
  El eterno femenino, 12, 27, 111-112, 116-117, 123-135, 143, 145, 150, 215, 217, 219, 222
Castillo, Debra, 85, 114, 123, 127, 134, 148
Castillo, Susana, 99
Chile, 27, 75, 91, 155, 158, 160, 183-184
Chocrón, Isaac
  La revolución, 12, 27, 192-193, 196, 204-208, 210-212, 215-216, 220
Coercion
  and exposure, 220
  and performance, 17, 48, 217-218
  and resistance, 20
  and space, 19
  and torture, 156
  and transgression, 227
  and translation, 24
  between actor and spectator, 17
  defined, 17

of audience, 209-210, 213, 226
of individual, 217
of performer, 194, 207, 213, 217-218
performance as, 200
Coetzee, J. M., 162-163, 187
Cohen-Cruz, Jan, 14
Colombia, 26, 30, 56, 76, 79, 87, 106
Confession, 51, 111, 164-165, 168, 183-184
  See also Interrogation
Costantino, Roselyn, 16, 25
Cross-dressing, 112-115, 118-120, 124, 126, 130, 143, 145, 150-151, 222, 225
  See also Transvestism
Cruz, Sor Juana Inés de la, 20, 85, 129-130
Cypess, Sandra, 59, 62, 64-65, 130

Derrida, Jacques, 195
Desaparecidos, 158-159, 165, 197, 222
Despojamiento, El (Gambaro), 27, 192-194, 199-201, 211-212, 215, 217, 220
Diamond, Elin, 14-15, 22
Díaz, Jorge, 75, 78, 81, 193
Dictatorship, 14, 48, 77, 91, 103, 161, 172, 182-183
Díez, Luys, 169
Disappearance, 21, 122, 158-159, 195, 197, 220
Displacement, 18, 21, 46, 99, 124, 145, 150, 153, 196, 217, 219, 221-223, 227
Display, 18, 109, 119, 145, 150, 153, 156-159, 161, 182, 208, 218, 220
Documentary theater, 33, 47, 73-74, 219-220
Dolan, Jill, 114
Donoso, José, 114
Dorfman, Ariel
  La Muerte y la Doncella, 27, 155-156, 183-187, 191
Dragún, Osvaldo, 78, 96, 194, 199, 210
Dramatic irony, 34, 55, 109
duBois, Page, 156

Ecuador, 11-12, 30, 223
Eidelberg, Nora, 144, 177, 190
Elam, Keir, 22
Enclosure, 75, 77-78, 86, 107, 150, 162
Escudero, María, 223-226
Eterno femenino, El (Castellanos), 12, 27, 111-112, 116-117, 123-135, 143, 145, 150, 215, 217, 219, 222

Falsa crónica de Juana la Loca (Sabido), 26, 29, 34, 51, 59, 65-74, 80
Feitlowitz, Marguerite, 187
Femininity, 12, 72, 78, 97, 112, 115-116, 118-119, 121, 130, 145, 147-148, 161, 182, 192, 219
Féral, Josette, 19, 211
Fetterley, Judith, 129, 143
Fiestas, 11-12, 16, 108, 222-227
Fletcher, Lea, 183
Foley, Barbara, 31
Foucault, Michel, 50
Franco, Jean, 80, 115-118, 120, 122, 133, 150, 152, 160-161, 170, 180
Fuentes, Carlos, 29, 59

Gambaro, Griselda, 13, 79, 86, 120, 128, 160, 163, 188, 190, 226
  El campo, 27, 47, 73, 79, 120-121, 155, 177-183, 188-190, 193, 213, 221
  El desatino, 79
  El despojamiento, 27, 192-194, 199-201, 211-212, 215, 217, 220
  Información para extranjeros, 17, 174, 189, 192-193, 197, 207-210, 212-215, 217, 219-221
  Las paredes, 79
  "Voracidad o canibalismo amoroso," 22-23, 127-128, 151, 219
Games, 67, 73-74, 107, 109
  and authority, 80
  and gender, 124, 139, 147
  and oppression, 77, 84, 99
  and patriarchy, 84, 96-97
  and reality, 94-95, 98-99
  and representation, 73, 96
  and resistance, 85, 97
  and script, 82, 99
  and theater, 96
  as liminal space, 99
  as performance, 77
  constitution of, 77, 99
  defined, 82
  literary, 84
  ritual, 27, 75, 81, 217
  roles in, 80, 98
  rules, 80, 82, 84
  violent, 26, 76, 96, 99, 107, 166
Garber, Marjorie, 112-113, 115, 120, 204
García, Luis Alberto, 30, 52

García, Santiago, 25
Gender
　ambiguity, 104, 135, 139
　and performance, 105, 112, 151
　and space, 19, 160
　and violence, 155, 181
　as category, 142, 145
　as performance, 24, 26, 111-113, 116-117, 120-122
　constraints, 122
　construction, 153
　identity, 14, 111, 118, 121, 151, 221
　imposition of, 116
　instability, 115, 140, 149, 152
　oppression, 178
　performance of, 111, 116, 132, 156, 159, 218
　representation of, 113, 116-117
　roles, 14, 28, 103, 111-112, 117, 123-124, 137, 143-144, 151-152, 217
George, David, 19, 58, 113, 195, 197, 211-212
Gerdes, Dick, 215
Gómez-Peña, Guillermo, 24-25
González, Patricia, 107
Gorostiza, Carlos, 75, 81, 83, 97
Graham-Jones, Jean, 143
Graziano, Frank, 158-159, 163-165, 173-174, 188
Gregory, Stephen, 167-169, 187, 190
Grotowski, Jerzy, 199, 213

Hart, Lynda, 121
Heise, Ursula, 118-119
History
　alternative, 47, 69-70
　and historical theater, 30-31, 33-35, 55, 59, 73, 222
　as performance, 30, 73-74, 215, 222
　as text, 33-37, 44, 50, 52, 129
　construction of, 29-31, 54
　official, 32, 42, 46, 49, 51, 54, 63, 69, 111, 154, 219-221
　performance of, 30, 52, 58
History play, 31, 58, 65, 71, 218, 221
Holzapfel, Tamara, 182, 190
Homosexuality, 90, 101, 142, 147-149
Huizinga, Johan, 82-83, 99
Hutcheon, Linda, 31, 54

Identity, 14, 27, 100, 104, 111, 113, 118, 127, 130, 138, 145, 149, 151, 167, 180-181, 192, 194, 217, 221-222, 227
Immobility
　and games, 75
　and wheelchair, 87, 91
　as resistance, 78, 85, 100
　false, 85, 100, 103, 109-110
　feminine, 78, 80, 97-98, 100, 115
　imposed, 85, 106-107
　in Gambaro, 79
　performance of, 110
　psychological, 78
　representation of, 109
Improvisation, 18, 22, 28, 37, 55, 65, 75, 81, 98
Inamoto, Kenji, 119
Información para extranjeros (Gambaro), 27, 174, 189, 192-193, 197, 207-210, 212-215, 217, 219-221
Insilio (inxile), 171-172
Instability
　of gender, 115, 140, 149, 151-152
　of performance, 12, 53, 67-69, 110, 116
　of the script, 48, 56, 218
　of theatrical space, 172
Interrogation, 51, 155, 163, 165-168, 180, 213, 219
　See also Confession
Invisibility, 119, 127, 156, 162, 169, 201

Jones, Marion, 119
Juego, El (Romero), 26-27, 73, 75-104, 106-107, 109, 115, 154, 160, 218, 220

Kintz, Linda, 125-126
Kubiak, Anthony, 194-195, 197, 216-217

Larson, Catherine, 84-85, 96-98
Leñero, Vicente, 13, 66
　Martirio de Morelos, 26, 29-30, 32-47, 49-51, 54, 59, 62, 73, 154, 163, 219
　La ruta crítica de "Martirio de Morelos," 37-38, 43
León-Portilla, Miguel, 59, 74
Lesbianism, 90, 104, 120, 144-145, 149
Lichtblau, Myron, 86, 90
Lindenberger, Herbert, 31, 35, 42, 73-74

Lispector, Clarice, 78
Ludmer, Josefina, 85, 91, 109

Madness, 57, 67-69, 72, 102
Madres de la Plaza de Mayo, 118, 122, 161-162, 222
Magnarelli, Sharon, 30, 34, 55, 68-70, 103, 192
Mahieu, Roma, 77
Malinche
  and marginality, 72
  as myth, 60, 72, 129-130
  as traitor, 59
  as translator, 59, 61-62
  reinterpretation of, 24, 59, 65, 131, 223
Mama Negra, 12, 223-227
Marqués, René, 29
Márquez, Rosa Luisa, 24, 84
Martirio de Morelos (Leñero), 26, 29-30, 32-47, 49-51, 54, 59, 62, 73, 154, 163, 219
Masculinity, 116, 137, 140-141, 143, 145, 148, 151
Meléndez, Priscilla, 33, 44-45, 47, 62-64
Mena, Karel, 86, 91
Metatheater, 14, 42, 75, 86, 133, 213
Mexico, 12, 20, 24-26, 29-30, 33, 38, 58, 60, 71-72, 76, 101, 111, 130, 192
Milgram, Stanley, 213-214, 221
Millett, Kate, 157
Moretta, Eugene, 76, 96, 179, 182, 196, 202, 206
Muerte y la Doncella, La (Dorfman), 27, 155-156, 183-187, 191

Narration, 29, 31, 38, 46, 60, 69, 73, 89, 137, 145, 218
Narrator, 38, 60-61, 68-70, 198, 224
Navajas, Esteban
  La agonía del difunto, 26, 76, 100, 106-109, 218
Nichols, Mike, 185-186
Nightingale, Benedict, 185
Nigro, Kirsten, 34, 49, 57, 101, 125, 127-128, 203-205, 207, 211, 215
Niño, Jairo Aníbal, 87
Noakes, Susan, 122
Noche de los asesinos, La (Triana), 75, 77, 81-83, 86, 96-97, 99, 192-193
Nonperformance, 13, 27, 47, 121, 177-178, 180, 189, 193-197, 202-203, 206, 208, 210-211, 216-218

Olivera-Williams, María Rosa, 171

Paralysis
  and oppression, 75
  and performance, 77
  and resistance, 78, 85
  and violence, 87, 89
  feigned, 26, 73, 76, 85-86, 92, 97-98, 100-101, 103, 109, 172
  female, 78, 97
  of audience, 191
  of nonperformance, 218
  performance of, 100
  refusal of, 115
  representation of, 78, 93, 96
  within games, 76, 78
Parody, 101-102, 114, 120, 122, 132-133, 150, 179, 219
Partnoy, Alicia, 158
Pavlovsky, Eduardo, 13
  El señor Galíndez, 27, 155-156, 172-177, 181, 185, 187, 190, 208, 219-220
  Paso de dos, 187
Pedro y el Capitán (Benedetti), 27, 155-156, 165-172, 174, 177, 181, 185, 190
Pequeña historia de horror (y de amor desenfrenado) (Vilalta), 26, 76, 100-106, 109, 113
Performance
  ambivalent, 15, 28, 76, 78
  and authority, 44, 160, 218
  and coercion, 17, 49, 218
  and gender, 105, 112, 151
  and liberation, 99, 115-116, 120, 123, 151-152, 194
  and reading, 45, 47, 122
  and repetition, 218
  and text, 13, 21-23, 30, 37, 44, 58-59, 82, 99, 127-128, 195, 218
  and theatricality, 18
  and translation, 59
  as destabilizing practice, 32
  as event, 19
  as mediation, 69
  as metaphor, 23, 122, 153, 180
  as process, 28
  as reproduction, 53
  as resistance, 21, 220
  as violence, 17, 90, 96, 99, 103, 120, 177, 195, 201
  coercive, 13, 180, 182, 192, 200, 210, 217

compelled, 47, 127, 151, 155, 178-179, 219
contingency of, 63
co-optation of, 156
defined, 14, 18-19
dramatic, 21, 130
elements of, 18, 77
empty, 193, 220
feminine, 151
impossible, 160, 193-195, 202, 217
instability of, 12, 37, 53, 68-69, 74, 110, 116
of documents, 35, 38
of gender, 111, 116, 132, 159
of historical material, 30, 33
of torture, 173
of violence, 154-155
paratheatrical, 16
private, 134
public, 178
representation of, 14, 26, 32, 206
role of spectator, 196
self-conscious, 23, 73-74, 124
self-reflexive, 75, 196, 210
space, 12-13, 19, 193
stage, 12, 121, 134
temporality of, 31, 33, 58, 110
theatrical, 48, 75, 114, 154-155, 177-178, 189, 191
unrealized, 47, 53, 128, 177-178, 192, 198, 217
visibility of, 50
Performative, 28, 57, 65, 71-72, 74, 79, 92, 94, 110-111, 117, 123, 132, 136, 138, 160-161, 182, 197, 223
Performer
and audience, 217
and role, 195-197, 199, 204, 221
and script, 122, 127
body of, 17
coercion of, 194, 213, 216-218
danger to, 13, 116, 196
degradation of, 199
dependence, 206, 210
exposure, 153, 220-221
female, 119, 122-124, 133, 144
gender of, 120
isolation, 174, 203
jeopardized, 189
site of violence, 195
spectator as, 20
unwilling, 48

vulnerability, 17, 220
woman as, 122, 127, 151-152
Peters, Edward, 159
Play within the play, 14, 21, 30, 48, 63, 182, 192, 212
Postma, Rosalea, 209

Rape, 87, 90, 95, 98, 103, 160, 170, 183-185, 191
Reenactment, 22, 39-40, 42, 46-47, 76, 91, 93, 130, 203, 218, 221
Rehearsal, 38, 47, 49, 53, 56, 58, 82, 213-214, 218
Rejali, Darius, 164
Repetition, 13, 18, 22, 24, 31, 53, 55, 70, 75, 77, 81-83, 89, 91, 99, 101-102, 139, 161, 164, 212, 214, 218, 221, 224-225, 227
Representation
and games, 76
and performance, 18, 25, 212
and terror, 195, 216
and transvestism, 113-114
coercive, 17
construction of, 71
ethics of, 155-156, 187
historical, 32-33
impossible, 179, 195, 200, 212
of gender, 113, 116-117, 122, 151
of performance, 14, 26, 32, 206
of torture, 27, 154-156, 162, 176, 191, 195, 208, 217
of violence, 78
of women, 87
parameters of, 154
paratheatrical, 222
political, 122
possibility of, 226
representación, 24
ritual, 87
stage, 189, 219
theatrical, 24, 113, 153, 179, 213
Revolución, La (Chocrón), 12, 27, 192-193, 196, 204-208, 210-212, 215-216, 220
Reyes, Carlos José, 52
Rial, José Antonio, 48
Bolívar, 16, 26, 29-30, 32, 41, 47-58, 64, 68, 70, 73, 80, 99, 154, 188-189, 193, 203, 218, 220
Ritual, 14, 18, 24, 27, 57, 68, 75-78, 80-81, 87, 100, 106, 159, 174-175, 177-178, 180, 190, 192, 213, 217, 225

Rodríguez, Jesusa, 25
Rogers, Pat, 119
Rohter, Larry, 184-186
Role playing, 14, 18, 76-77, 134, 155, 165, 178-179, 196, 201, 204-205, 207, 211, 215
Romero, Mariela, 13, 79
  El juego, 26-27, 73, 75-104, 106-107, 109, 115, 154, 160, 218, 220
Ruffinelli, Jorge, 161, 169-170

Sabido, Miguel
  Falsa crónica de Juana la Loca, 26, 29, 34, 51, 59, 65-74, 80
Sáez, Ñacuñán, 164-165
Sánchez, Luis Rafael, 193
Sarduy, Severo, 114
Sayre, Henry, 18, 218
Scarry, Elaine, 157, 159-160, 162-165, 172, 175, 179, 188
Schechner, Richard, 18, 58
Schmidhuber, Guillermo, 30
Schmitt, Natalie, 19, 83-84, 98, 227
Schulz, Bernhardt, 149
Script
  absent, 202, 204, 221
  and authority, 46, 219
  as convention, 16, 218
  instability of, 48, 56
  within games, 77, 80
Seda, Laurietz, 142, 149
Seduction, 88, 90, 103, 122-124, 135-138, 141-142, 146-147, 152, 178, 180-181
Self-consciousness, 46, 74, 101, 139, 179, 193
Self-reflexivity, 12, 30-31, 134, 189, 194, 196, 210, 213
Senelick, Laurence, 116-117
Señor Galíndez, El (Pavlovsky), 27, 155-156, 172-177, 181, 185, 187, 190, 208, 219-220
Space
  ambiguous, 155, 174, 177, 208, 219
  domestic, 201
  feminine, 19, 115, 150, 160
  imaginary, 77, 95-96
  masculine, 19, 118-119, 150, 160
  of performance, 13, 19, 28, 109, 126, 152, 193-194, 196, 204, 210
  of procession, 226
  of resistance, 85
  of spectator, 18
  of torture, 172-173
  private, 19, 117, 119, 122, 126, 134, 150, 159-161, 166
  public, 19, 117-119, 121, 124, 134, 150-151, 159-161, 166, 185
  theatrical, 14, 19, 24, 77, 79, 116, 121, 125, 157, 174, 193, 202, 204, 217, 219
Spectacle
  "abstract," 158-159 161, 163, 174-175, 182, 188, 194, 208, 221
  and audience, 191, 204, 208
  military, 158, 162
  of absence, 158
  of torture, 155-156, 163, 176, 217
  political, 163
  theatrical, 156, 163
Spectator, 50, 100, 104-106, 111, 121, 125, 144, 152, 172, 175, 178, 182, 186, 188, 192-193, 195-196, 206, 221, 223, 225, 227
  ambivalence of, 28
  coercion of, 210
  complicity, 209
  confrontation of, 16
  female, 90, 119, 209
  male, 118
  performance of, 20
  presence of, 17
  role of, 19-21, 196
  seduction of, 205
  space of, 18
  theatrical, 58, 119, 124
  vulnerability of, 13, 156, 177, 189
  within the play, 63
  See also Audience
Stage
  boundary of, 14, 155, 173-174, 182, 214, 217, 227
  demarcation of, 12, 16-17, 19, 219
  public, 117, 123, 139, 150, 153, 159, 162
State terror, 14, 16, 185, 194, 220
States, Bert, 23-24
Stover, Eric, 183
Suplicio del placer, El (Berman), 12, 27, 111, 116, 119, 123, 135-142, 145-146, 150-152, 218, 221
Szurmuk, Mónica, 127, 133

Tavira, Luis de, 40
Taylor, Diana, 15, 18, 25-26, 28, 32, 67,

81, 122, 153, 159-163, 174, 177, 181-182, 185, 187, 189-190, 197, 209-210, 213-214
Terror
  and representation, 195, 216
  and terrorism, 195
  cathartic, 156
  of nonperformance, 194-195
  political, 216
Terrorism, 27-28, 188, 195, 197, 217
Theatricality, 12, 14, 17-18, 22-23, 28, 34, 57, 66, 69, 103, 116, 154-155, 163, 174, 182, 188, 191, 194, 213, 219
  offstage, 16, 22, 24, 219, 222, 224
  self-conscious, 72, 182
Toledo, Iván, 30, 224
Torres Molina, Susana, 134
  . . .Y a otra cosa mariposa, 27, 111-112, 116, 119, 123-124, 142-153, 219
  Extraño juguete, 75, 81, 83
Torture
  and performance, 121, 155, 178
  and sexual violence, 170, 183, 185
  audience of, 21, 157, 163, 172-175, 190, 207, 209
  history of, 156, 159, 164
  offstage, 33, 56, 165
  representation of, 27, 154-156, 162, 176, 191, 195, 208, 217
  spectacle of, 156, 176, 188
  theatricality of, 28, 155-156, 163, 189
  visibility of, 157
Translation, 13, 24-26, 58-61, 65, 73, 142, 185, 195
Transvestism, 112-113, 118, 134, 141, 149, 151, 204, 219, 224-225
  See also Cross-dressing
Triana, José, 75, 77, 81-83, 86, 96-97, 99, 192-193

Uruguay, 27, 155, 157-158, 160-161, 169-172, 183
Usigli, Rodolfo, 29-30

Valenzuela, Luisa, 78
Valle-Inclán, Ramón del, 55-56
Vanden Heuvel, Michael, 196-197
Venezuela, 12, 16, 26-27, 29, 48, 75, 91, 192
Versényi, Adam, 71
Vignar, Marcelo, 157, 172
Vilalta, Maruxa
  Pequeña historia de horror (y de amor desenfrenado), 26, 76, 100-106, 109, 113
Violence
  against women, 155, 166, 177, 183, 187, 201, 209
  between characters, 17, 97-98, 103, 105, 148, 218, 220
  effect on audience, 187, 189-191, 210
  historical, 32, 74
  of nonperformance, 196
  performance as, 17, 73, 90, 99, 201
  ritual, 27, 80, 192
  sexual, 155, 170, 183-185, 209
  staged, 13, 16, 154, 188, 190
  state, 15, 158, 197
  theatricality of, 163, 189
  within games, 26, 76-77, 86, 96-97, 107
Visibility, 51, 119-120, 122, 127, 153, 155-157, 161, 169, 174, 182, 189, 201, 220
Voyeurism, 17, 68, 137, 190, 209, 215

Weiss, Peter, 33-34
Weschler, Lawrence, 157, 171
White, Hayden, 30-31, 44, 66
Wiles, Timothy, 199
Worthen, W. B., 21

Y a otra cosa mariposa (Torres Molina), 27, 111-112, 116, 119, 123-124, 142-153, 219
Yarbro-Bejarano, Yvonne, 118

Zatlin, Phyllis, 78
Zee, Linda, 179

NORTH CAROLINA STUDIES IN THE ROMANCE LANGUAGES AND LITERATURES

I.S.B.N. Prefix 0-8078-

Recent Titles

THE "LIBRO DE ALEXANDRE". MEDIEVAL EPIC AND SILVER LATIN, by Charles F. Fraker. 1993. (No. 245). -9249-1.
THE ROMANTIC IMAGINATION IN THE WORKS OF GUSTAVO ADOLFO BÉCQUER, by B. Brant Bynum. 1993. (No. 246). -9250-5.
MYSTIFICATION ET CRÉATIVITÉ DANS L'OEUVRE ROMANESQUE DE MARGUERITE YOURCENAR, par Beatrice Ness. 1994. (No. 247). -9251-3.
TEXT AS TOPOS IN RELIGIOUS LITERATURE OF THE SPANISH GOLDEN AGE, by M. Louise Salstad. 1995. (No. 248). -9252-1.
CALISTO'S DREAM AND THE CELESTINESQUE TRADITION: A REREADING OF CELESTINA, by Ricardo Castells. 1995. (No. 249). -9253-X.
THE ALLEGORICAL IMPULSE IN THE WORKS OF JULIEN GRACQ: HISTORY AS RHETORICAL ENACTMENT IN LE RIVAGE DES SYRTES AND UN BALCON EN FORÊT, by Carol J. Murphy. 1995. (No. 250). -9254-8.
VOID AND VOICE: QUESTIONING NARRATIVE CONVENTIONS IN ANDRÉ GIDE'S MAJOR FIRST-PERSON NARRATIVES, by Charles O'Keefe. 1996. (No. 251). -9255-6.
EL CÍRCULO Y LA FLECHA: PRINCIPIO Y FIN, TRIUNFO Y FRACASO DEL PERSILES, por Julio Baena. 1996. (No. 252). -9256-4.
EL TIEMPO Y LOS MÁRGENES. EUROPA COMO UTOPÍA Y COMO AMENAZA EN LA LITERATURA ESPAÑOLA, por Jesús Torrecilla. 1996. (No. 253). -9257-2.
THE AESTHETICS OF ARTIFICE: VILLIERS'S L'EVE FUTURE, by Marie Lathers. 1996. (No. 254). -9254-8.
DISLOCATIONS OF DESIRE: GENDER, IDENTITY, AND STRATEGY IN LA REGENTA, by Alison Sinclair. 1998. (No. 255). -9259-9.
THE POETICS OF INCONSTANCY, ETIENNE DURAND AND THE END OF RENAISSANCE VERSE, by Hoyt Rogers. 1998. (No. 256). -9260-2.
RONSARD'S CONTENTIOUS SISTERS: THE PARAGONE BETWEEN POETRY AND PAINTING IN THE WORKS OF PIERRE DE RONSARD, by Roberto E. Campo. 1998. (No. 257). -9261-0.
THE RAVISHMENT OF PERSEPHONE: EPISTOLARY LYRIC IN THE SIÈCLE DES LUMIÈRES, by Julia K. De Pree. 1998. (No. 258). -9262-9.
CONVERTING FICTION: COUNTER REFORMATIONAL CLOSURE IN THE SECULAR LITERATURE OF GOLDEN AGE SPAIN, by David H. Darst. 1998. (No. 259). -9263-7.
GALDÓS'S SEGUNDA MANERA: RHETORICAL STRATEGIES AND AFFECTIVE RESPONSE, by Linda M. Willem. 1998. (No. 260). -9264-5.
A MEDIEVAL PILGRIM'S COMPANION. REASSESSING EL LIBRO DE LOS HUÉSPEDES (ESCORIAL MS. h.I.13), by Thomas D. Spaccarelli. 1998. (No. 261). -9265-3.
'PUEBLOS ENFERMOS': THE DISCOURSE OF ILLNESS IN THE TURN-OF-THE-CENTURY SPANISH AND LATIN AMERICAN ESSAY, by Michael Aronna. 1999. (No. 262). -9266-1.
RESONANT THEMES. LITERATURE, HISTORY, AND THE ARTS IN NINETEENTH- AND TWENTIETH-CENTURY EUROPE. ESSAYS IN HONOR OF VICTOR BROMBERT, by Stirling Haig. 1999. (No. 263). -9267-X.
RAZA, GÉNERO E HIBRIDEZ EN EL LAZARILLO DE CIEGOS CAMINANTES, por Mariselle Meléndez. 1999. (No. 264). -9268-8.
DEL ESCENARIO A LA PANTALLA: LA ADAPTACIÓN CINEMATOGRÁFICA DEL TEATRO ESPAÑOL, por María Asunción Gómez. 2000. (No. 265). 9269-6.
THE LEPER IN BLUE: COERCIVE PERFORMANCE AND THE CONTEMPORARY LATIN AMERICAN THEATER, by Amalia Gladhart. 2000. (No. 266). 9270-X.

When ordering please cite the *ISBN Prefix* plus the last four digits for each title.

Send orders to: University of North Carolina Press
P.O. Box 2288
CB# 6215
Chapel Hill, NC 27515-2288
U.S.A.

The Department of Romance Studies Digital Arts and Collaboration Lab at the University of North Carolina at Chapel Hill is proud to support the digitization of the North Carolina Studies in the Romance Languages and Literatures series.

Made in the USA
Las Vegas, NV
24 October 2024